Christm

To Freda

you enjoy this,

Love Betty & Charles. XX

THE CRICKET ADDICT'S ARCHIVE

It was hit hard and high. But the bowler knew all about it. The Curate felt called upon.

The Colonel regarded it as his. His son thought it was up to him. The grocer had it all the **way.**

And the blacksmith shouted "Myern!"

OUR VILLAGE CATCH

THE CRICKET ADDICT'S ARCHIVE

EDITED BY

BENNY GREEN

ELM TREE BOOKS
HAMISH HAMILTON · LONDON

First published in Great Britain 1977
by Elm Tree Books/Hamish Hamilton Ltd
90 Great Russell Street, London WC1B 3PT

Copyright © 1977 by Benny Green

SBN 241 89610 X

For

Lionel Henry Weiser

(1928–1975)

Printed in Great Britain
by Ebenezer Baylis and Son Ltd
The Trinity Press, Worcester, and London

CONTENTS

ACKNOWLEDGEMENTS

The extract from *A London Family* by Molly Vivian Hughes is reprinted by permission of Oxford University Press; from *Sinister Street* by Compton Mackenzie by permission of Macdonald and Jane's Ltd.; from *Psmith in the City* by P. G. Wodehouse by permission of Barrie & Jenkins; from *The Proud Tower* by Barbara Tuchman (Hamish Hamilton Ltd.) by permission of A. M. Heath & Co. Ltd.; from *Masters of Cricket* by Jack Fingleton by permission of William Heinemann Ltd.; from *On Top Down Under* by Ray Robinson by permission of Cassell Australia Ltd.; from *A Pattern of Islands* by Arthur Grimble by permission of John Murray (Publishers) Ltd.; from *A Few Short Runs* by Lord Harris by permission of John Murray (Publishers) Ltd.; the extracts from *The Honeysuckle and the Bee* by J. C. Squire (William Heinemann Ltd.) are reprinted by permission of A. D. Peters & Co. Ltd.; the extract from *My Brother Evelyn and Other Profiles* by Alec Waugh (Cassell & Co. Ltd.) is reprinted by permission of A. D. Peters & Co. Ltd.; from *Allahakbarries C.C.* by J. M. Barrie by permission of the English Theatre Guild Ltd.; from *Experiment in Autobiography* by H. G. Wells (Victor Gollancz Ltd.) by permission of A. P. Watt & Son; from *The Old Century* by Siegfried Sassoon by permission of Mr. G. T. Sassoon; from *Carts and Candlesticks* by Alison Uttley by permission of Faber & Faber Ltd.; from *Love on a Branch Line* by John Hadfield by permission of Hutchinson & Co. Ltd.; from *The Greenwood Hat* by J. M. Barrie by permission of the English Theatre Guild; from *The Jubilee Book of Cricket* by Prince Ranjitsinhji by permission of William Blackwood & Sons Ltd.; 'C. B. Fry: classic in all respects' by Alan Gibson repro uced from *The Times* by permission; the extract from *Goodbye to All That* by Robert Graves (Cassell & Co. Ltd.) by permission of Robert Graves; from *Piccadilly Jim* by P. G. Wodehouse by permission of Barrie & Jenkins; from *Many Furrows* by Alpha of the Plough (A. G. Gardiner) by permission of J. M. Dent & Sons Ltd.; from *Open House* by J. B. Priestley (William Heinemann Ltd.) by permission of A. D. Peters & Co. Ltd.; from '46 Not Out' in *Crusoe on Cricket* ed. by Alan Ross by permission of London Magazine Editions;

from *Brightly Fades the Don* by Jack Fingleton by permission of William Collins Sons & Co. Ltd.; from *Batter's Castle* by Ian Peebles (Souvenir Press) by permission of Ian Peebles; 'Guilty, m'lud, to fiction if it serves higher Truth' from the *Guardian* 20 October 1967 and 'An urchin at Old Trafford' from the *Guardian* 29 May 1971 by Neville Cardus by permission of Miss M. Hughes; the extract from *A Fish Dinner in Memison* by E. R. Eddison by permission of Mrs. Latham and Ballantine Books Ltd.; from *Overthrows* by E. Sewell by permission of Hutchinson & Co. Ltd.; from *Hit for Six* by Gerald Brodribb by permission of William Heinemann Ltd.; from *Fireside and Sunshine* by E. V. Lucas by permission of Methuen & Co. Ltd.; Alan Richardson's letter to *The Times* 18 May 1963 by permission of Mrs. Phyllis Richardson; the extract from *Odd Men In* by A. A. Thomson by permission of Pitman Publishing Ltd.; 'Greyhounds in the slips, 1908' from the *Guardian* 24 June 1968 by Kenneth Gregory by permission of Kenneth Gregory; the extract from *Cricket Crisis* by Jack Fingleton by permission of Jack Fingleton; from *Australia 55* by Alan Ross by permission of Alan Ross; from *M.C.C.* by Colin Cowdrey by permission of Hodder & Stoughton Ltd.; from *Sort of a Cricket Person* by E. W. Swanton by permission of William Collins Sons & Co. Ltd.; from *The Face of England* by Edmund Blunden by permission of William Collins Sons & Co. Ltd.; from *Beyond a Boundary* by C. L. R. James by permission of Hutchinson Publishing Co. Ltd.; from *The Croucher* by G. Brodribb by permission of London Magazine Editions; from *Cricket All His Life* by E. V. Lucas by permission of Methuen & Co. Ltd.; from *Strangers' Gallery* by Marvin Cohen by permission of Marvin Cohen; from *A Year to Remember* by Alec Waugh by permission of W. H. Allen & Co. Ltd.; from *The Cricket Match* by Hugh de Selincourt (Jonathan Cape Ltd.) by permission of David Higham Associates Ltd.; the frontispiece by permission of *Punch*.

Every effort has been made to trace the copyright holders of the material used in this volume. Should there be any omissions in this respect, we apologise and shall be pleased to make the appropriate acknowledgement in future editions.

INTRODUCTION

WHY ANOTHER cricket anthology? Surely there are enough in existence already? The answer to the second of those questions is 'No, there
are not'. As for the first, so much writing about cricket deserves to be
preserved in some sort of permanent, or at least semi-permanent form,
that not even the existing collections of prose and poetry include every
item which has struck me as deserving of a second chance. So far from
attempting anything as absurdly presumptuous as the superseding of
previously published cricket anthologies, I hope this volume will be seen
as a modest addition to them, a snapper-up of unconsidered trifles which
either appeared once in some newspaper or magazine and were then
forgotten, or have been entombed for far too long inside volumes themselves forgotten by all but the most zealous cricketing bibliophiles.

As to the selections themselves, the best way of explaining their style
is perhaps with reference to the dedicatee of this book. Lionel Henry
Weiser, an exact contemporary of mine, was one of thousands of schoolboys I remember, myself among them, who acquired a rudimentary
batting and bowling technique on asphalt with a tennis ball, before
stumps chalked in quavering lines on a brick wall. We played together in
proper cricket matches, by which I mean on grass with twenty-two
players, two umpires and a scorer, from our fourteenth to our twentieth
years and if my memory serves me as accurately as I hope it does, he was
the first team-mate of mine to score a half-century. He was also a
modestly efficient medium-pace bowler who discovered very early in
life that on the fiendishly unprepared pitches of adolescence, all you
need do to be a destroyer is to bowl straight. By the time he was twenty-
one, rotundity and fatherhood had begun to catch up with him, and he
used to say that his career figures had been summarised at a record
early age.

However, it was not until his retirement from action that Weiser
really began to study the game. He was one of those men whose idea of
a good read is any edition of Wisden, cover to cover, including the
advertisements. (*Especially* the advertisements; one of his beliefs was
that you could chart the commercial history of England by studying the

steadily diminishing claims on behalf of Dr Collis Browne's Chlorodyne.) Over the years we spent perhaps a thousand afternoons at Lord's and the Oval, half-watching the cricket as we related it to its historical context. In the Lord's match between Middlesex and Glamorgan in 1948, after Compton and Edrich had both been dismissed with scandalous lack of respect, and a visiting Welshman was exulting in the row in front of us, Weiser, with the fervour of adolescence to excuse him, leaned forward and politely asked the interloper where Glamorgan had finished in the County Championship in 1914. Perhaps that was the last partisan gesture he ever made; long before he was old enough to vote he had stopped 'supporting' this side or that, and simply went from ground to ground in search of an innings or a bowling spell which had about it an element of beauty, or pathos, or comedy. The one theme on which he remained admirably biased was Denis Compton. To the day he died, Weiser could never bring himself to study in any close detail the England–Australia series of 1950–1; if he happened to come across a reference to that terrible nightmare, he would hastily turn over the pages or fling the book aside. Such reversals of the natural order of things were simply not to be contemplated. It was bad enough that they had happened at all; there was no point in dwelling on them.

But the reason why I had no choice but to dedicate this book to his memory is that it was Weiser who showed me what cricket really was. Had I never enjoyed all those conversations with him, I might never have come to see as clearly as I do now that cricket, no less than anything else, takes its character from the social environment which nurtures it. When I first encountered somewhere in the pages of Sir Neville Cardus the idea that nations get the cricket they deserve, the very idea took my breath away, and I put it down to the idle fancy of a romantic. Of course what the theory really embodied was the starkest realism, and it took the tutelage of Weiser to bring the truth home to me.

I began with assumptions crude to the point of asininity, for instance that the reason for the decline in English cricket (English cricket is always declining, a most convenient fact for controversialists) was the decrease in the number of amateur batsmen. If a man is paid to bat, I would argue, it follows that he will perform with a less liberated spirit than the man who bats without relying upon it for his living. The crushing irony which escaped both Weiser and myself on the Saturday afternoon when I propagated my theory was that even as I was propagating it, Denis Compton, a professional, was putting them to the sword with the aplomb of an Edwardian sprig buttressed by an independent income. I remember that Weiser gently changed my mind for me by remarking, 'It's not as simple as that' and taking me to the first day of an Oxford–Cambridge match. And there, gazing upon the spectacle of twenty-two liberated spirits performing as though the work's foreman had his eye on them, I began to repair my theories.

Most of the items in this collection were once read over and discussed by the two of us together; a few of them, like those by Colin Cowdrey and Ray Robinson, were not published until after Weiser's tragically premature death, but I know he would have been particularly tickled by the Cowdrey anecdote, with its wry savouring of the Gentleman–Player joke. Almost the last book whose delights we shared was Swanton's *Sort of a Cricket Person*. I have included Swanton's unforgettable description of the antics of Sir Julien Cahn and his account of the curious destiny of J. H. Human, not only because they engage my own interest, but because they also engaged Weiser's. In fact this collection performs for at least one cricket-lover the identical function which Weiser always perceived that Wisden performs for all cricket-lovers; it preserves the spirit of a past cricket occasion. In this instance the occasion was a deep friendship of which cricket was one of the foundation stones, and which, had the Fates been less callous, would have endured for many more seasons than it did.

BENNY GREEN

Awareness of the existence of cricket comes to the English virtually simult-
aneously with an awareness of life itself. Like almost all children, Molly
Vivian Hughes (1867–1956), Islington-born author of the classic account
of Victorian urban life, could not remember a time when cricket was not
part of the family round. Her father was a keen club cricketer who sometimes
brought his team-mates home.

WHEN THERE was no outing possible, we played cricket in our back
garden, and broke windows frequently. Each smash was a joy to me,
because I loved to watch the glazier at his miraculous job. He always
gave me a lump of putty which I made into dolls' cups and saucers, and
snakes for Barnholt.

Among the many cricketers coming and going there was one who was
so constantly staying with us that I looked on him as a kind of uncle. But
we always called him by his full name, Charlie Absolom, so that I
thought it was one word. He was a well-known cricketer of the time, and
played I think for England against Australia. His travelling-kit was
extremely simple, and he used to say that his packing up was done in
two movements—gathering up his night-shirt with one hand and aiming
it into his portmanteau wherever that happened to be. His jolly face
made up for the fierceness of his black beard, which I fancy he cultivated
on the model of Grace.

Of course Charlie Absolom played cricket with the boys and me in the
back garden, gave me underhands when he bowled and easy catches
when he batted (not that I caught them), and broke his due share of
windows. I can hear his cheery voice calling out, 'Coosh! There goes
another!' Mother never scolded when anything whatever was broken. As
she justly remarked, 'People don't break things on purpose, and if you
blame them they get nervous, and are most likely to break more'. And
she was far too sensible to suppose that you can play cricket properly
with half your mind engaged in fearing what the ball may break.

From *A London Family*, 1934.

1

Because it insinuates itself into the affections so early, cricket later can become a device for locating days, weeks, years of the distant past with an exactitude for which a great many autobiographists have been grateful. Sir Edward Montague Compton Mackenzie (1883–1972), notorious for the elephantine proportions of his memory, used cricket as on other occasions he used snapshots, flowers, pantomine, omnibuses and butterflies, as a skeleton key to unlock the door to the past, and release its essence.

However, Mackenzie was honest enough to record the awkward fact that very often the schoolboy's obsession with the game is really an obsession for codification, the reduction of the chaos of life to the disciplines of elementary arithmetic.

CRICKET WAS in the same way made a mathematical abstraction of decimals and initials and averages and records. All sorts of periodicals were taken in—Cricket, The Cricketer, Cricketing amongst many others. From an exact perusal of these, Michael and the Macalisters knew that Streatham could beat Hampstead and were convinced of the superiority of the Incogniti C.C. over the Stoics C.C. With the collection of cricketers' portraits some of these figures acquired a conceivable personality; but, for the most part, they remained L. M. N. O. P. Q. Smith representing 36.58 an innings and R. S. T. U. V. W. Brown costing 11.07 a wicket. That they wore moustaches and lived and loved like passionate humanity did not seem to matter compared with the arithmetical progression of their averages. When Michael and Norton (who was staying with him at St. Leonards) were given shillings and told to see the Hastings Cricket Week from the bowling of the first ball to the drawing of the final stump, Michael and Norton were very much bored indeed, and deprecated the waste of time in watching real cricket, when they might have been better occupied in collating the weekly cricketing journals.

From *Sinister Street*, 1913.

Sir Pelham Grenville Wodehouse (1881–1975) was one of millions of schoolboys more interested in creating their own statistics than in cherishing other people's. He was a regular member of the Dulwich College side in 1899 and 1900, opening the bowling with the future Surrey and England player N. A. Knox. The school records describe him as 'a fast right-hand bowler with a good swing, though he does not use his head enough. As a bat very much improved and he gets extraordinarily well to the pitch of the ball. Has wonderfully improved in the field, though rather hampered by his sight.' In his last season at Dulwich, Wodehouse scored 48 runs in ten innings and took seven wickets for 114 runs, later using his experiences as the basis for a cricketing hero called Mike Jackson, youngest of a prolific family resembling in some respects the Fosters of Worcestershire. It was in his Mike Jackson books that Wodehouse found himself graduating inadvertently from school yarns to the adult market. In the course of his long and triumphant life he was gradually to lose his love for cricket, as we shall see, but for the moment the Dulwich fast bowler reigns supreme. Psmith in the City *opens with Mike Jackson and the eponymous hero suspended in the limbo between Public School and University.*

Mr Bickersdyke Walks behind the Bowler's Arm

CONSIDERING WHAT a prominent figure Mr John Bickersdyke was to be in Mike Jackson's life, it was only appropriate that he should make a dramatic entry into it. This he did by walking behind the bowler's arm when Mike had scored ninety-eight, causing him thereby to be clean bowled by a long-hop.

It was the last day of the Ilsworth cricket week, and the house team were struggling hard on a damaged wicket. During the first two matches of the week all had been well. Warm sunshine, true wickets, tea in the shade of the trees. But on the Thursday night, as the team champed their dinner contentedly after defeating the Incogniti by two wickets, a pattering of rain made itself heard upon the windows. By bedtime it had settled to a steady downpour. On Friday morning, when the team of the local regiment arrived in their brake, the sun was shining once more in a watery, melancholy way, but play was not possible before lunch. After lunch the bowlers were in their element. The regiment, winning the toss, put together a hundred and thirty, due principally to a last wicket stand between two enormous corporals, who swiped at everything and had luck enough for two whole teams. The house team followed with seventy-eight, of which Psmith, by his usual golf methods, claimed thirty. Mike, who had gone in first as the star bat of the side, had been run out with great promptitude off the first ball of the innings, which his partner had hit in the immediate neighbourhood of point. At close of play the regiment had made five without loss. This, on the Saturday morning, helped by another shower of rain which made the wicket easier for the moment, they had increased to a hundred and forty-eight, leaving the house just two hundred to make on a pitch which looked as if it were made of linseed.

It was during this week that Mike had first made the acquaintance of Psmith's family. Mr Smith had moved from Shropshire, and taken Ilsworth Hall in a neighbouring county. This he had done, as far as could be ascertained, simply because he had a poor opinion of Shropshire cricket. And just at the moment cricket happened to be the pivot of his life.

'My father,' Psmith had confided to Mike, meeting him at the station in the family motor on the Monday, 'is a man of vast but volatile brain. He has not that calm, dispassionate outlook on life which marks your true philosopher, such as myself. I—'

'I say,' interrupted Mike, eyeing Psmith's movements with apprehension, 'you aren't going to drive, are you?'

'Who else? As I was saying, I am like some contented spectator of a Pageant. My pater wants to jump in and stage-manage. He is a man of hobbies. He never has more than one at a time, and he never has that long. But while he has it, it's all there. When I left the house this morning he was all for cricket. But by the time we get to the ground he may have chucked cricket and taken up the Territorial Army. Don't be surprised if you find the wicket being dug up into trenches, when we arrive, and the pro. moving in echelon towards the pavilion. No,' he added, as the car turned into the drive, and they caught a glimpse of white flannels and blazers in the distance, and heard the sound of bat meeting ball, 'cricket seems still to be topping the bill. Come along, and I'll show you your room. It's next to mine, so that, if brooding on Life in the still hours of the night, I hit on any great truth, I shall pop in and discuss it with you.'

While Mike was changing, Psmith sat on his bed, and continued to discourse.

4

'I suppose you're going to the 'Varsity?' he said.

'Rather,' said Mike, lacing his boots. 'You are, of course? Cambridge, I hope. I'm going to King's.'

'Between ourselves,' confided Psmith, 'I'm dashed if I know what's going to happen to me. I am the thingummy of what's-its-name.'

'You look it,' said Mike, brushing his hair.

'Don't stand there cracking the glass,' said Psmith. 'I tell you I am practically a human three-shies-a-penny ball. My father is poising me lightly in his hand, preparatory to flinging me at one of the milky cocos of Life. Which one he'll aim at I don't know. The least thing fills him with a whirl of new views as to my future. Last week we were out shooting together, and he said that the life of the gentleman-farmer was the most manly and independent on earth, and that he had a good mind to start me on that. I pointed out that lack of early training had rendered me unable to distinguish between a threshing-machine and a mangel-wurzel, so he chucked that. He has now worked round to Commerce. It seems that a blighter of the name of Bickersdyke is coming here for the week-end next Saturday. As far as I can say without searching the Newgate Calendar, the man Bickersdyke's career seems to have been as follows. He was at school with my pater, went into the City, raked in a certain amount of doubloons—probably dishonestly—and is now a sort of Captain of Industry, manager of some bank or other, and about to stand for Parliament. The result of these excesses is that my pater's imagination has been fired, and at time of going to press he wants me to imitate Comrade Bickersdyke. However, there's plenty of time. That's one comfort. He's certain to change his mind again. Ready? Then suppose we filter forth into the arena?'

Out on the field Mike was introduced to the man of hobbies. Mr Smith, senior, was a long, earnest-looking man who might have been Psmith in a grey wig but for his obvious energy. He was as wholly on the move as Psmith was wholly statuesque. Where Psmith stood like some dignified piece of sculpture, musing on deep questions with a glassy eye, his father would be trying to be in four places at once. When Psmith presented Mike to him, he shook hands warmly with him and started a sentence, but broke off in the middle of both performances to dash wildly in the direction of the pavilion in an endeavour to catch an impossible catch some thirty yards away. The impetus so gained carried him on towards Bagley, the Ilsworth Hall ground-man, with whom a moment later he was carrying on an animated discussion as to whether he had or had not seen a dandelion on the field that morning. Two minutes afterwards he had skimmed away again. Mike, as he watched him, began to appreciate Psmith's reasons for feeling some doubt as to what would be his future walk in life.

At lunch that day Mike sat next to Mr Smith, and improved his acquaintance with him; and by the end of the week they were on excellent terms. Psmith's father had Psmith's gift of getting on well with people.

On this Saturday, as Mike buckled on his pads, Mr Smith bounded up, full of advice and encouragement.

'My boy,' he said, 'we rely on you. These others'—he indicated with a disparaging wave of the hand the rest of the team, who were visible through the window of the changing-room—'are all very well. Decent club bats. Good for a few on a billiard-table. But you're our hope on a wicket like this. I have studied cricket all my life'—till that summer it is improbable that Mr Smith had ever handled a bat—'and I know a first-class batsman when I see one. I've seen your brothers play. Pooh, you're better than any of them. That century of yours against the Green Jackets was a wonderful innings, wonderful. Now look here, my boy. I want you to be careful. We've a lot of runs to make, so we mustn't take any risks. Hit plenty of boundaries, of course, but be careful. Careful. Dash it, there's a youngster trying to climb up the elm. He'll break his neck. It's young Giles, my keeper's boy. Hi! Hi, there!'

He scudded out to avert the tragedy, leaving Mike to digest his expert advice on the art of batting on bad wickets.

Possibly it was the excellence of this advice which induced Mike to play what was, to date, the best innings of his life. There are moments when the batsman feels an almost superhuman fitness. This came to Mike now. The sun had begun to shine strongly. It made the wicket more difficult, but it added a cheerful touch to the scene. Mike felt calm and masterful. The bowling had no terrors for him. He scored nine off his first over and seven off his second, half-way through which he lost his partner. He was to undergo a similar bereavement several times that afternoon, and at frequent intervals. However simple the bowling might seem to him, it had enough sting in it to worry the rest of the team considerably. Batsmen came and went at the other end with such rapidity that it seemed hardly worth while their troubling to come in at all. Every now and then one would give promise of better things by lifting the slow bowler into the pavilion or over the boundary, but it always happened that a similar stroke, a few balls later, ended in an easy catch. At five o'clock the Ilsworth score was eighty-one for seven wickets, last man nought, Mike not out fifty-nine. As most of the house team, including Mike, were dispersing to their homes or were due for visits at other houses that night, stumps were to be drawn at six. It was obvious that they could not hope to win. Number nine on the list, who was Bagley, the ground-man, went in with instructions to play for a draw, and minute advice from Mr Smith as to how he was to do it. Mike had now begun to score rapidly, and it was not to be expected that he could change his game; but Bagley, a dried-up little man of the type which bowls for five hours on a hot August day without exhibiting any symptoms of fatigue, put a much-bound bat stolidly in front of every ball he received; and the Hall's prospects of saving the game grew brighter.

At a quarter to six the professional left, caught at very silly point for eight. The score was a hundred and fifteen, of which Mike had made eighty-five.

A lengthy young man with yellow hair, who had done some good fast bowling for the Hall during the week, was the next man in. In previous matches he had hit furiously at everything, and against the Green Jackets had knocked up forty in twenty minutes while Mike was putting the finishing touches to his century. Now, however, with his host's warning ringing in his ears, he adopted the unspectacular, or Bagley, style of play. His manner of dealing with the ball was that of one playing croquet. He patted it gingerly back to the bowler when it was straight, and left it icily alone when it was off the wicket. Mike, still in the brilliant vein, clumped a half-volley past point to the boundary, and with highly scientific late cuts and glides brought his score to ninety-eight. With Mike's score at this, the total at a hundred and thirty, and the hands of the clock at five minutes to six, the yellow-haired croquet exponent fell, as Bagley had fallen, a victim to silly point, the ball being the last of the over.

Mr Smith, who always went in last for his side, and who so far had not received a single ball during the week, was down the pavilion steps and half-way to the wicket before the retiring batsman had taken half a dozen steps.

'Last over,' said the wicket-keeper to Mike. 'Any idea how many you've got? You must be near your century, I should think.'

'Ninety-eight,' said Mike. He always counted his runs.

'By Jove, as near as that? This is something like a finish.'

Mike left the first ball alone, and the second. They were too wide of the off-stump to be hit at safely. Then he felt a thrill as the third ball left the bowler's hand. It was a long-hop. He faced square to pull it.

And at that moment Mr John Bickersdyke walked into his life across the bowling-screen.

He crossed the bowler's arm just before the ball pitched. Mike lost sight of it for a fraction of a second, and hit wildly. The next moment his leg stump was askew; and the Hall had lost the match.

'I'm sorry,' he said to Mr Smith. 'Some silly idiot walked across the screen just as the ball was bowled.'

'What!' shouted Mr Smith. 'Who was the fool who walked behind the bowler's arm?' he yelled appealingly to Space.

'Here he comes, whoever he is,' said Mike.

A short, stout man in a straw hat and a flannel suit was walking towards them. As he came nearer Mike saw that he had a hard, thin-lipped mouth, half-hidden by a rather ragged moustache, and that behind a pair of gold spectacles were two pale and slightly protruding eyes, which, like his mouth, looked hard.

'How are you, Smith,' he said.

'Hullo, Bickersdyke.' There was a slight internal struggle, and then Mr Smith ceased to be the cricketer and became the host. He chatted amiably to the new-comer.

'You lost the game, I suppose,' said Mr Bickersdyke.

The cricketer in Mr Smith came to the top again, blended now, however, with the host. He was annoyed, but restrained in his annoyance.

'I say, Bickersdyke, you know, my dear fellow,' he said complainingly, 'you shouldn't have walked across the screen. You put Jackson off, and made him get bowled.'

'The screen?'

'That curious white object,' said Mike. 'It is not put up merely as an ornament. There's a sort of rough idea of giving the batsman a chance of seeing the ball, as well. It's a great help to him when people come charging across it just as the bowler bowls.'

Mr Bickersdyke turned a slightly deeper shade of purple, and was about to reply, when what sporting reporters call 'the veritable ovation' began.

Quite a large crowd had been watching the game, and they expressed their approval of Mike's performance.

There is only one thing for a batsman to do on these occasions. Mike ran into the pavilion, leaving Mr Bickersdyke standing.

From *Psmith in the City*, 1910.

Do writers like Wodehouse tend to exaggerate the importance of cricket? A revealing response to this eternal question has been provided by the American historian Barbara Tuchman, who, in writing The Proud Tower, *a portrait of the world before the War, 1890–1914, disclosed an interesting fact about Henry Mayers Hyndman (1842–1921). Hyndman was an old Etonian and a cosmopolitan gentleman who, having been converted to the cause of revolution by Karl Marx in person, formed the Socialist Democratic Federation, and was reported by Bernard Shaw as saying 'I could not carry on unless I expected the revolution at ten o'clock next Monday morning'. The same impatience appears to have blighted Hyndman's considerable skill as a cricketer. He played several times for Sussex, and in 1864, the year of the great disappointment which Miss Tuchman records, scored two half-centuries for the county side.*

HYNDMAN COMPLAINED of the peculiarly British technique by which the ruling class absorbed rising labour leaders who proved only too willing to sell out to the dominant minority (that is, the Liberals) after they had 'obtained their education from well-to-do Socialists who have been sacrificing themselves for their sake'. The tone suggests some justification for the friends who said that Hyndman, a cricketer, had adopted Socialism out of spite against the world because he was not included in the Cambridge eleven.

From *The Proud Tower*, 1966.

A year after Hyndman's rebuff, W. G. Grace scored his first first-class century, and by 1872 was spreading the gospel of the game around the Empire. One of Grace's cronies was Robert A. Fitzgerald (1834–1881), honorary secretary of the MCC from 1863 until ill-health obliged him to stand down in 1877. Fitzgerald did much to improve amenities at Lord's, both on and off the field; Sir Pelham Warner describes him as 'sagacious, cheery and amusing', and Grace adds that he was 'an assiduous and energetic official'. He must also have been intrepid, for in 1872 he took a side to Canada, for which Grace performed prodigies, off the field as well as on, as Fitzgerald describes.

IT MUST not be supposed that the Twelve were allowed to subside into private life on leaving the cricket ground; their real work commenced with the last ball bowled. Cards were found on the table when they returned to their hotel, with the inscription,

BANQUET
to the
GENTLEMEN OF ENGLAND,
August 22nd, 1872, Montreal.

It was sumptuously carried out. After dinner, the President indulged in a speech, the political bias of which provoked hostile demonstrations; and at one time the Captain, who sat next him, was in expectation of an apple or other missile intended for the worthy President. However, a calmer tone soon prevailed, and the toast of the evening, 'The English Cricketers', met with the heartiest reception. The Captain delivered Speech No. 2. It was a comprehensive speech; it dealt with the past; it played with the present; it prophesied pleasantly of the future; it complimented everybody; it did not forget himself; it left out, as most speeches impromptu do, all the good points it had carefully prepared; it gave utterance to other good things it would never have thought of but for the champagne and company around. It had one great merit; it soon came to an end. Great confusion prevailed in the company as to the particular people who should reply to the toasts. Canada is evidently a country of orators. Everybody speaks at a public meeting, not unfrequently everybody at once. Appleby was called on to reply for the 'Navy', we never discovered why, unless the slight connection between bowline and bowling secured him the honour. He unaffectedly alluded to his services on the sea, better known to others than to himself, and after quoting several of Dibdin's odes sat down amidst general applause. The speech of the evening was W. G.'s. It had been looked forward to with impatience, not to say a tinge of envy, by the Eleven. He replied to the toast of the 'Champion Batsman of Cricketdom'. He said, 'Gentlemen, I beg to thank you for the honour you have done me; I never saw better bowling than I have seen today, and I hope to see as good wherever I go'. The speech took longer to deliver than you might imagine from its brevity, but it was greeted with applause from all who were in a proper position to hear it. . . .

As we have previously hinted, cricket presented by no means the only field of action where the Twelve exhibited themselves and their prowess. 'Knife and Fork' was played at Ottawa in the Parliament Square. The banquet was of the most recherché character. Tables were laid in a capacious tent. The arrangements were perfect, even to the proverbial shower which always falls on public dinners in the open air. The tent let in a little rain, which soon evaporated in steam under the warmth of British and Canadian eloquence. Mr Wright presided. He gave the usual loyal toasts. The speaker was fervid and his periods were rounded—too much so, perhaps, as his turn to speak came round very often. The Captain was emotional, but he spoke from the heart, and he may be excused a little warmth, as the ventilation was by no means good, and the occasion was a good one for a stump-orator. W. G. made his second speech; he said, 'Gentlemen, I beg to thank you for the honour you have done me. I never saw a better ground than I have seen today, and I hope to see as good wherever I go'. A similiarity may be traced to his Montreal speech, but that does not affect its originality to a different audience. The chairman had got into a difficulty as to sex in a classical allusion to the three Graces. He did not bring it in very cleverly, and Gilbert was puzzled how to reply, but taking the allusion as intended for the female portion of his family, he was understood to regret that his sisters were not present to return thanks for themselves. . . .

The Twelve were invited to a grand banquet given by the members of the Royal Canadian Yacht Club, whose club-house is on the shore of Lake Ontario. W. G. was of course called upon, and replied in speech No. 3 (see pages 52, &c; and for 'bowling' and 'ground' read 'batting' and you have it). . . .

In Hamilton Mr Swinyard entertained the Twelve at his house, and a large party assembled to do honour to the occasion. A few speeches were delivered, or it would not have been a Canadian banquet. W. G. uttered his fourth; this time in reply for 'The Ladies'. It was breaking new ground for the Unapproachable; but he acquitted himself with his usual brevity, and reading 'ladies' for 'bat, ball, and ground', and consulting his previous orations, you will have speech number four in its integrity. . . .

A dinner at the Travellers' introduced the Twelve to many of the leading sportsmen of New York. A very pleasant evening was spent. Hearty toasts were given and responded to. W. G. was, of course, put up once more. He was rather at a loss for something new, but luckily bethought him of the last thing in season—so for 'Batting, Bowling, Ground, and Ladies', read 'oysters' this time, and Speech No. 5 lies before you. . . .

From *Wickets in the West*, 1873.

Fitzgerald's account is suffused with the larky high spirits of an overgrown Victorian schoolboy, but diarists like him tended to minimise the more horrific aspects of such a tour. A much later writer, Jack Fingleton (b. 1908), has been one of the few reporters of the jet-age to cast himself back imaginatively into the situation of a cricketer of Fitzgerald's era, and to consider the awesome challenge of inter-continental travel. We will be meeting Fingleton again later in his capacity of shrewd and scrupulously fair judge of cricketing politics, but for the moment, here he is casting himself out on to the inhospitable waters of the late nineteenth century.

On the Strain of Cricket Travel

'Travel crowds a Test tour in Australia and imposes a tremendous strain upon the players.' So said MCC captain F. R. Brown at the end of the 1950–51 tour of Australia, in which all travelling was by air.*

IT WAS January 13, 1885. Arthur Shrewsbury's team of Englishmen had just finished a match against a batch of 22 at Candelo, on the far south coast of New South Wales. The next game, also against a team of 22, was against the Shoalhaven district at Nowra.

A crow would have made quick work of the distance between Candelo and Nowra, but on such a day it would have been difficult to get the crow to try. The sky was black and intensely moody; the wind was on the make; and the band of Englishmen looked apprehensively at the little steamer of 500 tons as they gathered on the wharf at Tathra. Bags of potatoes and numbers of squealing pigs were being hustled aboard.

No road over the mountains connected Candelo and Nowra. A long sea trip of 200 miles to Sydney in the slow little vessel lay ahead of the Englishmen; and the irony of the business was that they would have to cover more than half that distance again as they came south by train and coach back to Nowra. They had one hope—a tentative arrangement had been made that, if conditions were suitable, a Government tug

*Brown's team grew to 19 when Tattersall and Statham were flown out from England. With such numbers, Brown and the leading professionals took it in turns to have a week's rest. Brown went to a sheep station. Hutton sailed leisurely from Sydney to Adelaide between the Third and Fourth Tests.

would put to sea off the mouth of the Shoalhaven River, tranship the cricketers, and bring them in to Nowra. But the weather made that arrangement seem very unlikely.

The captain of the little coastal tub met the cricketers as they came aboard, putting their cricket bags under a big spread of tarpaulin.

'Sorry to give you such a nasty day, Mr. Shrewsbury,' said the captain. 'I'm afraid, too, it will get worse. I don't think we will be seeing that tug.'

The weather did get worse. Land was soon lost to view in the low clouds and pelting rain. The winds lashed into stinging spray the tops of large Pacific rollers. Terrified, the pigs in their pens squealed louder and louder.

The English cricketers huddled like a group of bedraggled fowls under what cover the bridge could give. All were violently sea-sick. Lunch-time came and went with nobody venturing below to the pokey little dining-room. In fact, the odours from there made them the more wretched.

About mid-afternoon a sailor approached Shrewsbury.

'Message from the cap'n, sir,' he said. 'We are about off the Shoal-haven now but the skipper doesn't think the tug will come out.'

Shrewsbury grunted. He didn't care much what happened. Long ago he had cursed the little steamer, the tug, the Shoalhaven, and the very cricket tour of Australia. Also the squealing, squawking pigs. He wished, with all his heart, that he had left Australian tours to the one he had made five years earlier. On this January day there would be a big, roaring fire in the Trent Bridge Inn and he could have been standing there, pewter pot of ale in hand, yarning with his fellows of the Nottinghamshire eleven.

There remained eight hours more of this bouncing, jolting voyage to Sydney. It was almost dark now, but the passengers could see the rollers coming and could brace themselves against their charge. It would be worse in the dark, pitching and plunging; but even this could be preferable to changing at sea into the tug and then bouncing shorewards.

Shrewsbury had neither the heart nor stomach for anything more. He grimaced when he thought of his stomach. It had let him down long ago. In its place was a ball of pain. He wasn't exactly scared—just sick, sick of everything.

Five minutes later the same sailor came to him.

'The skipper would like to know, sir,' he said, 'if you could come up on the bridge and see him?'

Shrewsbury nodded. Holding tight to stanchions and rails, he timed his wobbly feet to the pitch of the vessel and scrambled up slippery steps to the bridge.

The engines had been cut down. Straining eyes on the bridge were sweeping the sea for a sight of the tug. There was now little daylight left.

'I'm afraid I will have to take you on to Sydney, Mr. Shrewsbury,' said the captain. 'I don't think the tug has come out. And I don't blame 'em, do you?'

Shrewsbury agreed. But just then came a shout, 'Tug on the starboard bow, sir.'

They looked and there, dimly, was the tug, a minute affair, riding high one moment and out of sight in the trough the next. Shrewsbury was sure he had seen bigger pleasure craft on the Trent.

The steamer changed course and lurched towards the tug but, obviously, it wouldn't be possible to get close.

Shaw, the English manager, was now on the bridge. He and Shrewsbury looked at each other, doubt and apprehension in their eyes.

'What about it, gentlemen?' asked the sea-captain.

'What do you think?' asked Shaw.

'It will be a difficult job getting you across,' said the skipper, 'but the tug has come out—and it will save you many more hours of this. I'll give it a go, if you will.'

England's cricket fields seemed to belong to another world as Shaw and Shrewsbury talked matters over. 'I think we should try it, Alfred,' said Shrewsbury, and added with a wry grin, 'if we go down, we take the honours of the rubber with us.' (They had already won Tests at Adelaide and Melbourne.)

Shaw turned to the captain. 'Very well,' he said, 'we are willing to try it.'

They slipped and stumbled back to their fellows beneath the bridge. 'We are going to the tug,' said Shaw. 'Each man will take his cricket bag and be responsible for it. And—England expects that every man in the next half-hour or so will do his duty.'

Shaw counted out six men to do the first trip—himself, Read, Bates, Flowers, Briggs and Ulyett. They formed a line across the deck and handed six bags into the lifeboat, swaying on its davits.

'Just a minute, Johnny,' called Shrewsbury to Briggs. It had suddenly crossed Shrewsbury's mind that Briggs had hit 121 in the First Test. No need to throw discretion to the winds and the sea altogether. It would be policy to divide his stars. He pulled Briggs back and pushed the stonewaller Scotton to the deck-rail.

The davits were now letting the lifeboat down. Deftly, with their oars, the crew kept it from smashing against the side of the parent vessel; and then, again, when it hit the water.

Two by two, the cricketers stood on the rail, reached for the davits, and then went smartly, hand under hand and legs entwined around the ropes, to the craft below.

Smartly, ever so smartly, the davits were cast off, and away went the lifeboat from the lee of the steamer. The remaining cricketers could barely watch as the cockle-shell ran up and down and, sometimes, out of view. They feared for their fellows; they feared, even more, for their own turn, soon to come.

A Yorkshireman, Joe Hunter, was the only one who didn't cheer when, finally, the six cricketers were seen on the deck of the tug and the lifeboat appeared again from the other side of the tug. Joe had lost his voice completely!

Back came the lifeboat and huddled in the lee of the steamer. Oars were out again to hold it from smashing on the side. This time the cricket bags were slung overboard and the remaining six cricketers prepared to slide down the ropes. Joe Hunter, with Shrewsbury, stood near the rail, ready to go over.

'Are you all safe down there?' Joe called to the lifeboat.

'Yes.'

'Well,' said Joe, 'you stay where you are and I'm going to stay where I am.' He meant every word. He spoke from the bottom of his heart.

W. Barnes was another who declined to move at the last moment.

Off went the cockle-shell, back it safely came and was hauled aboard. The steamer tooted, the tug tooted, and each went its way, soon lost to the view of the other.

In less than an hour, the 10 Englishmen had landed at Nowra.

Hunter and Barnes continued their nightmare journey to Sydney, 90 miles away. Next day, still sore and ill from the voyage, they caught a train to go some 90 miles to Moss Vale. There they entered a coach to ride 50 miles over a bumping, winding track down the mountains. 'Keep an eye out,' the coachman told Hunter, as he shut the door on him. 'There may be bushrangers about.'

Twenty-one hours after they had left their comrades, Barnes and Hunter saw them again in Nowra. When Bobby Peel saw them he squealed like a pig, climbed to the cross-bars of a lamp-post and, assuming a voice stricken with terror, called out to Hunter, 'You stay where you are; I'm going to stay where I am.'

From *Masters of Cricket*, 1958.

Contemporary with his fellow-Australian Fingleton is Ray Robinson (b. 1908), author of several books of cricket essays and an award-winning collective biography of every man ever to captain Australia. Among Robinson's heroes is one of the members of the amazing Trott family.

Postman's Knock

G. H. S. Trott

IF A boy with a talent for sport asked which job would most help fit him for international rank what would you suggest? Vocational guidance could scarcely recommend an occupation more favourable than postman. Long daily walks are just what the doctor orders for everyone these days. Uphill, downdale, upwind, downwind, delivering letters gives leg-strengthening exercise in sunshine and shower while the lungs gratefully breathe air as fresh as the locality permits. To back theory with fact, one of cricket's most-admired captains, Harry Trott, was a postman. As an equivalent of a private's knapsack holding a field-marshal's baton Trott's leather bag held letters stamped with names of places which his skill as a player and gifts as a skipper would take him to see.

Born in the Melbourne inner suburb of Collingwood on 5 August 1866, George Henry Stevens Trott was the third of eight children of Adolphus Trott. Stevens was his mother's maiden name. Scouts who saw Harry at 17 playing with park juniors, the Capulets, recruited him to South Melbourne in 1885. At 20 he scored 200 for South against St Kilda and in his first intercolonial match for Victoria was as cool as the underside of a cucumber. It was the first time a youth making his debut at Adelaide Oval had hit George Giffen over the heads of on-lookers standing outside the chain that then marked the leg boundary.

Rapidly developing into Victoria's most attractive batsman, he scored mainly in front of the wicket, yet his late-cuts were close to perfection. Bowlers grew to fear a swinging-on drive that often he was not afraid to lift. 'Let his side be under the whip and you see him at his best', said Giffen. 'He wields a wide blade and no matter how he may stonewall he

17

never loses his elegance of style.' Harry folded his shirtsleeves as formally as banquet serviettes around elbows that knew how to bend after a hot day's play.

A man of middle height, 175 cm (5ft 9in), he weighed 70 kg (11st) when he made 0 on his Test debut at twenty-one. At 22 he set Sydney talking by scoring 172 for the 1888 Australian XI against New South Wales. At 23 he married buxom Violet Hodson at Fitzroy in February 1890 before his second successful tour of England and New Zealand. By the mid-twenties he was one of those fuller figures in flannels, like Queensland all-rounder Tom Veivers in the 1960s.

His wide well-nourished moustache could never mask his good-natured smile but batsmen had no right to expect Australia's best leg-spinner to be friendly to them at the wicket. When a young batsman hit a slow leg-side full-toss to the fence Harry commended him with 'I see you know how to deal with that rubbish'. Not long afterward a ball that looked similar but had different flight yielded a catch in the outfield. 'That first one was to give you confidence, son', he told the batsman. 'The next was to teach you a lesson.' Like later spinners Mailey and Fleetwood-Smith, he put wicket-taking before economy. It was hard to get much turn from Sydney tracks as shiny as the marble pillars of the GPO but, varying pace and flight, he obtained whip from the pitch. At Leicester on his third tour, 1893, he made 100 in 130 minutes and took 11 wickets.

Driving at Lancashire spinner Johnny Briggs, Trott was stumped while scrambling back but Umpire West ruled him not out. Harry repeated the shot next ball and walked to the pavilion. Tackled about having thrown his wicket away, he replied 'Little Briggsy had bowled himself inside out trying to trap me. Why should he be robbed because West was out late last night?'

Trott's fielding at point caused the position to be called strong-point when he occupied it. His interceptions earned the imprecations of square-cutting forerunners, Barnes, Burge, Stackpole and Walters.

In days when few grounds had shower facilities, tired cricketers soaked in baths. When Trott climbed out and towelled himself the first thing he put on was his felt hat. Harry was instantly recognizable by this habit regardless of other unveiled means of identification.

Trott captained Victoria with striking success and not always with the best sides to handle. He was 28 when he sent an English XI in and won by seven wickets. His eight wickets for 63 in 1895 still form the best average for Victoria against an English Test side.

When some other public servants complained about the frequent absence of Trott the postal chief replied 'Harry Trott is a national institution'.

On four tours of England from 1888 to 1896 he exceeded 1,000 runs on each visit and totalled 145 wickets. Six of his ten centuries were made there. Yet it is as captain that he is best remembered, an understanding judge of human nature and character. Studying players' whims and fancies, he got the best out of his men. Firmly bound by the cords of his good nature, they grew fond of this genial man, never known to have a downright quarrel with a player. They called him Trotty or Joe and all were resolved never to let him down.

Harry's quizzical grey eyes missed nothing, or if they did no other eyes spotted it. His seemingly drowsy top lids deceived nobody once play began. The more intense the battle the more flexible his mind became. He gave the impression of being a more intuitive captain than the others. Intuition impelled him to act promptly without waiting for confirmation. Dumping the textbook, some called it. If he did act on hunches they were the sort of hunches endorsed by his teams, beneficiaries of his quick perception and subtlety of strategy.

We have the word of fellow players that, himself a regular bowler, he had a fuller knowledge than batsman-captains of his bowlers' powers and limitations. They felt his handling showed a closer understanding of the arduous nature of their work. He changed them more frequently, for their own and their side's benefit, knowing the value of nursing them to keep them at their best. Players thought him an uncanny judge of who was likeliest to get most out of the pitch whichever way the turf was behaving—not only which wicket but which end. Far from being an egotist who bowled too much, he gave himself an average of a dozen overs a Test innings. When his tossed leg-breaks separated pairs who had frustrated other bowlers he would promptly bring on someone else to carry on the good work. In his Test career he took 29 wickets and 21 catches in 24 matches; in addition to making 921 runs.

By direction of an Australian Cricket Council the selectors chose the 1896 team early before the season's main games. One result was the staggering omission of cheerful Albert Trott, who at 21 had made a match-winning debut in the 1895 Adelaide Test when Harry was twenty-eight. Middlesex snapped up Albert, who quickly won recognition as one of the world's best all-rounders.

Though not eager to undertake the captaincy Harry Trott accepted election by the players. Several of his team came from higher up the social scale and had the advantage of better education. Among them were three college boys, an engineer, a solicitor, a secretary and a bank officer. As usual, there was no room for class distinction when they elected this cricket-wise postman their skipper, a man of personality and homespun humour, the Will Rogers of cricketers. One of the college boys, Clem Hill, said, 'As a captain Harry Trott was in a class by himself—the best I ever played under'. (Before he became captain himself Hill played for his country under Trott, Darling, Trumble and Noble, and for his State under Giffen.) Hill continued:

> Harry was quick to grasp a situation. He saw an opponent's weakness in a second. He knew in a moment when a crack bowler was having an off day. Time and again he got a champion batsman's wicket by putting on a bowler whom he knew the batsman did not like. His seeming experiments were not confined to lesser games. Confident in his own convictions, he applied them in Tests.

In his book *The Golden Age of Cricket* Robert Trumble, one of Hugh's sons, says his father found Trott in every way a born leader.

> In the opinion of many players associated with him, Australia never had a better captain and, with his understanding of the personalities and problems of members of his team he had a unique advantage over some later leaders of Australia's Test elevens.

When he became captain at 29 Australian enthusiasm for international cricket had waned from its early fervour under Gregory and Murdoch. England had won 19 to seven of the preceding 30 Tests. To tour Britain with a team of 14 containing nine players new to English conditions was called ridiculous.

When Hill dropped Grace at 40 off Trott's bowling he shamefacedly told his skipper he was sorry. Trott: 'Don't let that upset you, son. Every one on this field has dropped catches. Better luck next time!' He spilt few himself—and never missed a chance for a practical joke. Nothing seemed to upset him. Going to bat in a game at Lord's he put a lighted cigar aside. The next man scarcely had his pads on when Harry returned, out first ball. He calmly walked to pick up the cigar, saying 'Glad it hasn't gone out'. Mostly he smoked a pipe with a bowl like an embryo incinerator.

A ball bowled by Ernie Jones against Marylebone Cricket Club at Lord's knocked a sparrow to the ground. Onlookers called 'Kill it, kill it.' A man ran on the field to end the injured bird's suffering. As he approached the sparrow flew away (more fortunate than the swallow that deflected a ball from Greg Chappell on to John Inverarity's middle stump at Adelaide in 1969). On the eve of a Test Harry remarked to Jones that critics were saying he was losing some of his pace, leaving England's Tom Richardson the fastest bowler of the year. Jones replied 'I'll show them tomorrow Joe, that they are a bit out in their reckoning'. The conversation was Trott's way of bringing his speedman up to concert pitch.

Against Richardson's phenomenal bowling at Lord's on the fastest wicket for weeks Harry was one of five out for blobs in Australia's calamitous 53. The second innings was slumping until Trott and Syd Gregory astonished all by the effrontery of their batting. In face of impending defeat on a pitch where 13 Australian wickets had gone for 120 they clapped on 90 in 65 minutes. Bowlers who had been on top saw the ball faring no better than a watchdog's nose against a postman's boot. The intransigent pair carried on to 221 at almost 80 an hour. Their fourth-wicket stand could not win the Test but batting of such valiant quality set the series aglow, assuring success for the tour. Trott's 143 was his highest Test innings.

A notoriously nervous starter, tall Frank Iredale was depressed by low scores. One morning at Trent Bridge Trott told this teetotaller, 'Look here, Noss, what you need is a tonic. I often have one myself. I'll mix you one.' Iredale had just buckled on his pads to open an innings when Harry brought him an unidentified drink. The result reminded the watching team of the fable of the mouse that, after drinking spilt whisky, squeaked 'Now bring out your cats!'. Iredale batted at his best. Repeats of the prescription brought more successes, including 108 in an Old Trafford Test. Not until long afterwards did Trott let anyone know it was brandy and soda.

Doubts about the propriety of choosing an Indian in England's team caused the authorities to write asking whether the Australians had any objection. Captain and manager said they would be pleased to allow Ranjitsinhji to play, accepting that he was part of English cricket. They saw Ranji scintillate for 154 not out, highest innings of the three-Test series.

Having noticed that Grace's footwork at 48 was becoming laboured and Stoddart, 36, had not played leg-breaks well, Darling suggested that in the second innings of a Manchester Test Harry should go on opposite Jones for the first over against the breeze. While others stared at a slow leg-spinner sharing a new ball, his fieldsmen reckoned it would be a rewarding innovation. Confronted so soon with leg-spin, both batsmen floundered and Jim Kelly stumped them in Trott's first two overs.

Tossing the ball to Trumble, Harry said, 'I felt I could wheedle those two out, now you have a go'.

When seven batsmen's failures at Old Trafford left wicketkeeper Kelly to help Trumble get 27 runs to win against the dreaded Richardson, Trott could watch no longer. Boarding a cab outside the ground, he told the cabby to drive anywhere. It was the only time the team knew Trott had nerves like the rest of them.

Trott's team adopted a couple of music-hall ditties. One from The Country Girl was 'Peace, peace, let us have peace!'. When a wicket fell, a group of fielders awaiting the next batsman would sing a parody

> 'Peace, peace, two innings apiece,
> But nobody stayed very long.'

MacLaren told them he would give anything to play the game as keenly yet as light-heartedly as they did. They used to tease England's star cover-point, Gilbert Jessop, if they got a single by him.

Not even a collapse for 18 depressed Harry. The slump caused Spofforth, then living in London, to come to the Oval to commiserate. 'Terrible isn't it', Trott agreed. 'Things could hardly be worse. But tell me, Spoff, are there any decent leg shows on at the theatres?'

On a fiery track Jones was so alarming that Yorkshire batsmen unashamedly declined singles that would have made them face his next over. Seeing Moorhouse struck on the thigh, the crowd began chorusing 'Tek 'im off, Trott!'. As if heeding them, Harry threw the ball to Charles Eady. On so unfriendly a pitch the Tasmanian giant was almost as dangerous. The crowd protested anew. Moorhouse, waving his bat at Trott, objected 'Tha tek off wonn and put on 'nother fasst as t'other'.

Wisden felt that even in a season of ill-fortune he would have earned just as great a reputation: 'Blessed with a humour that nothing could ruffle, he was always master both of himself and his team, whatever the position of the game'. It says much for his leadership that the tour should have risen above reactions to the deliveries of Jones and spinner Tom McKibbin. *Wisden* classed their bowling actions as unfair and noted that no umpire called them.

Under Trott's benign captaincy and theatre director Harry Musgrove's management the 1896 team regained prestige that Australian cricket in England had not enjoyed for a dozen years. Their play in a well-contested rubber proved that a tour could be an over-all success without being boosted by triumph (England won two Tests to one, though Grace said luckily). They finished 25 of their 34 first-class matches in Britain where their skipper allowed himself only one game off. They continued to be a happy band throughout 11 more games in the United States and New Zealand on their way home. The Boston *Transcript* sent a reporter to Philadelphia to ask the captain had the Australians ever heard of baseball. Trott: 'Of course we have'. Reporter: 'Then why don't you play it?' Trott: 'Running around in circles makes us giddy'.

Booking rail sleepers between Chicago and San Francisco Harry and his men could not buy single berths but had to pay for two, with the right to resell one. Iredale said:

> The embarrassing thing about the sleeping arrangement is one never knows who your neighbour is, male or female. Well, cricketers are not bashful as a rule but it is, to say the least, rather uncomfortable to find your upper or lower berth inhabited by a female! Considering that one has to disrobe behind the same curtain, the privileges are stretched rather too far.

Yet they have been calling the 1970s the permissive age!

From the Maoris' ceremonial haka Harry Trott quickly borrowed something to round off his response to NZ mayors and other dignitaries who proposed the team's health. After voicing his side's appreciation, he stepped a pace forward and, imitating the traditional invocation to a haka, exclaimed 'What's the matter with the Mayor of Invercargill?'. In unison the team replied 'He's all right'. Trott: 'Who's all right?' The team chorused 'The Mayor of Invercargill'.

His players had admired his natural ease of manner as he chatted in London with the Prince of Wales (later Edward VII) who wound up a long talk by handing him a cigar. Asked what he had done with this, Harry replied, 'I smoked it', to the surprise of some who thought it should have been preserved as a souvenir. This led to a practical joke on his return to Melbourne. He handed a friend a butt of a cigar which he said had been smoked by the Prince. Others were given similar butts, each being begged not to mention it in case it aroused jealousy. When that request was broken, it came out that he had collected the souvenirs from ashtrays the night before the ship berthed.

Harry often put on hypnotic acts on ships and at parties. Once he fixed heavy-lidded eyes on a young man and made occult passes with his hands. The man appeared to sink into a trance. When Trott ended his hypnotism and told him to come to, there was no response. Trott slapped him, pricked him with a pin. The man did not move. Fearing the mesmeric effect had been overdone, Trott went to call a doctor.

This satisfied the young man who got up and walked off, grinning. English batsmen, however, did not find it easy to laugh off the hypnotic effect of Trott's flighted leg-breaks.

Harry Trott was Australia's Man of the 90s. With the deference of worshippers at a shrine, men taking their families to the beach would pause outside his double-fronted weatherboard house, 40 Phillipson Street, Albert Park, three doors from Marine Parade. They murmured good wishes before moving on. Harry's home was conveniently situated 200 paces from the Victoria Hotel with its shady colonnade.

Players who had brought a revival of interest were still being paid only £15 a match despite a leap in profits. Before the Englishmen arrived in 1897 five South Australians signed a request for £200 for the five-Test series. Parleys with the Melbourne Cricket Club and Sydney ground trustees lifted pay to £25 a Test. (There it stood for 23 years until after World War I when it was raised to £30 a Test.)

Called a 'team of all the talents' Stoddart's side was regarded as unbeatable. Yet Trott led Australia to win four Tests out of five. His tactics included rapid changes of bowling to prevent batsmen settling down and new field settings. Ranji called him the finest tactician ever to skipper a side.

Editors castigated the public for showing no interest in a convention of 50 politicians discussing federation of the colonies. Another editorial defended the people for preferring the cricket, saying 'Our cricketing eleven forms the best example of Federation yet achieved . . . We believe Harry Trott and his ten good men and true have done more for the federation of Australian hearts than all the big delegates put together.'

Fielding with cheetah-like speed, the side stirred the crowds to roars of admiration. The dash and anticipation of Jones at mid-off and Syd Gregory at cover enabled Trott to do without an extra-cover and place him elsewhere. Horan described Trott's team as 'the finest combination of players I have ever seen in action. They played as if the eleven had one mind and that a master-mind of cricket.' Trott is the only skipper who has ordered England to follow-on in three consecutive Tests. He had the luck to win three of the five tosses and it stuck with him when smoke from bushfires around Melbourne was densest when the Englishmen batted.

Wicketkeeper in five Tests against him, William Storer gave reasons why English professionals did not think much of Trott's captaincy: 'I like a captain to have a settled plan. He just seemed to do whatever he thought of at the moment. Some of our chaps found it rather upsetting.'

Very likely. With all due disrespect to orthodox strategy every one of his eight Tests as skipper was finished, with a winning ratio of five to three.

The eupeptic skipper's girth grew until at 102 kg (16st) he was likened to Falstaff in bulk as well as humour, though never near Colin Milburn's top weight. Carrying so much made Trott subject to over-heating. He suffered sunstroke at Sydney in 1898 and lost the sight of one eye before his last Test innings, 18, at the age of 32. An ailment that baffled doctors left him with phobias that unhinged his reason. That such a warm-hearted member of the brotherhood of man should be so afflicted—with pitiless cruelties soon to rend the Trott family—strained orthodox beliefs. They were the sort of outrageous incongruities that today could support Nobel Prize laureate Jacques Monod's contention that much occurs through the mindless workings of chance, not by direction that could be called divine. After a long period in a mental hospital Trott went to Bendigo, a semi-invalid.

Love of cricket helped him fight back to strength and sanity. In 1902 he strolled on to Bendigo United Cricket Club's ground and asked could he join in net practice. Within weeks he was scoring well for the Buccs, the club that later produced the Nagel twins. After six years out of first-class cricket Trott reappeared as Victoria's captain against the English XI in 1904. In his last big match for his State against another English side in 1908 at the age of 41 he took 5 for 116. At 44 he headed both South Melbourne's averages, for the fifth time as batsman and third as bowler. No all-rounder has since approached this, though Bill Cornelius, John Shaw and Keith Kendall have topped South's batting six times.

A few days before Trott turned 48 came the shock of the pistol-in-mouth suicide of Albert, 41, mistakenly believing he had cancer. A week later World War I began carnage in which younger relatives and friends were dying. The man who was everybody's friend died gauntly at 51 on 9 November 1917 while slaughter on the Western Front was bereaving millions. Men from other States hurried to pay respect to a leader all admired. M. A. Noble arrived from Sydney in time to be a pallbearer. As the cortege moved from Albert Park towards Brighton cemetery it became greater at every part of the journey.

Trott's only child had been eight when his father's first illness began this harrowing chapter of events, which unsettled his son, leaving him irresolute. Harry's daughter-in-law Myrtle and his widow Violet were left to bring up seven grandchildren. The Victorian Cricket Association gave Violet Trott £1 a week pension for life and Myrtle went out to work to feed her family. One evening in the depression of the 1930s a passer-by saw half a dozen girls and boys playing against a pole in a street, waiting for their mother's return from work. They were using one of Harry Trott's bats, autographed by Grace, Ranji and others but split at the bottom from contact with the road. The stranger asked who they were. After Myrtle came home he called and paid her £50 for the bat. 'We ate on that for a year', one grandchild told me.

Despite that traumatic trough in the family's history Harry Trott's spirit lives on today. Now married, one of the street players, Mrs Frankie Brown, is a vivacious and popular A Grade rink skipper in Albert Park bowls.

At 15 great-grandson Stuart Trott batted throughout Frankston Colts' innings for 104 not out against Baxter one Saturday morning. Driven to Mornington, he kicked seven goals that afternoon against Chelsea's under-16 team. As a 19-year-old police trainee he appeared as a St Kilda winger in the Victorian Football League and won the 1972 club championship at 24 after two years as runner-up. He is named after the flotilla leader *Stuart* in which his father (G. H. S. Trott II) served in World War II. Stuart gave up cricket for professional running and football because the earnings were a greater help toward home-buying by a young married man with two daughters. As a star in football finals he has sped along the wing before crowds up to 120,000, four times as large as any that cheered his famous forebear.

From *On Top Down Under*, 1975.

Not all touring players were involved on the same exalted level as men like Grace and Trott. When the English colonised the earth, cricket came in the baggage train of the conquerors, and to this day a schoolboy need have no difficulty in remembering where the British Empire was once located; wherever cricket flourishes today, there was the Empire. And it flourishes in some surprising places. Arthur Grimble (1888–1956), having placed himself at the disposal of the Edwardian Foreign Office, soon found himself in the Gilbert and Ellice Islands, where he eventually became the British Resident. Cricket flowered under the Pacific sun, even if its blooms were a little unexpected.

THE BEGINNINGS of cricket in the Pacific were not invariably attended by the spirit of brotherhood that this noble sport was once believed to inspire. Something went wrong from the start in Samoa, for example. A match there was an affair of hundreds, not elevens; no tally of sides was kept, no amiable warnings of visits were issued; one village simply arose on a day and set forth to give battle to another. 'Battle' is the key word. The marching crowd paraded around the village of its chosen enemies with taunts and brandished bats until these emerged to accept the challenge. The bats, which were made of local hardwood and weighed eleven pounds apiece, were carved into shapes suited at once to conditions of war and peace. Competition was so terrific in the field that winning was a hazardous business. The position of the batsman who scored the winning hit was peculiarly trying. His was the heart of oak who, ringed around by a hoard of furious fieldsmen, dared slog his side to victory. Those earliest Samoan matches lasted for weeks at a time and often ended in considerable slaughter. It was excellent for courage but poor for the moral score-board. The Missions rather understandably banned the game for their converts as one unsuitable for aspiring Christians, however militant their church. But I think it had been revived on more neighbourly lines by the early nineteen-hundreds.

Cricket was certainly going strong on Ocean Island when I arrived there. In the fair-weather season from late March to early October, there were a dozen or more native police out for practice every day from

27

4 pm to sundown, and either a pick-up game or a match with the Company's team billed for every Saturday at 2.30 pm. The Old Man had notions derived from the very choicest public schools of his epoch about how often an officer and gentleman of the European staff should turn up at the nets. Every day, barring acts of God or the Resident Commissioner, was the rule for a good little cadet. It was lucky for me, in the circumstances, that I dearly loved the game for its own sake.

The cricket field was still very much in the making at that time. Starting with little but a pitch of tamped earth, over which a strip of coconut matting was laid, Methven and his prisoners had gradually cleared and levelled about three acres of stony flat around it on the Residency plateau. He heartily despised cricket, but he wanted a parade ground for his police. The south and west sides commanded a tremendous view of the Pacific, while palms and forest trees screened the north and east boundaries; but a dozen years were yet to run before any kind of grass began to grow cheerfully on that torrid waste of phosphate dust and rock. Every known variety was tried, and practically everything throve in the wet season, but nothing survived more than a month of the dry spell. When the effort was abandoned after many failures, the flat was triumphantly invaded by the tussocky grass of the island. That looked better to the ladies, but the man never lived who could drive a clean ball through more than sixty yards of it. The consequence was, we all became deliberate moonshooters and cowshotters. It was deeply immoral cricket and, for that very reason, highly amusing. Nevertheless, I preferred the stone age, when a batsman could score along the ground and even a wicked fluke off the edge of the bat could roll as sweetly (for me) to the boundary as the most accomplished leg glance.

The Company had an all-Australian team; the Government could put only two or three Europeans in the field; but half a dozen policemen —and especially the Fijian NCOs—batted and bowled well up to the best of an average English club eleven. Despite that, I don't remember our ever winning a Government–Company Test rubber (for of course we played five Test Matches a season). It struck me then, and I verified it later in other places, how notably higher the performance of average Australian cricketers was, age for age, than that of their English equivalents. But the ale we drank together after five hours of it under the equatorial sun tasted no less sweet for that. Maybe that was because the Australian ale was almost as good as the Australian cricket, and Australian good fellowship even better than either or both.

The Old Man was anxious to spread the gospel of the game more widely among the Gilbertese. He told me one Saturday to give the first lesson to twenty-two of the Company's labourers whom the police had enveigled up to the field. At the end of the practice, which had not proved very enthusiastic, I asked them if they would like another trial some time. 'Sir', replied their spokesman with courtesy, 'we shall be happy to come, if that is your wish.' I explained that there was no enforcement, but put it to him that the game was a good game: didn't he think so too? 'Sir', he said again, 'we do not wish to deceive you. It seems to us a very exhausting game. It makes our hearts die inside us.'

I naturally asked why, in that case, he had said they were willing to have another go. He whispered seriously for a while with his companion. 'We will come back', he answered at last, 'on acount of the overtime pay which the Government, being just, will give us for playing on its ground'.

Those early teaching days provided some pretty problems of umpiring. In one case at least, no decision was ever reached. Ari, a little quick man, and Bobo, a vast and sluggish giant, were in together when Ari hit what he judged to be an easy two. He proceeded to run two, paying, as usual, not the slightest heed to his partner's movements. The gigantic Bobo ran only one, with the result that both players were at Ari's original crease when the ball was thrown in. But it was overthrown; seeing which, Ari hurled himself upon Bobo, started his great mass on a second run, and then himself careered away on his third. Bobo finished his second, but by that time Ari was back at his original crease again, having finished his fourth. He started on his fifth, but collided with Bobo, who was making heavy work of his third, in mid-pitch. Both collapsed there, Ari on top of Bobo, and Ari's original wicket was thrown down. Which of the two was out? In point of fact, it was Bobo whom we sent back to the pavilion, but that was not on an umpire's decision. It was because Ari's head had butted with great force into his diaphragm and left him gasping for medical aid.

Another case was much discussed. One Abakuka (Habakkuk) so played a rising ball that it span up his arm and, by some fluke, lodged inside the yellow and purple shirt with which he was honouring our game. Swiftly the wicket keeper darted forward and grappled with him, intending to seize the ball and so catch him out. After a severe struggle, Abakuka escaped and fled. The whole field gave chase. The fugitive, hampered by pads donned upside down (to protect his insteps from full-pitchers) was overtaken on the boundary. Even handicapped as he was, he would hardly have been caught had he not tried there, by standing on his head, to decant the ball from his shirt-front; and though held, feet in air, he resisted the interference with such fury that it took all that eleven masses of brown brawn could do to persuade the leather from his bosom. After so gallant a fight, it would have been sad to judge him out. Fortunately, we were saved the pain, as he was carried from the field on a stretcher.

Ten years later, cricket was popular everywhere, and a better grasp of its finer points was abroad, but odd things still happened now and then to keep us alert. When I became, in my turn, the Old Man on Ocean Island, there was a game between two Police teams in which the umpire of the fielding side, for no obvious reason (since nobody had appealed), suddenly bawled 'Ouchi', which is to say, Out. We were interested to hear what he meant, especially the batsman, but all the answer he gave was, 'Sirs, you know not how bad that man is. O, beere!' The expletive usually denotes disgust at a nasty smell. We decided that a man's personal odour had little to do with the laws of cricket, and that batsman continued his innings. But, an over or two later, there was a legitimate appeal against him. In attemping a leg hit, he had flickered a strap of his pad and it looked from point's angle as if he had been caught at wicket.

'Ouchi!', yelled the umpire with splendid gusto.

'Ouchi?', queried his victim, 'and for what reason, O eater of unclean things, am I ouchi?'

'Rek piffor wikkut!' The decision was rendered to the sky, resonant with triumphant conviction.

We decided again that the batsman had better continue, but he was so shaken by that time that his stumps were pushed back by the very next ball, a deplorable long-hop. 'Ouchi!', gloated the umpire, 'ouchi-ouchi!' and followed his retreat, prancing with glad hoots, to the very pavilion.

We learned later that the complex behaviour of a light-hearted village girl was at the bottom of this regrettable business. But the sequel to the story has a nicer flavour for cricketers. Both men gave up playing for a while; a few weeks later, however, they came to the Residency hand in hand, with garlands on their heads, to say they wanted to be taken into practice games again. But by that time, I knew the background of their quarrel, and said something severe about umpires who imported private feuds into their cricket. 'Yes, Old Man, of a truth', the offender answered, 'our sin was to play this game while we were contending over that female person. It is not expedient for men at variance about women to be making *kirikiti* against each other, for behold! it is a game of brothers. But now we are brothers again, for we have turned away from that female!' As a matter of cold, hard fact, it was *she* who had turned away from *them*. But that aspect of the matter was, after all, beyond the cognizance of the MCC, whereas his finding that cricket is a game of brothers was sound beyond all argument.

From *A Pattern of Islands*, 1952.

Grimble is the perfect specimen of the successful colonial administrator but he is dwarfed by the likes of George Robert Canning, 4th Lord Harris, (1851–1932; Eton, Oxford, Kent and England), the great Major-General of the Golden Age of English cricket. Captain of Kent, 1875–89; Captain of England in four Test matches; President of the MCC, 1895; Trustee of MCC, 1906–16; Hon. Treasurer of MCC, 1916–32. Sometime Under-Secretary for India, Under-Secretary for War, Governor of Bombay, he insisted that there were no rules for cricket, only laws: 'Rules', he said, 'are made to be broken, laws are made to be kept'. Harris did valiant work on behalf of the game during his governorship of Bombay, even though some of his attitudes appear to have been a shade eccentric.

ABOUT 1895 the Bombay Gymkhana had a Hindu lad as bowler in their employ, a very well-behaved, useful young fellow whom the members liked very much. At the end of the season he gave notice to leave. They expressed their regret, offered to raise his pay, and to do anything they could to induce him to stay. Nothing could change his intention, and after much trouble they ascertained his reason—viz., that he had been warned he would lose caste if he continued to play with beef-eating Englishmen. So much for the native. Now for the Englishman, and I will tell what I had personally to put up with by a brief paraphrase of a speech I made at a function to which I was invited in 1911—after His Majesty King George's Durbar at Delhi—by the students of the Ferguson College at Poona, to this effect: I imagined from their inviting me to take part in a meeting which had to do with athletics that they did not realize how I was treated when Governor some twenty years previously; that I was abused by the native Press as if I had done all I could to lead youth astray; that because I occasionally took part in a game of cricket—at the outside, ten days in the year, on the private ground of Government House at Poona—I was grossly neglecting my duties. Whereas I might have been lying on a sofa, smoking cigarettes, and reading French novels; and because they would not have known what I was doing I should have been free from condemnation; but because I took part in an honest, healthy, active pastime, thereby encouraging Indian youth to do the like, I was not fit for my position.

I saw a Parsi named Writer bowl against the Presidency Eleven and against Lord Hawke's Eleven, and considered at the time that for a few overs he was quite as difficult as that distinguished Nottingham bowler, George Wootton, and the action was extremely similar; but he could not keep it up as an English professional does, and it is in the matter of patience that I think the Indian will never be equal to the Englishman.

When I first went there the amount of time wasted in the calls for, and the drinking of, water by the Parsi batsman was quite ridiculous, but they got over their weakness, and I suppose are as well able to play a long innings in their own climate without constant resort to drinks as an Englishman. Where I was disappointed with the Parsis was in their fielding. I should have thought that with their activity and what appeared to be rather long arms they would have been specially good fields, but they were not, I consider, as good as Englishmen, and nowhere near as good as Australians.

From *A Few Short Runs*, 1921.

Towards the end of his long life Harris was spotted, out of his accustomed milieu, by the critic and poet Sir John Squire (1884–1958), one of that exclusive band of sedentary Englishmen whose love for the game overcomes a congenital inability to excel at it. Squire found his lordship cornered by one of the pillars of the New Journalism, and not enjoying the experience very much.

A NIGHT or two afterwards I spent one of the oddest evenings of my life. Another man and I stayed on in Bath, and my eldest son also happened to be there; a message came from T. P. O'Connor, who was staying at the Grand Pump-Room Hotel, asking us to come over after dinner. When we got to his private sitting-room we found him with Lord Harris: the incongruity of the pair, although they had age and long political experience in common, was startling—but they had both taken their aged bones to Bath and come together, the impish Irish journalist with his shapeless face and sly eyes and the tall, austere, aquiline, bewhiskered, correct cricketer and Indian governor. Lord Harris, who at nearly eighty had recently been making runs and taking wickets on the Fourth of June at Eton, welcomed every attempt to turn the conversation to cricket or imperial history, but T. P. was too much for him and for some hours monopolized the talk with reminiscences of Victorian worthies of the Jubilee Plunger type, and stories of the what-the-lady's-husband-said-to-the-duke sort, relating to past ornaments of Burke. Now and again, as he produced an especially impudent piece of ancient scandal, he turned with his brogue and said: 'Ye'll remember that, Lord Harris?'. Lord Harris was the perfect gentleman, and perhaps he was really enjoying the relaxation from decorum; but his nods of assent were of the slightest and his smiles had a trace of effort to them. It was rather as though an Archbishop should have found himself supping with the chorus, and was making the best of it.

From *The Honeysuckle and the Bee*, 1948.

Squire's reputation as a critic and versifier is in some danger of being dwarfed by his posthumous fame as the leader of the Invalids C.C.; that band of rabbits immortalised by A. G. MacDonell in England, Their England. *One of the advantages of forming an occasional cricket club composed more or less of professional writers is that there is very little danger of your deeds remaining unsung. One of the several members of Squire's side who subsequently committed his recollections to paper was the novelist Alec Waugh (b. 1898).*

No two men could have been more different than Bax and Squire. They were very different too, as captains of a cricket side.

It might have been expected that Bax, who had shown little sense of stage-management in his career as a writer, would have been a vague and casual captain of a cricket side and that Squire, who had such a marked sense of self-direction, would have been on the field a brisk, military martinet. Not at all; though Bax looked like an Elizabethan poet, he was a business-like manager. The staff work of his tours was smooth, and his teams arrived on time with an umpire, a scorer and a twelfth man in flannels.

The Invalids were very different. *England, Their England* is dedicated to Squire. He figures in its pages as Mr Hodge. The book is comic and the comedian's licence to exaggerate is freely used. Into the famous cricket match are crowded the high spots of a dozen matches, and no real game could have ended in that kind of a tie with half the fielders colliding in mid-wicket. It is full, rich caricature. But in the presentation of Mr Hodge's captaincy and management there was no caricature at all. It really was like that.

I first met the Invalids as an opponent in the summer of 1921. I was living in Ditchling and captained the village side. Squire had wanted to make it a whole-day match. But it was harvest time, the villagers could not get away, so we agreed on a one-thirty start with a buffet lunch first for the visitors in my bungalow. I expected my guests around midday, but the first opponent appeared at half past nine, in the belief that it was a whole-day match. I have forgotten his name. I have never seen him since, he was a very silent man. I soon began to hope that

35

other members of the side would be under a similar misapprehension, but the slow passing hours of the morning were only broken by a couple of telegrams for Squire from players who had been delayed. Noon came, half past twelve, one o'clock; then the solitary arrival and myself ate a portion of the lunch, covered over the remains in the hope that they would be reasonably fresh at suppertime, and made our way to the ground where the villagers were patiently waiting for the 'toffs from London'. Eventually the game began at five to four, with the last two places filled by an eleven-year-old schoolboy and the taxi driver who had driven half the side from the remote station to which they had been misdirected.

I will not call that a typical experience—but it was an effective introduction to the Invalids. Squire was at that time the busiest man of letters in the country: more often than not he was forced to leave the writing of his Sunday article for the *Observer* till the Saturday morning, and most regular members of his side can recall fidgeting in his study, beside the messenger who was waiting to take down his manuscript to the printer, while the Invalids, one by one, were assembling forty miles away in a Sussex pub. Every regular Invalid has his own pet story of a side six short without its captain being put in to bat and desperately trying to hold out till lunch when a further instalment of players might be expected.

No side can have been managed more capriciously off the field and its management in the field was unexpected. Squire, unlike Bax, had not had, well, how shall I put it—the conventional grooming of a cricketer, and he captained his sides, as Hitler led his armies, not from a study of the textbooks but by the light of poetic intuition. In a half-day game once against a good side on a good wicket, he opened his attack with his second and third change bowlers. At tea, with the score at 165 for two, he explained his plan. 'I thought I would get two or three quick wickets, then loose my good bowlers, when they were fresh, against the tail'.

He enjoyed bowling, and some maintained that his tactics in the field were dictated by the subconscious need to create a situation when he would be justified in putting himself on to bowl. He had, as a bowler, some curious idiosyncrasies. The average captain, when deciding from which end he will prefer to bowl, studies the slope of the ground and gauges the direction of the wind with a wetted finger. Squire looked at the sun. 'I'll go on this end', he would say. 'At the other end the glint of the sun upon the stumps would put me off.' 'Mr Hodge', A. G. MacDonell wrote, 'was a poet, and therefore a theorist and an idealist.

Every ball that he bowled had brain behind it, if not exactness of pitch.'
He took a four-step trot, and tossed high into the air a ball guileless of
spin and swerve. It was astonishing how often he broke a partnership.

But the most remarkable feature of a remarkable eleven was Squire's
capacity to get the best play out of his side. Was it an innate gift of
leadership or did the memory of an earlier Sir John who would not
'march through Coventry with that', inspire or rather goad a reasonable
club cricketer, who recognised how hopelessly the odds were laid
against him, into a desperate resolve to put a face on things? Something
of both most likely. Certainly most regular Invalids will admit that they
played ten per cent above their normal form for Squire and two high
victories stand upon his records—against a strong RAOC side Aldershot,
when that fine musician Walton O'Donnell took seven wickets and
made over 80, and at the Oval against the Lords and Commons largely
owing to the three-figure partnership between Clifford Bax and that
sound writer of detective stories, Milward Kennedy, who appeared on
the score card disguised by his baptismal name, M. R. K. Burge.

It is one of the anomalies of leadership that Squire, untrained as a
cricketer, with no skill at the game and little knowledge of it, should
have been able to get the best out of his team, while as editor of the
London *Mercury*, with his great knowledge of literature and feeling for
the humanities of literature, he should not have been able to get the best
work out of his friends. The rates of pay on the *Mercury* were low but
most writers would sooner have £10 from a paper they respect and an
encouraging editor who takes pleasure in their work than £30 from an
impersonal, commercially-minded magazine. Over the years a number
of excellent poems, essays and stories appeared within the yellow covers
of the *Mercury*, but few of Squire's juniors felt when they had reached a
final sentence, 'This really is rather good. I'll let Jack have first look at
it'.

From *My Brother Evelyn and Other Profiles*, 1967.

Squire and Waugh represent the second generation of cricketing writers; all the precedents had been set many years before by Sir James Matthew Barrie (1860–1937), who defined himself as a slow bowler 'so slow that if I don't like a ball I can run after it and bring it back'. It was Barrie who enshrined forever the ideal of a group of gentlemen splashing about in the homely backwaters of the end of the nineteenth century, finding in cricket a device for prolonging the schooldays so dearly coveted. Barrie's humorous history of his club is the prototype for comical cricket books of its kind.

Broadway as a Cricket Centre

IN THE leafy month of June, when old Sol progresses to his height of passion and sluggish draughts move gently through the vibrating light of a drowsy noontide, ruffling the dainty plumage of sweetly trilling songsters performing their ablutions in shaded pools, it is then that the panting climber of the precipitous paths of Parnassus longingly looks with lingering gaze over the seething masses of the madding crowd toiling intently in dusty thoroughfares to green fields dotted with white figures on reasonable terms.

Such a place is Broadway. The ozone of this village, which is charmingly situated between Court Farm and Russell House, dates back to the time of the Romans, who, with the help of Balbus, built a wall here. The name Broadway is of Roman origin, and is believed by the cognoscenti to be compounded of two words, *broad* and *way*. However this may be, it was certainly to Broadway that Caius retired when he fled from the city. Here Caesar probably played many fine innings of a Saturday afternoon. But all this was long ago, in the days of top hats and underhand bowling. Coming to more recent times, and entering the village by the Evesham Road, the first object of interest at which we pause is Mr Frank Millet. He is standing a little to the off. Immediately after leaving Mr Millet, which we do with reluctance, but time is short and there is much to see, we scatter over his garden, strolling through the beautifully kept flower beds until we come to the Millet which is one of the sights of Broadway. The Quackuary is a sort of rustic steam-press in which the eggs laid by the Allahakbarries and their rivals are hatched by machinery. On the morning of a match all the female members of Russell House are up betimes hieing them to the cricket ground with aprons, into which they may be seen gathering the eggs. Many of the ducks which come waddling toward us are Allahakbarries, and they are quacking excitedly at the prospect of more little brothers and sisters.

We now return to our conveyance, and the courteous Jehu whipping up his horses we soon reach the

VILLAGE GREEN.

Pause here for a moment to observe the quaint house on the left, whose walls are well-nigh hidden by a magnificent specimen of the wisteria. H. J. Ford, O. Seaman, and A. E. W. Mason have stayed in that house. Almost directly opposite it is a more modern edifice, the erstwhile abode of A. Conan Doyle and S. Pawling. A straight line drawn between these two houses would represent the shortest way from the one to the other. Better, however, than stopping to draw this line, accompany us up the long street which now opens before us to the village hostelry, an ancient structure, heavy with historic associations. To the leg-side of the entrance is the

BANQUETING HALL OF THE ALLAHAKBARRIES

and on the off is a narrow passage in which the first memorable meeting of the two captains took place. The stair leads to the chambers above. In one of these a Stuart king slept immediately before being caught and bowled for nothing. Edward T. Reed has also slept in this room.

Continuing our journey up the village street we pause for a moment at the shop where Gilmour bought a hat for a shilling. Well worth a visit also is the Curiosity Emporium across the way, where, if we are lucky, we may pick up some interesting relics, such as the spectacles left behind last year. We have now reached Court Farm, the

HEADQUARTERS OF THE BROADWAY GANG,

and are shown over it by the mistress of the house, who, however, is looking a little pale to-day. That is Antonio de Navarro leaning against the wall for support. He looks pale. Messrs. Herkomer, Greene* and

---

* Plunket Greene, the singer.

Alfred Parsons form an interesting group in the Badminton Court. They are none of them feeling very well to-day. As we bid good-bye to our charming hostess, reminding her that we shall meet anon on the field, we notice that her hand trembles.

And now for the third Test Match.

THE TEAM

For the 1899 Test Match

When the spring of 1899 broke into summer it found the Allahakbarries already at the nets. Broadway had won the first Test Match (1897) by 1 run, Herkomer being responsible for the winning hit, and in the following year the Allahakbarries made hay of their opponents to the tune of 6 wickets, winning hit by O. Seaman, Esq. Feeling this year, therefore, ran very high, and in the exceptional circumstances the Allahakbarrie captain thought himself justified in arranging some trial matches for the first time in the history of the club. The first of these matches, which was played against the Artists, came off at Denmark Hill, on a sullen wicket, and was remarkable for some tall scoring. Pawling made 34, Ford 32, and Pritchard 26. Others who played themselves into form in this match were Partridge (4) and Barrie (3). Reed (the popular Queen's Club pro.) and Mason were unfortunate with the bat, but they missed several catches in the field. Ford had the following highly creditable bowling analysis: 3 overs, 3 wides, 43 runs and o wickets. On the other side Mr Swinstead made a fair score.

Soon thereafter Mr Barrie called a committee meeting to consider the composition of the team for the 1899 Test Match, present, himself and Reed. After a careful exchange of views the following were elected as a nucleus of the eleven: J. M. Barrie, Esq., Reed (E. T.). At the next meeting H. J. Ford and S. Pawling, with Partridge, were chosen; A. Conan Doyle was also mentioned at this meeting, but it was stated on authority that he had decided to devote himself henceforth to second-class cricket. These five are all Homeric men with the bat, and Ford, as he has shown this year, can trundle a bit, but so far the weak spot in the eleven (if any) is the bowling. It seemed wise to select someone for his bowling only, and after considering the claims of Pritchard, the choice fell on A. E. W. Mason. Now for a wicket-keeper. Hornung and Meredith have both kept the sticks at Broadway, and each had his backers. Another good man is G. MacGregor, the Middlesex amateur, but the general feeling was in favour of a pro., and Meredith was finally fixed upon. We have as yet no suspicion of a tail, and to remedy this, O.

Seaman was elected. We now want a hard hitter. Shall it be Gilmour or A. E. Stoddart? It was decided to play Gilmour if the pitch was treacherous, and Mr Stoddart if it was sticky. For the tenth place a good all-round player who is at home on all kinds of wickets was the desideratum. Augustine Birrell is the very man. These with A. N. Other complete the team, which is thus composed as follows:

J. M. BARRIE, ESQ. (Forfarshire) (*Capt.*).
H. J. FORD, ESQ. (Middlesex).
S. PAWLING, ESQ. (Berkshire).
A. E. W. MASON, ESQ. (Kent).
O. SEAMAN, ESQ. (Surrey).
A. BIRRELL, ESQ. (Lancashire).
A. N. OTHER, ESQ. (Yorkshire).

with

REED, E. T. (Kent).
MEREDITH, W. (Surrey).
PARTRIDGE, J. B. (Middlesex).
GILMOUR, THOMAS (Lincolnshire).

Reserves: Messrs. Pritchard, MacGregor and Stoddart.

FORECAST

Of the Allahakbarrie Score in the 1899 Test Match

This annual engagement, which is now recognised as a first-class fixture, came off to-morrow at Broadway in ideal cricketing weather. By 11.15 the pavilion was thronged with beautiful women and brainy men.

A perfect wicket, a little on the creamy side, had been prepared by the groundsmen, Millet and Navarro.

Barrie (Capt.) again won the toss, and after examining the wicket elected to go in. He did not go in himself.

The Broadway team took the field at 11.30. They look a gamey lot.

I have just learned that Barrie (Capt.) expects the wicket to play queerly.

Amid loud cheers Seaman and Gilmour now strode to the wickets.

Barrie is being severely criticised for sending Gilmour in first.

Seaman is carrying his bat over his shoulder, which creates a favourable impression.

Gilmour is to take first over. He looks pale but determined.

In a strange silence Plunket Greene, who is trundling from the Bramall Lane end, sends down the first ball.

The next man in is Ford.

Ford stands seven feet in his stockings, and meets all balls in the middle of the pitch. Curiously enough, Ford was originally played as a bowler.

Ford has opened his account by pulling Greene beautifully all round the wickets for 3.

A complete change has now come over the game.

It is Seaman's turn to face the music. Seaman shapes very badly. I fear he will not be a stayer.

The last ball of the over was lifted by Seaman over his head for 2 (all run).

Seaman is now well set.

Ford has hit Smith all along the ground for 1.

The bowling is now tied in a knot.

Seaman is very uncomfortable with Smith's curly ones. He made some shocking strokes. I expect to see him go at any moment.

Seaman has cut Smith for 3, and driven him to the ropes for 4. I shall be surprised if Seaman does not give Broadway more trouble to-day.

The separation, however, came from the other end. In lifting a ball to deep mid-off, Seaman was smartly caught by Parsons at square leg standing back. He had compiled a very stylish 9 in twelve and a half minutes, and received an ovation.

13 for 2. It is still anybody's game.

Meredith is Ford's next partner. He is a graceful bat.

13 for 3.

Pawling is the next to wield the willow.

The score now reads 13 for 4. It is Ford who is out.

Reed has joined Pawling, and from his third ball he gave a palpable chance to Herkomer at cover point, but it was not held. Profiting by this escape, Reed fluked the ball finely through the slips for 2, and manipulated it to the on for a dainty single. He was then out l.b.w. The let-off has cost Broadway dear.

The next man in was Barrie (Capt.). On returning he received an ovation.

Partridge and Pawling now came together. Partridge is wearing his new pads, but they impede his progress to the wickets, and I fear he will not be a stayer.

Pawling is playing with his scoring bat.

The long innings of Pawling has been at last brought to a close. He has scraped together 6. His wickets were spread-eagled by Navarro. Pawling retired much dissatisfied with the ruling of the umpire.

On Mason's joining Partridge the score stood thus: 22 for 7.

The stand of the innings now took place.

Partridge opened the ball by bagging a brace of lovely cuts, each for 3 and both off his pads.

Partridge has just despatched the sphere to the boundary. It was a glide off his pads. I am confident that Partridge's pads will stand him in good stead to-day.

Mason is content to keep up his end and leave the scoring to Partridge.

The score rises so rapidly that the figures dance on the telegraph board.

Smith is bowling with his head. He has just sent down a very hot one, but Partridge opened his pads to it and a 4 accrued.

The 50 is now up, and the scoring is terrific. Partridge had laid aside his bat and is kicking out.

With two 3's and a beauty to the ropes for 4, Partridge has sent up the 60. All bowling is alike to him to-day. The 70 is now up.

Partridge is twenty-one years of age. He played many good games for his school, and first attracted the attention of Barrie when practising at the nets. He made his first appearance for the Allahakbarries in 1893, and got his blue in the same year. He stands 5 feet 10½ inches in his pads.

The 80 is now up. In a single over from Parsons Partridge snicked him to mid-off, smashed him to leg, hurled him among the crowd, and

43

twice lifted him in the air and banged him hard against the pavilion. This sent up the 100 amid loud applause.

There was an interval of a few minutes at this point to enable Partridge to be photographed.

I have had a brief conversation with Partridge. He tells me that he never played his own game until to-day. He resides in the N.W. district, and is qualified for Middlesex, but cannot afford the time for three-day matches. His telegraphic address is "PADS, LONDON".

On the game being resumed Mason appeared without his bat, and Partridge, who is much annoyed, appealed to the umpire. The decision was given against him, however, and Mason is trying to play Partridge's game.

Partridge continues to give them beans. Off two overs he has scored three 4's and four 3's. The 130 is now up.

In winter Partridge is by profession an artist. He is on the ground staff of *Punch*. He is a modest, unaffected fellow, and very popular among his brother pros. According to *Who's Who* he has as yet published nothing, but contemplates a work to be entitled 'A New Way to Play Old Cricket'. He is fond of all outdoor sports. He also bikes, but whether in pads, I cannot say. He is a non-smoker. His position at the wickets is easy and alert, and he has a large variety of strokes, but he is perhaps best with his right leg. He plays with a very straight pad.

Mason is out, caught and bowled, and has lent invaluable assistance, which must not be judged by the amount of his runs. His full score stands thus: 1.

The remaining batsmen are Birrell and Tother. The end is now close at hand.

Herkomer is deputed to bowl, and is mixing them all he knows. The first ball Birrell got went through him. The second, third, and fourth hit him on the chest. Herkomer has found the spot.

Birrell is out.

Tother now whipped in. He evidently means to lay on the wood.

Tother missed his first ball and ran, but he was given out. His has been a short but merry innings.

The tenth wicket fell with the total at 132.

Partridge carried out his pads for a superb 110.

Lest the Forecast should be wrong in some of its details this page has been left blank, so that the fortunate possessor of this work may append the scores actually made.

HINTS

To the Team by their Captain

1

Don't practise on opponent's ground before match begins. This can only give them confidence.

2

Each man, when he goes in, to tap the ground with his bat.

3

Should you hit the ball, run at once. Don't stop to cheer.

4

No batsman is allowed to choose his own bowler. You needn't think it.

5

Partridge, when bowling, keep your eye on square-leg.

6

Square-leg, when Partridge is bowling. Keep your eye on him.

7

If bowled first ball, pretend that you only came out for the fun of the thing, and then go away and sit by yourself behind the hedge.

From *Allahakbarries C.C.*, 1899.

Like the rest of the cricketing authors in his side, Barrie tended to neglect the game when it came to his own professional work. One exception was his first stage success 'Walker, London', which opened at Toole's Theatre in 1892, and included a young male character so obsessed with the game that his title in the cast-line is simply 'W. G.', and who is told by one of his lady friends 'You call yourself W. G. because you think you are a great cricketer, and I can bowl you myself'. Ironically, the author with the most impressive cricketing testimonials of all was someone who ignored the game altogether in his work. He was H. G. Wells (1866–1946), whose father retains his niche in Wisden to this day, for reasons which the following extract makes plain.

MY MOTHER used to accuse my father of neglecting the shop for cricket. But it was through that excellent sport as it was then, that the little menage contrived to hold out, with an occasional bankruptcy, for so long before it was finally sold up. He was never really interested in the crockery trade and sold little, I think, but jam-pots and preserving jars to the gentlemen's houses round about, and occasional bedroom sets and tea-sets, table glass and replacements. But he developed his youthful ability to play cricket which he had kept alive at Up Park, he revived the local club and was always getting jobs of various duration as a professional bowler and cricket instructor in the neighbourhood. He played for the West Kent Club from 1857 to 1869 and bowled for the County of Kent in 1862 and 1863. On June 26th, 1862, he clean bowled four Sussex batsmen in four successive balls, a feat not hitherto recorded in county cricket. Moreover his cousin John Duke at Penshurst, whom he had once got out of danger when they were swimming together, let him have long and considerate credit for a supply of cricket goods that ousted the plates and dishes from half the shop window. Among the familiar names of my childhood were the Hoares and the Normans, both banking families with places near Bromley, for whom he bowled; and for some years he went every summer term to Norwich Grammar School as 'pro'.

From *Experiment in Autobiography*, 1934.

It would seem that Wells was not quite as detached as he pretended from the game his father loved so dearly. If Wells was perhaps slightly puzzled by the intensity of that love, he evidently regarded it as deeply significant, perhaps in a sociological sense. In a letter to a friend written from France in August, 1932, Wodehouse says, 'I like Wells, an odd bird, though. The first time I met him, we had barely finished the initial pip-pippings when he said, apropos of nothing, 'My father was a professional cricketer. If there's a good answer to that, you tell me'. No such ambivalence ever clouded the view of Siegfried Sassoon (1886–1967), yet another of those late Victorian rural children who could never recall the absence of cricket from their lives. Sassoon learned the art of cricket in the remote villages of the Kentish Weald, and later played for sides with names like the Blue Mantles.

AFTER LUNCHEON I got into my brown velveteen riding suit and waited for Richardson to bring the horses up to the house. He always made going out for a ride seem an important event and looked very smart in his livery. He would have considered it a disgrace to have worn his stable clothes when taking me out, and I never saw him drive even a pony-cart without looking as though it was a carriage and pair. Like Sportsman he had perfect manners. When he had assisted me into the saddle, which was rather a long way up, my mother came out with a note in her hand which she wanted him to leave at Major Horrocks's house. I knew already that the note was to say that she couldn't come to tea that afternoon. It wasn't much more than a mile to the Major's; but it was too hot for walking, she said, and if Richardson were to drive her I shouldn't get my ride. I now asked Richardson which way we were going; he suggested that we might go round by Brenchley and leave the note on our way home. There was an all-day match at Brenchley and we could watch some of it over the hedge. This was exactly what I'd wanted. Tom had a way of anticipating one's wishes. So off we trotted, up the hill, in the opposite direction from Major Horrocks's house. At the top of the hill we met a traction engine, which with some horses might have meant the possibility of tumbling off. But Sportsman passed it as though it wasn't there, and I patted his neck appreciatively. Sylvia, a harmless character who usually went in the dogcart, gave a sort of curtsey to the traction-engine, which was politely standing still. As we went along I hoped we should meet somebody who knew me, for I was very proud of being seen on such a big horse.

But we saw no one until we got to the cricket ground, except when we overtook the curate, whose opinion I didn't value much, though he always made great efforts to be pleasant. 'He'd look a sight better in that black straw hat without his Monkey Brand beard', remarked Richardson; to which I callously agreed. A few minutes later we were watching the match; by standing up in the stirrups I could see quite well over the high hedge. Brenchley were batting and the little scoring board on the other side of the ground showed that they had been making plenty of runs. We weren't the only spectators in the road. As usual, the brewer's dray had pulled up and looked like being there for the rest of the afternoon. The drayman, whose horses were half-asleep, was watching the game with a heavy indolent attitude which seemed suitable to the barrels of beer behind him, while the youth who drove the baker's van appeared conscious that he ought to be continuing his round though always unable to tear himself away until he had seen what had happened next. A little further along the hedge was the tea-tent, which was full of talkative local ladies and would soon contain the curate. Most of the Brenchley players were sitting under the chestnut trees on the far side of the field, and at a respectful distance from the tea-tent was the Rose and Crown beer-tent, well patronized by the villagers, one of whom bawled, 'Call that ker-ricket!' whenever the Horsemonden fast bowler sent down a bumpy one. Horsemonden being the next village to Brenchley, there was strong local rivalry in the match, and feeling in the beer-tent ran high. Every time one of the batsmen made a good stroke I envied the apparent ease with which he did it, particularly when it was George Collins, who had played for Kent as a professional before I was born and still walked six miles each way to play for Brenchley. When Collins had completed his fifty and the church clock struck four, Tom said, 'We'd better be jogging on now if we're going to leave the mistress's letter at Mascalls'. Reluctantly I rode away, wondering whether *I* should ever make a fifty for Brenchley. . . .

For Mr Hamilton's batting average I felt an eager and almost proprietory concern. He began by knocking up a dashing thirty in an important Brenchley match. Richardson, who was captain of our rustic team, expected much of him, and I myself had hopes of seeing him make at least fifty in his first match for Matfield. But fifties, as I well knew, were seldom made on Matfield Green; in fact when I'd played there for the first time, a few weeks before, the other side had been all out for thirteen, though I'd scored eight runs myself, owing to them bowling underhand at me. Mr Hamilton, indeed, seemed none too sure about his fifty when he was putting on his pads to go in first wicket down after Richardson had won the toss; he was aware that the mown piece in the middle of the Green looked better than it really was. The turf was quite decent, but when people ran about on it there were hollow-sounding thuds, almost as if there was a cellar underneath. In dry weather the wicket could without exaggeration be described as dangerous, and Mr Hamilton was about to bat on a very dry wicket indeed. 'Which cap are you going to wear?', I inquired, as he rummaged in his bag for his batting gloves. For he was both a Butterfly and a Crusader, and I was wondering which colours would be likely to overawe our opponents most. But one club cap was much the same as another to the opposing players, several of whom had both braces and belts to sustain white trousers which were so high in the waist that, as a local humorist remarked, they 'looked as if they cut 'em under the arms'.

The game now began, and some lively hits into the rough grass were made off the old-fashioned round-arm bowling. It took a long time to get into double figures at Matfield unless you skied the ball, and scientific strokes along the ground only resulted in singles. Would C. H. Hamilton's batting be too stylish for the Green?, I speculated, when the first wicket had fallen and he was wending his way toward the crease in his Crusader cap. The question remained unanswered, for his actual bat played no part in the proceedings. The bowler, who had grim black whiskers and very long arms, took two steps up to the wicket and delivered a fast ball which rose sharply and whizzed past C. H. Hamilton's nose. The next ball did the same but struck him in the ribs. The third one never rose at all. It shot under his bat and knocked his middle stump down. 'Them toffs never do no good on the Green', remarked a bandy-legged old labourer who was standing behind the scorer's table. Quite pleased about it, he seemed, though I eyed him angrily. In consequence of this and a few somewhat similar experiences, the Beet decided that he preferred playing for Brenchley, and did so with gratifying results. He made sixty-four in the Flower Show Match. Meanwhile he lit his pipe with an air of relief rather than regret that his innings were over so soon.

Authentic details of the distant past being difficult to recapture, I take this opportunity of relating that Mr Hamilton's pipe reminded me of an episode in his University career which he had amusingly described to me. One day he was in G. L. Jessop's rooms; for that famous man had been a college friend of his. Jessop's pipe—a large one—had become clogged, and he was blowing into it for all he was worth. Mr Hamilton, with sympathetic interest, was looking over his shoulder. The climax came, and a clot of tobacco flew into one of his eyes, causing inflammation for some days afterwards. In my opinion, however, there was nothing inglorious in having tobacco blown into one's eye by Jessop, who hardly ever played in a county match without smiting at least one ball clean out of the ground. Anyhow, the anecdote has stuck in my mind, so I see no harm in repeating it.

From *The Old Century*, 1938.

Students of the game as assiduous as Sassoon would have acknowledged John Nyren (1764–1837) as the father of all cricket literature. Nyren played for the Hambledon club and wrote two classic works, The Young Cricketer's Tutor *and* The Cricketers of My Time *from which the following reminiscence is taken.*

UPON COMING to the old batters of our club, the name of John Small, the elder, shines among them in all the lustre of a star of the first magnitude. His merits have already been recorded in a separate publication, which every zealous brother of the pastime has probably read. I need, therefore, only subscribe my testimony to his uncommon talent, shortly summing up his chief excellences. He was the best short runner of his day, and indeed I believe him to have been the first who tried the short hits to account. His decision was as prompt as his eye was accurate in calculating a short run. Add to the value of his accomplishment as a batter, he was an admirable fieldsman, always playing middle wicket; and so correct was his judgement of the game, that old Nyren would appeal to him when a point of law was being debated. Small was a remarkably well-made and well-knit man, of honest expression, and as active as a hare. He was a good fiddler, and taught himself the double bass. The Duke of Dorset, having been informed of his musical talent, sent him as a present a handsome violin, and paid the carriage. Small, like a true and simple-hearted Englishman, returned the compliment, by sending his Grace two bats and balls, also *paying the carriage.* We may be sure that on both hands the presents were choice of their kind. Upon one occasion he turned his Orphean accomplishment to good account. Having to cross two or three fields on his way to a musical party, a vicious bull made at him; when our hero, with the characteristic coolness and presence of mind of a good cricketer, began playing upon his bass, to the admiration and perfect satisfaction of the mischievous beast.

From *The Cricketers of My Time*, 1832.

An attitude strikingly similar to Sassoon's is revealed by Alison Uttley (1884–1976) although throughout the length of her volume of childhood reminiscences, the creator of Grey Rabbit never once reveals which part of Britain she is describing. Close scrutiny of her text, however, and the casual remark about having been brought up 'in the north', suggests Lancashire, or perhaps Cheshire. But who was the county captain whose sisters had their own team?

DOWN BY the river, in the water meadows, smooth and green, there was a portion roped off from the cattle. It was the village cricket ground. The hills rose on all sides, and the circle of fields lay in the bottom like green water in a cup. The cricketers walked along the road from the village, and the opposing team came in a horse-brake. Two horses drew this vehicle, and it rumbled proudly through the village, past the barber's shop, past the brewery where they waited to load up with some boxes of beer, by the wharf-yard to the gate of the meadows. There the brake stopped for a minute or two while little boys held the white gate open. Slowly it went on the rough path under the elms where rooks cawed in their rookery. The path ended, the cricketers tumbled out with their green baize bags and walked the rest of the way across the open fields to the cricket ground. We, who had watched their arrival with great interest, drove home to spread the news that there was a cricket match.

From our own seat under the oak tree on the hill-side, we looked down over many fields and copses to the little green patch like a pale handkerchief, laid out in the valley, where the white-clad cricketers played 'the finest game, bar none'.

'We didn't mind whether the ball was on the off or the on, we hit it for six,' said one of them.

We were so far away, the cricketers looked like diminutive clockwork toys, but we sat in the shade of our tree and watched with the deepest interest. The click of the bat came long after the men had made their run, the ball was caught and the faint shout of applause reached us later. It was an interesting phenomenon, that slow speed of sound, as if we were watching a play in another dimension. When the match was over we did not hear the result till the servant boy came back with the milk cart the next morning. Even then we never talked much about it, as it was Sunday, and we were getting ready for church.

There they were, fair-haired John Gold, who came for orders for cattle foods, young Dick, who went by train to a bank each day, Tom Fletcher and all. Most of them were in the choir on Sunday, their white flannels changed for surplices, their voices singing 'Glory be to God' instead of 'How's that, Umpire?' When a man had made a good score he must have felt particularly happy in church, and we gazed at him with admiration.

Cricket and church were alike holy. The flight of the ball, the swift, graceful movements of the men, the swing of the bat, were as full of praise as were the hymns we sang. Cricket and church were near each other in many ways. The curate played with the village team. He couldn't preach, but we forgave him because he played cricket. When he prepared me for Confirmation, we always began with a cricket talk. This broke the religious ice, and made it easy for him. The vicar sat smiling down there. Round the ropes were a few wooden forms, and there sat old whiskered men and young boys with bottles of ginger pop, and sometimes the squire joined them. The field was his, and he was the president of the club. The spectators were never many, perhaps a score on special days.

Cricket had been the centre of our lives ever since I remember. When my brother was about seven and I was nine my father brought us from the market town a set of yellow stumps and bails and a real bat. We had begged and cajoled and wheedled him to get them. Before that we played with a bat my father made, the stable door as a wicket, and the stumps chalked upon it. This involved much argument as to whether the wicket had been hit, much peering at the chalk to see if any was rubbed away. It was a great day when the six brightly painted wickets came out of the market basket, and we held the little bails in our hands and stroked the bat. The smell of the twine on the handle went to our heads like wine. We were nearly delirious with joy as we rubbed the bat with linseed oil from the barn.

My father measured out a small pitch on the little enclosed lawn near the house. We made a hole for the bat, which we euphemistically called the crease, and we began to play a game that never ended. In imagination I still bat there and play tip-and-run, and call to the echoes.

Behind the batting end was the garden wall, the strong old wall with its massive rough stones. It acted as long-stop and saved a fielder. On the off side was our beloved, familiar, friendly wall, where we played see-saw, with a plank over it; where we ran as trains, puffing up and down; where we leapt and flew our kites, played shop and five-stones. It, too, was a fielder, but beyond it was the house with its many windows, and we had to make a rule that no ball went over it. Once I brought the doctor's sons home from school with me to play cricket. When three windows had been broken, my father stopped the game and I was shamed before them. The 'on' side had the orchard, which was 'six and out'. It took a long time to climb down the steep face of the wall and to search for the ball in the thick grass under the apple trees, with the pony trotting there, alarmed at the missile, or the cade lamb butting its hard little head at one's legs. There was a time when a hit in the orchard disturbed the bees in the hives and sent them buzzing round our heads. It was not a popular place, and the cricketer immediately put his bat down and helped to find the ball.

We played with the servant boy, and sometimes with the servant girl, with anybody staying with us, and with children we brought home from school for tea and cricket. Cricket bat and wickets were kept in the home barn, with the rakes and besoms, all reared up in the corner of that well-swept, strong-walled, hay-scented home of good things.

We moved our cricket ground to a more spacious territory when the hay was carried and the big field near the house was cleared. After the last load of sweet scented hay had gone to the stackyard, and the Bonny-rake had swept up the remnants, and the Irishmen had had their Harvest Home and were leaving us, we prepared for cricket. The newly shorn field looked like a lawn. I always felt very proud as I gazed at it, and conceited, as if I were the squire with a smooth cricket ground laid out, rolled and prepared. It was like that from a distance. When we ran through the big gate, rushing across the grass to the only level part in in that lovely, pale green field, we always felt surprised. There didn't seem to be a really smooth spot in it. The short grass, which looked as smooth as silk, was harsh and rough as sack-cloth. There was no level piece as in the water meadows.

The ball wouldn't roll in it, the strong newly-cut stalks checked its flight, but we could hit freely, when the ball managed to arrive at the wicket. We could hit a mile if we liked, for there were no boundaries, except the ends of the earth. Solemnly, portentously, with deep excitement, we pitched the wickets, and marked the crease and shooed away the cows. We tossed for first innings, and the fun began. We played till it was dark every night of summer. Down in the water meadows we could catch a glimpse of the other cricketers in their white flannels, practising on a weekday, playing a match on Saturday, but we went on.

Swallows flew low over the field, cows frisked their tails near us, the cart horses, released from work, grunted and neighed and rolled on the ground with enjoyment. Schoolboys joined us. An old labourer tried his hand at bowling. He called it 'bowelling'. The ancient oak tree with its heavy boughs and the swing hanging there, the spreading ash tree, near which we played, the three great oaks on the hill-side above us and woods surrounding us, all seemed to take part in the game. Surely the trees were watching, they had eyes for us, they moved their branches in approval and nodded their green heads. Laughter and shouts were caught in their leaves, and sometimes the ball was thrown up in sheer exuberance among the boughs. Could we hit the evening star, up there in the sky?

We were cricket mad; we played every day, and we would have played on Sunday, but my father wouldn't allow us. We talked cricket and we dreamed about it. I left the most entrancing book to play cricket. The game had no rival. The farm boy brought back the latest scores of county cricket when he went to the station with the evening milk. We had only a weekly paper, so we couldn't study the scores until Friday or Saturday. Later, when we had the luxury of a daily paper, I knew all the scores by heart. I read through the cricket and could at once reel off the totals for each county and the scores of all our favourite cricketers.

C. B. Fry was one hero of early days, and so deep was our affection for him that when we had a little money we took in his magazine, *The Captain*, which cost a whole shilling. We had never seen any first-class cricket and only occasionally had we been to the village matches, for we preferred to play ourselves, but we took the keenest interest. We practised spin bowling, and when 'googlies' were heard of, then googlies were our desire. I bowled underhand, the boys bowled overarm with a good run and a hard delivery. I developed a break in my slow bowling, which aggravated them as they swiped and missed. The ground was bumpy and sloping, and very hard with the rock so near its surface, so it was difficult to hit the wicket. We played with a composition ball, an unyielding, unkind ball which had little pieces chipped out of it as the season advanced. When it was new it was glorious, we thought it was a county ball, but its splendour soon waned with the impacts on stone. For a long time we dreamed of a real leather ball, and at last my brother had one for his birthday. The feel of the leather, the stitching round it, the faint gold letters stamped upon it, the touch of the seam, the smell of it, all affected me so deeply that I still have that ache of beauty when I hold a cricket ball.

Our cricket received a strong impetus when a family of real cricketers came to live in the next valley. The eldest son was the county captain. His sisters formed a team of girls, and we played up and down the county against other teams. One of the girls could stump a batsman with such speed and call 'How's that?' with such venom, that the opposing teams were intimidated by her. Sometimes the famous man condescended to coach us, and once a year Lord Hawke brought down a team of well-known players to play a mixed team. I was one of the team of white-garbed cricketers, watched by my father from the oak tree on the distant hill.

Sometimes we went by train, or drove in a brake to far-away villages high in the hills, or we went to country houses where a cricket team had been raised to play against us. We had a printed fixture card with a long list of engagements.

The cricket ground by the river was very different from our own bumpy, daisy-strewn, wall-bounded pitch, where the horse wandered up and down and the pony shied at the ball. The grass was shorn to a velvet texture, such as I had never seen before. It was a delight to step upon that turf, and in running it gave us wings. From far away I had watched the horse-mower moving up and down, and the horse wore leather shoes. Now I saw the reason. There was a little pavilion and a score-board with tin figures and deck-chairs for our captain's parents and friends. They drove down in an open carriage with a big tea-basket for the team, and all the paraphernalia of wickets and pads, gloves and balls, and a selection of beautiful bats.

In the far distance I could see my own hill-side and the farm under the trees, and I knew that somebody was sitting on the seat under the oak tree looking down at the white-clad figures on the square of pale green, listening to the click of the bat, the gnat-like cheers when a good catch was made, and the same person was also watching the vast movements of the sky where the clouds ranged in white masses; his eyes were regarding the hawk hovering above the tree-tops and looking with interest at the brakes and charabancs which seemed to swim along the opposite side of the valley on the turnpike road, with its stone walls. Cricket was only part of the scene to him, a game played for a couple of hours and then forgotten, but the other was life itself.

As I think of those cricketing days I believe that the greatest joy in life was playing in the home meadow by the river on that soft turf, with the echoing hills guarding the circle of green. Batting was a hazardous job, but bowling and fielding I loved above everything. I felt on top of the world as I waited, loose-limbed, free, on tip-toe, ready to dart forward, concentrated upon the game, yet aware of those hills and the shining, tossing river, of the scent of hay from the meadows around us, and the blue sky above. Sometimes the telegraph boy came walking over the fields with a yellow telegram for the captain, with her brother's score, or the position of the county. We felt part of the great world of cricket as she tore it open and told us the news. Then back we went to the match or to the practice, for each was as full of delight as the other.

When the cricket season was over I felt a deep sadness. It was like the end of harvest and saying good-bye to the Irishmen.

Sometimes we played in a country town, with hills surrounding the green cricket ground and bare limestone crags against the sky. On the way we drove up a long green valley between steep limestone hills, where flocks of sheep were grazing. In the valley bottom by the white road flowed a narrow river with water forget-me-nots, meadowsweet and yellow monkey flower in its calmer reaches, and a wildness and beauty about it as it dashed over stones in the little gorges. There were meadows of mowing grass with blue wild geranium and the bloody cranesbill, the two colours intermingling and tempting us to stop, but the driver whipped his horses and we went clattering on through the rocky defile to the small hilly town.

Sometimes we played in villages, with fields of uncut grass around the pitch, when the ball was lost among dog-daisies and sorrel. Bulls and cows, horses and sheep, we played cricket among them as if they were part of the game, and so they were. It was a contest without rancour, for whether we lost or won, we went home pleasurably excited. I climbed the hill and entered my home to tell them all about it, and it seemed that I had been away on the Crusades from the welcome and attention I received.

From *Carts and Candlesticks*, 1948.

It is a sad thought indeed of all those cricket matches in which Sam Pig makes the winning hit and the fielding standards are compromised by the number of grey, or greying rabbits in the deep, which Miss Uttley has never written about. A few ladies have written coherently about cricket, and there are surely many thousands like the one in Love on a Branch Line *by John Hadfield (b. 1907), who was indoctrinated into the game by assorted brothers to the point where she accosts strange men on trains and bemoans the passing of the past.*

THE WOMAN opposite me in the train put down her needlework and leaned forward with a hesitant gesture of inquiry. 'I see you are looking at the cricket scores', she said. 'Forgive my intruding, but could you tell me how Leicestershire are getting on?'

I read out the scores. 'You follow county cricket?' I asked.

'I love it!', she exclaimed, with a schoolgirlish titter that came incongruously from someone of uncertain years and unmistakably greying hair. 'My brother used to keep wicket for Clifton, you see, and my sisters and I used to bowl and field for him on the lawn at home. I wasn't much of a bowler myself. But'—she smiled—'I was rather good at retrieving the ball from the shrubbery.'

I smiled too. 'Leicestershire are not doing very well just now,' I said.

'No, they have no amateurs. It isn't quite the same when they're all professionals, is it? Not that I'm snobbish about it. I always used to think Hobbs and Sutcliffe two of the nicest men you could possibly meet. And some of the other ones—the rough diamonds like Parkin or Macaulay—they all fitted in somehow, didn't they? Just like the village blacksmith or the poacher on the village green. But all that is a thing of the past now, isn't it?'

From *Love on a Branch Line*, 1959.

Meanwhile, the captain of the Allahakbarries is inclined to take a much less complimentary view of ladies and cricket. What Barrie would have thought of the idea of English and Australian ladies contesting Test series with the same grave preoccupation as the men can hardly be imagined. But Barrie must secretly have cherished the very idea of girl cricketers, for he was one of those men whose affection for the game was governed very strongly by the degree of ineptitude with which people played it.

I LAY BENEATH a cherry tree, the idle spectator of a cricket match between a ladies' school and eleven young women of the neighbourhood. Not long before, I had seen two teams of the softer sex scrimmaging over a football, hardly an edifying spectacle; but here they made a pretty picture, those happy girls, flitting and darting in print and flannel, and the field was vocal with them. The elevens wore at their waists a rose, a red rose of the school girls, for the others a Maréchal Niel; and the victorious side were to leave the field with the rose of the vanquished at their belts.

The captains tossed for first innings in a professional manner; but, owing to a little peculiarity in one of them, who could not toss the coin without throwing up the other arm also, the penny was lost and a postage stamp had to be used; it answered all requirements and was slow in coming down, thus adding to the suspense. Then the Maréchal Niels went to the wickets, of course padless, carrying their bats beneath their arms, while the tail of the 'out' side gathered round the crease to hem in the ball and have a little chat until it came their way. The first representatives of the yellow rose were Miss Rawlins and Miss Thoms, who both played at least as well as a junior boys' team and with fairly straight bats, Miss Thoms getting the first cheer for going out and patting the ground with her bat. The attack was entrusted to Miss Mitchell (swift daisycutters) and a tall girl familiarly addressed as 'Georgie' (overhand). The first over was a maiden, but off Georgie's second ball Miss Rawlins scored; following it up shortly afterwards by lifting Miss Mitchell heftily to the on for two. The running between wickets was much faster than that of boys, once the batswomen started, but they lost time in watching the flight of the ball. Miss Thoms gave point a chance off a hard one, which was not taken, and then skied Georgie straight above short mid-on, who shouted 'Mary dear'. I found that 'Mary dear', at present cover point, was their great catcher, and that wherever the ball was lofted, the fieldswomen usually shouted for her. Several singles and a bye followed, and then Miss Mitchell found her way to Miss Rawlins' wicket (one for 11).

The next comer was Miss Philips, who immediately opened out to a tempting one from Georgie, and put her away to leg for 3. For this only 2 should have been scored; but long leg, instead of returning the ball, ran smartly with it to the stumps and put it personally into the wicket-keeper's hands. Miss Philips was now in superb form, and subjected the fielders to a rare piece of leather-hunting. Having driven Miss Mitchell for a brace, she cut another ball quite professionally, for which a couple was notched, and then running after a wide one, and overtaking it in the slips, hit it clandestinely for 3. This brought on Miss Coombes, *vice* Georgie; but runs still came, and the score stood at 25 after three-quarters of an hour's play. In stealing a run, however, the batswomen ran into each other, and before they could extricate themselves Miss Hibbert had told Miss Coombes what to do with the ball. (2 for 25.) Miss Epson, who came in second wicket down, did not seem at home with Miss Coombes, and having slipped her in a flukey manner for 1, had her wickets spread-eagled. Thirty was brought on soon afterwards in byes, no long-stop apparently being securable who would do more than hasten alongside the ball. Miss Hibbert was substituted for Miss Mitchell, in the hope of getting another wicket before luncheon; but both batswomen played carefully, never hitting out except when they felt confident of raising the leather high in the air to some place where Mary dear was not fielding.

Play was resumed at 1.45, when the two not-outs (Miss Thoms, 7, and Mrs Tetch, o) faced the bowling of Miss Hibbert and Miss Mitchell. Off the former's third ball Miss Thoms—who was now playing with more confidence—should have scored a pair; but Mrs Tetch, making a mistake as to her destination, rushed off in the direction of third man and was run out. (4 for 34.) Further disaster befell the 'in' side in the next over, Miss Thoms knocking off the bails with the skirt of her dress three times while turning to see whether Mary was fielding at long leg. She was then given out. Out she went in the jolliest way. They were all like that. Mary caught Miss Curson, and then the only altercation of the match arose, the Maréchal Niel captain coming out to complain that Mary was catching too many, and had no right to catch balls hit in the direction of another fielder. After consultation between the umpires the decision was given in Mary's favour. The two succeeding batswomen failed to score (also because of Mary). (Six, seven and eight for 35.) Mrs French, the next woman in, fell just as she was getting well set, and retired evidently under the impression that if you fall you are out. Things were now looking black for the the Maréchal Niels, but the last wicket gave a deal of trouble, and a change of bowling had to be again resorted to. Miss Leslie drove, lifted, cut and spanked Miss Hibbert hard for 2, 1, 2 and 2, after which the end soon came, owing to Mary. It was charming to see the not-out player who had scored one lifting her cap to the pavilion and the red and yellow roses alike cheering her; but indeed throughout the match the teams played like white men.

The innings of the red rose was opened by Mary dear and Miss Wace, to the bowling of Mrs French and Miss Leslie. Mary took the first over from Miss Leslie, who has a dangerous delivery, pitching her balls so high that it is extremely difficult to reach them. Mary, however, has a leap that can reach anything, and 10 soon went up. The scoring now became fast and furious, Mary obtaining a complete mastery of the bowling and becoming so excited that she attempted once to catch herself.

With the score at 20, Mrs Tetch was tried at the pavilion end, but was only allowed to bowl one over, Mary hitting her so hard that it took five fielders to bring the ball back.

At 26 Miss Wace, whose shoe-lace had become undone, hit her wickets while retying it, and the next comer got a blob. With two of the best wickets down for 26, the prospects of the 'in' side were now less bright. Mary continued to smite them; but was at last dismissed by a cup of cocoa brought to her amid applause, or at any rate by the next ball, which fell into the hands of Miss Leslie, who found it there after looking for it on the ground. After a short interval for what was evidently the most delicious conversation, play was resumed. The result seemed a foregone conclusion with the score at 35 for three wickets; but a remarkable change came over the aspect of the game when Miss Curson was put on to bowl. In her first over she almost did the hat trick, her delivery being so swift that even the slips fled. With only four wickets to fall and 8 runs to get to win there was still a possibility of the Maréchal Niels pulling the match out of the fire, and the fielding now became so smart and clean that Miss Mitchell was thrown out by Mary, who had come on as substitute for a fielder. Bets in gloves were offered and taken by the two fieldswomen nearest me. By byes and singles the score rose slowly to 41, when Miss Mousey was cleverly run out, the stumps being knocked down at both ends. Miss Curson had now gone completely off her form, and Mrs French was again tried. At 42 Miss Croall would have been run out if Mrs Tetch had not paused to dust the ball before returning it. This lost the Maréchal Niels the match, for at 5.30 Miss Croall made the winning hit, a dashing blow into the deep, which was caught by Mary but not until the needed 1 had been run.

The gaiety of them was a new delight on cricket fields. The most successful bowlers were Miss Curson, who took three wickets for 7 runs, and Miss Leslie (three for 14). When all is said and done, however, the match was Mary dear's, who, I am incredibly informed, is a schoolmarm and the mother of two. I was also told that she cried on the way home because she thought she was such a rotten catcher. The distribution of the roses of the fallen among the victors was delightfully formal but ended in a gay race to the pavilion. As for myself, I continued to eat cherries; it seemed the right thing to do, in thankfulness for the lingering sun and for merry ladies.

From *The Greenwood Hat*, 1930.

Albert Knight (1873–1946), was an opening batsman who played as a professional for Leicestershire between 1897 and 1912, a period which saw the county advance to first-class status. After scoring several centuries for the county, Knight became coach at Highgate School, where, no doubt the polysyllabic rococo of his prose style recommended itself to the Classics masters. Here he is on the theme of University cricket.

NOT MERELY as contributory forces to a greater manifestation or setting of the game in some larger and more widely appealing spectacle, but simply for themselves and by themselves, the schools and colleges of our land afford unequalled expositions of the game. Only the cynic will suggest that the cricket is the better part of their curriculum, only the very wise man will suggest that too much attention is given to it. The University game, the Oxford *v* Cambridge match at Lord's, is in so many ways the most interesting episode of each recurring year.

The social aspect of the game is that most calculated to impress the ordinary observer. The miles-long line of cabs and motors which stretch adown and around the neighbourhood of St John's Wood, roughly indicates what wealth and power, what fashion and influence, still interest themselves in a game which town slum and village green alike love. Within the ground, the family companionship, the evident camaraderie, the boisterous enthusiasm, give to the 'battle of the blues' characteristics rarely meeting in such combination elsewhere. A plebeian spectator, wandering amid the mighty and the great like some 'Jude the Obscure', may be pardoned for suggesting that on the occasions privileged to his witness, the game *per se* was not of a very extraordinary character. Quite possibly the lack was in the critic rather than in the exposition of these youths. The whole game, however, is in many ways unique, and has an influence upon thousands who have never had the inestimable good fortune of a university education, or who, perchance, have never seen the wonderful old city by the Isis banks or the town which borders the Cam.

Of these memorable matches, indeed, one may think as less disturbed than all else by the evolution of the modern game from a pastime, to a great spectacle largely governed by the considerations of commerce and business. Matthew Arnold, musing o'er the beautiful city which did not appreciate his interpretation of the Faith of the centuries, wrote of Oxford as 'The home of lost causes and forsaken beliefs, of unpopular names and impossible loyalties'. If this were true of theologies, that Oxford bent not her knee to the passing Zeitgeist, but set aloft her lonely light amid the mists of Tubingen criticism, she may do the same for sport. The Varsity match is the last stronghold of an amateurism well-nigh extinct in first-class cricket. It manifests what, in practice at least, seems an 'impossible loyalty' to the glow and glory of pure sport, and the continuous contribution, unhappily growing less, of great university and college players, is one of the most health-giving and invaluable which the modern game receives.

From *The Complete Cricketer*, 1906.

If Knight's is the most byzantine of all the cricketing prose styles, probably the most magisterial is the one favoured by Kumar Shri Ranjitsinhji, Maharajah Jam Sahib of Nawanagar (1872–1933; Cambridge University, Sussex and England). Scorer of 72 first-class centuries, twice scorer of 3000 runs in a season, an England player fourteen times, captain of Sussex 1899–1903; prominent member of the Indian Council of Princes, active at the League of Nations. On the eve of his highest score, 285 not out against Somerset at Taunton in 1901, he stayed up all night fishing. His Jubilee Book of Cricket, *published in 1897, is dedicated 'To Her Majesty the Queen-Empress'.*

IT HAS sometimes been objected that nearly all the pleasure derived from cricket is due not so much to the intrinsic merits of the game as to accidents of conditions and surroundings. That bright June sunshine and fine green turf are good settings for a game no one can deny. Then there is that grand old elm yonder to lie under while looking on. And there is all the pleasant companionship and salted wit of the pavilion and the railway journey. But I cannot help thinking that it is the spirit of cricket—of the game itself—that glorifies everything connected with it. No doubt when people play the game on a rough jumble of veldt-grass and mine-tailings in the outskirts of Johannesburg, half the pleasure they find is the result of association of ideas. The feel of a bat and its sound against the ball bring back memories of the green turf and cool breezes of England. Still, cricket is a gem fair in itself, apart from the beauty of its setting—a gem quite worthy of a niche in Queen Victoria's crown. . . .

Let us see what kind of man is produced by a life devoted to cricket. It has always seemed to me that those people are most fortunate whose work and pleasure are combined. I do not mean those who merely take a kind of side interest in their work while their real interests are otherwise directed, but those whose chief pleasure is their work. It is of course out of the question to compare playing cricket with the pursuit of art, science or literature. But in a far-off way a professional cricketer's life does somewhat resemble that of an artist. The true artist regards his art, not as a means to an end, but as an end in itself. For him his art

66

is not only his work but his pleasure. Now most cricketers would rather play cricket than do anything else, even though it is the means whereby they live. The large majority of professionals play cricket for cricket's sake, rather than because they get so much a year for appearing in so many matches or bowling for so many hours at nets. For this reason, I think I would rather be a professional cricketer than a man who toils to make a large income out of some business that he hates, in order to be able to spend it on something he likes. Such men have a divided life, half of which is not life at all in the true sense of the word. A cricketer is a far better exponent of the art of living than many men who are far richer and far more highly esteemed. Perhaps this is the reason why cricketers as a class are so remarkably happy themselves and so extremely pleasant to deal with. There are few worthier fellows in the world than the average professional of the better class. I remember hearing Mr Stoddart say—and I hope he will not mind my repeating it—'Well, I never want to meet three better fellows or more pleasant companions than Tom Richardson, Albert Ward, and Brockwell'. This was soon after he returned from his tour in Australia in the winter of 1895–6. It is true he happened to light on three particularly good specimens, but what he said of them is widely applicable among professionals. They are as a class good fellows and pleasant companions. And it would be curious if there was much wrong with the life that produces men who are happy themselves and make others happy too. . . .

Cricket is the best athletic food for the public. It is not so furiously popular as football, nor so much thought of in some districts. But it has a more even and firmer hold on people in general. Neither time nor money has tarnished it. There are very few newspaper readers who do not turn to the cricket columns first when the morning journal comes; who do not buy a halfpenny evening paper to find out how many runs WG or Bobby Abel has made. Many of these same people go to the Oval on Saturday afternoon to see Surrey play Gloucestershire. And the large majority of them would be doing nothing if they did not do this. The remembrance of a bright half-hour when Tom Hayward and Walter Read were in together makes the cricket news doubly interesting all the summer. It is a grand thing for people who have to work most of their time to have an interest in something or other outside their particular groove. Cricket is a first-rate interest. The game has developed to such a pitch that it is worth taking interest in. Go to Lord's and analyse the crowd. There are all sorts and conditions of men there round the ropes—bricklayers, bank clerks, soldiers, postmen, and stockbrokers. And in the pavilion are QCs, artists, archdeacons and leader-writers. Bad men, good men, workers and idlers, are all there, and all at one in their keenness over the game. It is a commonplace that cricket brings the most opposite characters and the most diverse lives together. Anything that puts very many different kinds of people on a common ground must promote sympathy and kindly feelings. The workman does not come away from seeing Middlesex beating Lancashire or vice versa with evil in his heart against the upper ten; nor the Mayfair *homme de plaisier* with a feeling of contempt for the street-bred masses. Both alike are thinking how well Mold bowled, and how cleanly Stoddart despatched Briggs's high-tossed slow ball over the awning. Even that cynical *nil admirari* lawyer caught himself cheering loudly when Sir Timothy planted Hallam's would-be yorker into the press-box. True, he caught himself being enthusiastic and broke off at once; but that little bit of keen appreciation did him no harm. Jones and Smith, who quarrelled bitterly over that piece of land, forgot all about the matter under the influence of Ford's hitting, and walked down to Baker Street quite familiarly. They will come up in the same carriage tomorrow morning, as they always used to do till last month. Yes; there is a world of good in cricket, even in cricket as played nowadays, though it does require so great a sacrifice of time that might be devoted to more obviously useful pursuits.

From *The Jubilee Book of Cricket*, 1897.

It is generally believed that part of the text of Ranjitsinhji's monumental work was in fact written by his great friend and batting partner in the Sussex side, C. B. Fry (1872–1956). Certainly in a prefatory note Ranji acknowledges Fry's assistance, and, knowing what nature of man Fry was, it is hard to imagine him 'assisting' an author without actually composing his text for him. Fry was perhaps the most extraordinary figure in the history of English sport, as Alan Gibson here conveys.

C. B. Fry: classic in all respects

C. B. FRY was born on April 25, 1872. He is a difficult man to write about, partly because so much has already been written about him, partly because he wrote so incomparably about himself. I have never enjoyed an autobiography more than *Life Worth Living*. Of the attempts by others to put him in print, perhaps Denzil Batchelor's account in the Phoenix *Cricketing Lives* series is the best. Denzil was Fry's secretary for several years (Agate called him Fry's 'Jock'), and one of the few men who could hold his end up in a conversation with the master.

Sir Neville Cardus often has written beautifully of Fry, though he has never given him a long study. Sir Neville also seems to have been equal to the conversational demands, on the 1936–7 tour of Australia. Indeed, he once scored a technical knock-out, breathing into his companion's ear the words, 'This'll irk you, Charles', just as the November 11 two-minute silence was beginning. I dare say Sir Neville will be repeating this story today, but he will agree we must never tire of quoting the classics.

Fry was also a classic. He was a classic academically, with his first in Mods. This was to show he could do it. He did not bother too much about Greats. He had done enough to show himself a scholar comparable with, possibly superior to, John Simon and F. E. Smith, his contemporaries at Wadham.

Someone will be saying, 'What are these Mods and Greats? Who are Simon and F. E.? Where is Wadham?' But these short-cuts have to be made in writing an article about Fry, or a man would find himself writing a whole newspaper to say nothing of breaking the rule that no sentence should exceed 25 words (he endeavoured to apply such a rule to contributors to *C. B. Fry's Magazine*, but so noticeably failed to observe it in his own writings that the contributors rebelled, whereupon he offered a dispensation to those who had benefited from a classical education, and therefore 'understood how to frame subordinate clauses'). Yet he was capable of a pithy sentence. Denzil Batchelor once said that when Fry was in an astringent mood he became the incarnation of the ablative absolute.

Fry was a classic cricketer. When he and Ranjitsinhji were batting together, there can never have been a better cricketing illustration of the difference between the classical and the romantic. At one end, Fry coming forward, left leg well down the pitch, perfectly balanced and controlled, but ready to move into attack should the ball offer the chance: at the other, Ranji's astonishing back play, with its misleading air of improvisation, the bumper flicked to long-leg from the lobe of the left ear.

They scored thousands of runs together for Sussex. It was said that Fry 'learnt all he knew' from Ranji, but this cannot be true: every picture shows their styles to have been different. I suspect that it was because Fry was conscious that he was in all respects a classic, that he turned down the kingdom of Albania. He would have had no place in an Anthony Hope romance.

Fry broke the world record at the long jump, and would have gone over to Athens to win it in the 1896 Olympics, had he known they were on. He scored six centuries in six successive innings, a feat which Bradman equalled but did not surpass. He won a Blue for football, and would have won one for rugby but for an injury (he preferred rugby, but played for Southampton in an FA Cup final). He represented India at the League of Nations, deputizing for Ranjitsinhji.

He increased, quite dramatically, the circulation of a London evening newspaper by writing cricket reports for it. He failed, however, despite several efforts, to make a success of a magazine for boys. The one which came nearest to establishing itself was *The Captain*, much of which still reads well enough. It was difficult to get enough advertising in the magazine. 'I have always thought', Fry wrote, 'that the disbelief of advertisers in the capacity of boys to absorb soap was the snag which eventually tripped up the career of *The Captain*'.

My own acquaintance with C. B. Fry, though treasured, was brief. I met him once on the training ship *Mercury*, which he commanded, in the Mamble river. Of that enterprise, F. E. Smith had said: 'This is a fine show, C. B., but for you a backwater'; and Fry replied: 'That may be, but the question remains whether it is better to be successful or happy'.

Fry's own political career was handicapped by his faithfulness to the Liberal Party. He polled very well at Brighton, but was never elected. At the age of 70, he told the Oxford University Liberal Club: 'I think I'll try again'. There was loud applause, but he never did.

It was at Oxford, which he loved, that I mostly saw him. He was still magnificently built, and he retained his habit, of which many have written, of playing strokes with an umbrella. Indeed, in the buttery of the Queen's College, the umbrella momentarily mislaid, he seized an assagai from the wall in order to demonstrate how Ranjitsinhji played. It was a slightly alarming moment, as the buttery was not very large, and the assagai sharp: in consequence I failed to absorb important information, for never to this day have I been quite sure how Ranji played the famous leg glide.

Fry played in 26 Tests, all in England except the first two, when he was a youngster with a side in South Africa well below England strength. As he had to earn his living, he never toured Australia except as a writer. There was a belief among his contemporaries that he would have scored hugely on Australian pitches. Yet in this country he was not an outstanding success against the Australians.

In 1899 he scored 187 runs in eight Test innings. In 1902, in four innings in three Tests, he scored 0, 0, 1 and 4, and then was dropped. Ranjitsinhji was dropped in the same series (13, 0, 2, 4). Yet they dominated the domestic scene so much then that it struck awe into every heart to leave them out.

These failures by Fry were no doubt partly the mere luck of it. But the Australians thought, with some reason, that they had him tied down, by cutting out his favourite strokes on the on-side. In 1905 he gave them an answer by scoring 144 at The Oval, mostly through the off-drive and the cut. In the end he averaged 32 in Test cricket, good in those days but not outstandingly so.

He led England, victoriously, in 1912 against Australia and South Africa, in the triangular tournament. In his career, which began in 1892 and finished in 1921, he scored over 30,000 runs at an average of over 50. In 1921, when England were in trouble against Armstrong's Australians, he was asked to consider leading the side again. After a successful outing against them for Hampshire, he probably would have done; but an injury prevented it.

He had looked set for another hundred against the Australians in the Lord's Test of 1905. But when he had scored 73 he was given out, caught at the wicket, by Jim Phillips. Phillips was an Australian umpire who had many years before no-balled Fry for throwing, to his intense and lasting irritation. On this occasion Fry maintained that he had hit the toe of his boot with the bat, well away from the ball. Phillips explained that he had heard a click. 'I asked him—of course, after the match—whether he was sure it was not the slamming of a door in the pavilion'.

In 1912, after he had won the rubber against Australia, the Oval crowd cheered him and called for him. Earlier in the same match they had booed him, because of his refusal to restart play after rain. Fry would not go on the balcony. 'Be your noble self', urged Ranjitsinhji. He replied, 'This is not one of my noble days'.

Ancedotes such as these suggest in his character not exactly an acidity but a certain mordancy, a classical disdain. Despite his politics, he was never a tribune of the people. On the other hand:

Omne tulit punctum qui miscuit utile dulci.
Lectorem delectando pariterque monendo.

This might be roughly translated: mingle profit and pleasure, delight your audience at the same time as you instruct them, and you will win all the votes. C. B. Fry did mingle profit and pleasure, did both delight and instruct, and he would get my vote every time.

From *The Times*, 25 April 1972.

Although characters like Fry—who captained Repton in 1891, Oxford University in 1894, Sussex in 1908, England in 1912, declined an England place in 1921 and remained a prominent figure for the next thirty years—create an impression of timelessness, the history of cricket does not quite present the unbroken sequence it should. The 1914 season was never completed: on 27 August of that year W. G. Grace sent his famous letter to The Sportsman *demanding that cricketers put aside their bats and balls and join the greater game in France. That Grace was wrong there can be no faint shadow of doubt, for not only is playing cricket perfectly compatible with national crisis, as the British Government was wise enough to acknowledge in the Second World War, but the flood of volunteers in 1914 embarrassed the enemy much less than it did the British War Office, which was not prepared for the onrush and had no idea what to do about it. But as the wartime chronicle of Robert Graves (b. 1895) shows, the British went on playing the game regardless.*

JUNE 24, 1915. Vermelles. This afternoon we had a cricket match, officers versus sergeants, in an enclosure between some houses out of observation from the enemy. Our front line is perhaps three-quarters of a mile away. I made top score, 24; the bat was a bit of a rafter, the ball, a piece of rag tied round with string; and the wicket, a parrot cage with the clean, dry corpse of a parrot inside. It had evidently died of starvation when the French evacuated the town. Machine-gun fire broke up the match.

From *Goodbye to All That*, 1929.

The Great War destroyed a great many aspects of British life involving cricket. The old rural existence celebrated by writers like Sassoon and Uttley gradually faded into the past, the days of the Gentleman-cricketer were now strictly numbered, and what has since been defined as the Golden Age finally met a violent end with the death in the war of players like Hutchings and Blythe of Kent. Just as significant in its way was the self-imposed exile in New York of the ex-Dulwich fast bowler P. G. Wodehouse, who by 1916 had been Americanised for long enough to be able to stand back and appreciate the degree of bewilderment facing the American investigator who tries to plumb cricket's mysterious depths. It was almost the last time Wodehouse was to incorporate cricket in the text of his fictions; so far as the game was concerned, a terrible fate awaited him. Its name was Baseball.

LONDON BROODED under a grey sky. There had been rain in the night, and the trees were still dripping. Presently, however, there appeared in the leaden haze a watery patch of blue; and through this crevice in the clouds the sun, diffidently at first but with gradually increasing confidence, peeped down on the fashionable and exclusive turf of Grosvenor Square. Stealing across the square its rays reached the massive stone walls of Drexdale House, until recently the London residence of the earl of that name; then, passing through the window of the breakfast room, played lightly on the partially bald head of Mr Bingley Crocker, late of New York, in the United States of America, as he bent over his morning paper. Mrs Bingley Crocker, busy across the table reading her mail, the rays did not touch. Had they done so she would have rung for Bayliss, the butler, to come and lower the shade, for she endured liberties neither from man nor from Nature.

Mr Crocker was about fifty years of age, clean shaven and of comfortable stoutness. He was frowning as he read. His smooth, good-humoured face wore an expression that might have been disgust, perplexity, or a blend of both. His wife, on the other hand, was looking happy. She extracted the substance from her correspondence with swift glances of her compelling eyes, just as she would have extracted guilty secrets from Bingley, if he had had any. This was a woman who, like her sister Nesta, had been able all her life to accomplish more with a glance than other women with recrimination and threat. It had been a popular belief among his friends that her late husband, the well-known Pittsburgh millionaire, G. G. van Brunt, had been in the habit of automatically confessing all if he merely caught the eye of her photograph on his dressing table.

From the growing pile of opened envelopes Mrs Crocker looked up, a smile softening the firm line of her lips.

'A card from Lady Corstorphine, Bingley, for her at-home on the twenty-ninth.'

Mr Crocker, still absorbed, snorted absently.

'One of the most exclusive hostesses in England. She has influence with the right sort of people. Her brother, the Duke of Devizes, is the Premier's oldest friend.'

'Uh?'

'The Duchess of Axminster has written to ask me to look after a stall at her bazaar for the Indigent Daughters of the Clergy.'

'Huh?'

'Bingley, you aren't listening! What is that you are reading?'

Mr Crocker tore himself from the paper.

'This? Oh, I was looking at a report of that cricket game you made me go and see yesterday.'

'Oh, I am so glad you have begun to take an interest in cricket. It is simply a social necessity in England. Why you ever made such a fuss about taking it up I can't think. You used to be so fond of watching baseball, and cricket is just the same thing.'

A close observer would have marked a deepening of the look of pain on Mr Crocker's face. Women say this sort of thing carelessly, with no wish to wound; but that makes it nonetheless hard to bear.

From the hall outside came faintly the sound of the telephone, then the measured tones of Bayliss answering it. Mr Crocker returned to his paper. Bayliss entered.

'Lady Corstorphine desires to speak to you on the telephone, madam.'

Half-way to the door Mrs Crocker paused, as if recalling something that had slipped her memory.

'Is Mr James getting up, Bayliss?'

'I believe not, madam. I am informed by one of the housemaids who passed his door a short time back that there were no sounds.'

Mrs Crocker left the room. Bayliss, preparing to follow her example, was arrested by an exclamation from the table.

'Say!' His master's voice. 'Say, Bayliss, come here a minute. Want to ask you something.'

The butler approached the table. It seemed to him that his employer was not looking quite himself this morning. There was something a trifle wild, a little haggard, about his expression. He had remarked on it earlier in the morning in the servants' hall.

As a matter of fact, Mr Crocker's ailment was a perfectly simple one. He was suffering from one of those acute spasms of homesickness which invariably racked him in the earlier summer months. Ever since his marriage, five years previously, he had been a chronic victim to the complaint. The symptoms grew less acute in winter and spring, but from May onward he suffered severely.

Poets have dealt feelingly with the emotions of practically every variety except one. They have sung of Ruth, of Israel in bondage, of slaves pining for their native Africa, and of the miner's dream of home. But the sorrows of the baseball enthusiast, compelled by fate to live three thousand miles away from the Polo Grounds, have been neglected in song. Bingley Crocker was such a one, and in summer his agonies were awful. He pined away in a country where they said, 'Well played, sir!' when they meant 'At-a-boy!'

'Bayliss, do you play cricket?'

'I am a little past the age, sir. In my younger days—'

'Do you understand it?'

'Yes, sir. I frequently spend an afternoon at Lord's or the Oval when there is a good match.'

Many who enjoyed a merely casual acquaintance with the butler would have looked on this as an astonishingly unexpected revelation of humanity in Bayliss, but Mr Crocker was not surprised. To him, from the very beginning, Bayliss had been a man and a brother, who was always willing to suspend his duties in order to answer questions dealing with the thousand and one problems which the social life of England presented. Mr Crocker's mind had adjusted itself with difficulty to the niceties of class distinction, and though he had cured himself of his early tendency to address the butler as 'Bill', he never failed to consult him as man to man in his moments of perplexity. Bayliss was always eager to be of assistance. He liked Mr Crocker. True, his manner might have struck a more sensitive man than his employer as a shade too closely resembling that of an indulgent father toward a son who was not quite right in the head; but it had genuine affection in it.

Mr Crocker picked up his paper and folded it back at the sporting page, pointing with a stubby forefinger.

'Well, what does all this mean? I've kept out of watching cricket since I landed in England, but yesterday they got the poison needle to work and took me off to see Surry play Kent at that place, the Oval, where you say you go sometimes.'

'I was there yesterday, sir. A very exciting game.'

'Exciting? How do you make that out? I sat in the bleachers all afternoon, waiting for something to break loose. Doesn't anything ever happen at cricket?'

The butler winced a little, but managed to smile a tolerant smile. This man, he reflected, was but an American, and as such more to be pitied than censured. He endeavoured to explain.

'It was a sticky wicket yesterday sir, owing to the rain.'

'Eh?'

'The wicket was sticky, sir.'

'Come again.'

'I mean that the reason why the game yesterday struck you as slow was that the wicket—I should say the turf—was sticky—that is to say, wet. Sticky is the technical term, sir. When the wicket is sticky the batsmen are obliged to exercise a great deal of caution, as the stickiness of the wicket enables the bowlers to make the ball turn more sharply in either direction as it strikes the turf than when the wicket is not sticky.'

'That's it, is it?'

'Yes, sir.'

'Thanks for telling me.'

'Not at all, sir.'

Mr Crocker pointed to the paper.

'Well, now, this seems to be the boxscore of the game we saw yesterday. If you can make sense out of that, go to it.'

The passage on which the finger rested was headed Final Score, and ran as follows:

SURREY—First Innings.

Hayward	c. Woolley b. Carr	67
Hobbs	Run Out	0
Hayes	st. Huish b. Fielder	12
Ducat	b. Fielder	33
Harrison	Not Out	11
Sandham	Not Out	6
	Extras	10
	Total (for four wickets)	139

77

Bayliss inspected the cipher gravely.

'What is it you wish me to explain, sir?'

'Why, the whole thing. What's it all about?'

'Its perfectly simple, sir. Surrey won the toss and took first knock. Hayward and Hobbs were the opening pair. Hayward called Hobbs for a short run, but the latter was unable to get across and was thrown out by mid-on. Hayes was the next man in. He went out of his ground and was stumped. Ducat and Hayward made a capital stand considering the stickiness of the wicket, until Ducat was bowled by a good length off-break and Hayward caught at second slip off a googly. Then Harrison and Sandham played out time.'

Mr Crocker breathed heavily through his nose.

'Yes!' he said, 'Yes! I had an idea that was it. But I think I'd like to have it once again, slowly. Start with these figures. What does that sixty seven mean, opposite Hayward's name?'

'He made sixty seven runs, sir.'

'Sixty seven! In one game?'

'Yes, sir.'

'Why, Home-Run Baker couldn't do it!'

'I am not familiar with Mr Baker, sir.'

'I suppose you've never seen a ball game?'

'Ball game, sir?'

'A baseball game?'

'Never, sir.'

'Then, Bill,' said Mr Crocker, reverting in his emotion to the bad habit of his early London days, 'you haven't lived. See here!'

Whatever vestige of respect for class distinctions Mr Crocker had managed to preserve during the opening stages of the interview now definitely disappeared. His eyes shone wildly and he snorted like a warhorse. He clutched the butler by the sleeve and drew him closer to the table, then began to move forks, spoons, cups, and even the contents of his plate, about the cloth with an energy little short of feverish.

'Bayliss?'

'Sir?'

'Watch!' said Mr Crocker, with the air of an excitable high priest about to initiate a novice into the mysteries.

He removed a roll from the basket.

'You see this roll? That's the home plate. This spoon is first base. Where I'm putting this cup is second. This piece of bacon is third. There's your diamond for you. Very well then. These lumps of sugar are the infielders and the outfielders. Now we're ready. Batter up! He stands here. Catcher behind him. Umps behind catcher.'

'Umps, I take it, sir, is what you would call the umpire?'

'Call him anything you like. It's part of the game. Now here's the box, where I've put this dab of marmalade, and here's the pitcher winding up.'

'The pitcher would be equivalent to our bowler?'

'I guess so, though why you should call him a bowler gets past me.'

'The box, then, is the bowler's wicket?'

'Have it your own way. Now pay attention. Play ball! Pitcher's winding up. Put it over, Mike, put it over! Some speed, kid! Here it comes, right in the groove. Bing! Batter slams it and streaks for first. Outfielder—this lump of sugar—boots it. Bonehead! Batter touches second. Third? No! Get back! Can't be done. Play it safe. Stick round the sack, old pal. Second batter up. Pitcher getting something on the ball now beside the cover. Whiffs him. Back to the bench, Cyril! Third batter up. See him rub his hands in the dirt. Watch this kid. He's good! Lets two alone, then slams the next right on the nose. Whizzes round to second. First guy, the one we left on second, comes home for one run. That's a game! Take it from me, Bill, that's a game!'

Somewhat overcome with the energy with which he had flung himself into his lecture, Mr Crocker sat down and refreshed himself with cold coffee.

'Quite an interesting game,' said Bayliss. 'But I find, now that you have explained it, sir, that it is familiar to me, though I have always known it under another name. It is played a great deal in this country.'

Mr Crocker started to his feet.

'Is it? And I've been five years without finding it out! When's the next game scheduled?'

'It is known in England as rounders, sir. Children play it with a soft ball and a racket, and derive considerable enjoyment from it. I have never heard of it before as a pastime for adults.'

Two shocked eyes stared into the butler's face.

'Children?' The word came in a whisper. 'A racket?'

'Yes, sir.'

'You—you didn't say a soft ball?'

'Yes, sir.'

A sort of spasm seemed to convulse Mr Crocker. He had lived five years in England, but not till this moment had he realized to the full how utterly alone he was in an alien land. Fate had placed him bound and helpless, in a country where they called baseball rounders and played it with a soft ball.

He sank back in his chair, staring before him. And as he sat the wall seemed to melt and he was gazing upon a green field, in the centre of which a man in a grey uniform was beginning a Salome dance. Watching this person with a cold and suspicious eye stood another uniformed man, holding poised above his shoulder a sturdy club. Two Masked Marvels crouched behind him in attitudes of watchful waiting. On wooden seats all round sat a vast multitude of shirt-sleeved spectators, and the air was full of voices.

'Pea-nuts! Get y'r pea-nuts!'

Something that was almost a sob shook Bingley Crocker's ample frame. Bayliss, the butler, gazed down upon him with concern. He was sure the master was unwell.

From *Piccadilly Jim*, 1917.

*By the time Wodehouse described that touching scene, the father-figure of
English cricket, W. G. Grace, was already dead. Whether or not Grace was
really an author, or whether all the volumes bearing his name are in fact the
work of zealous ghosts is uncertain, but certainly the authentic ambience
rises from some of his reminiscences.*

TRUE, THERE were important clubs in such large towns as Liverpool,
Manchester, and one or two others; but the members were mostly in
good positions, and were usually elected by ballot. At the weekly
meetings of those clubs, the younger members came to play, the older
ones to criticise, and sides were picked. A few matches were played
during the season with clubs of the same strength who were within
driving distance. The dinners played no insignificant part at those
gatherings, and many a good bottle of port was cracked before the
evening was over. It is related that the Kingscote club nearly ruined
itself by its hospitality to the Epsom club after a friendly match. Three
haunches of venison were consumed, besides other delicacies, and the
cellar ran dry. The chairman is said to have closed the innings of the
claret with the remark: 'Gentlemen, I am sorry to say there is only one
bottle left, and as it would be ridiculous to divide that among so many,
with your permission I'll drink it myself.' That sort of social cricket
existed, and very enjoyable cricket it was; but cricket amongst the
people was scarcely known until the All-England Eleven appeared.

The spring and dash of life have somewhat abated in me, and perhaps I
am less careful today in the matter of sleep than I was ten or fifteen
years ago; but I cannot remember when I did not at the beginning or
middle of the season take care to have a fair amount of rest. Every player
must judge for himself whether he requires six, eight or ten hours. It
has happened on many occasions that I have been up half the night, and
scored heavily next day; but that proves nothing, unless, perhaps, that I
possess exceptional physical powers.

    A good story comes to mind, which, while it goes against my theory,
is too good to be lost. It occurred during the Scarborough week, where
good cricket and good cheer go hand-in-hand. Three or four of us were

on the way to our rooms in the early morning, after an enjoyable dance; and being more in the mood for chatting than sleep, we, with one exception, decided to spend an hour or two longer comparing reminiscences. The 'exception' had commenced his innings that day, and was not out when play stopped. 'You can do what you like', said he; 'but I'm off to bed, as I mean to make a hundred tomorrow.'

I forget how long we sat up—certainly later than we should have done in the beginning of the season—but next day every one of us scored largely; while our friend was out first over, without adding to his overnight's score. I sincerely hope young players will not follow our example, though it was not attended with disastrous results.

Saturday was one of the hottest days of a very hot month, and I thought I might as well put my best foot forward in the early morning. My partner was Mr P. C. Crutchley, and he being in the scoring mood also, we kept the ball travelling at a great pace. The ground was in rare order, and from noon till luncheon-time we put all we knew into our hitting, only stopping for a few minutes while I borrowed a bat, having broken the one which had served me so well. The new bat was a good one, but much too small in the handle for me, and the pace slackened slightly; however, during the luncheon hour the Hon. Spencer Ponsonby Fane very kindly got hold of some thick twine, which he wrapped round it and brought it up to the right size. Tired nature began to tell its tale during the afternoon: but relief came from the officers' tent in the form of champagne and seltzer; and at it we went again, and were not parted until we had put on 227 runs, and raised the total to 430 for five wickets. The opinion of the Kent Twelve, Mr Absolom's in particular, was, 'that it had been a very hot day!'

It is an old story, but will bear repetition, how Jupp and Southerton tried to get me in a fix when the ball bounded into an opening of my shirt while I was running in the Gloucestershire v Surrey match at Clifton College in 1878. Townsend and I were batting and had run three when the ball lodged there, and after we had run three more, Jupp and Southerton collared me. 'We don't know how many runs you mean to run, sir; but you might give us the ball.' 'No, thank you; take it out for yourself, Jupp,' I said, laughing. 'You don't get me out in that way!'

He had rather a liking for a glass of champagne, but objected to dilution. When the United South played Walsall on a certain occasion, I was the guest of Mr Russell, a great supporter of the game. He invited

82

the professionals of the team to look in upon him in the morning, when he would crack a bottle or two before they began the day's play. Jupp turned up with the others, and when asked to have seltzer with it said, 'No, thank you, sir; I have always found champagne good enough by itself.'

From *Cricket*, 1891.

The student picking up the story of international cricket on its resumption in 1921 senses a profound change, something much subtler than the mere fact that for the moment England were no match for the Australians. One fortunate difference, hardly noticed at the time, was the steady rise of the idiosyncratic match report. Cardus was one writer for whom the 1921 series was his first. Another was the essayist Robert Lynd (1879–1949), whose work appeared regularly in the New Statesman *and* John o' London's Weekly *among others.*

A Row at the Oval

IT WOULD be easy to make too much of the scenes that occurred at the Oval on Saturday, when the fifth Test Match was begun. But at least they brought a few minutes' dramatic excitement into as tedious a day's cricket as it would be possible to imagine.

It all came of too much inspection of the wicket. The crowd got tired of sitting round an empty field with nothing happening but half-hourly strolls on the part of the two captains in their blazers from the pavilion to the wicket and back again.

Armstrong would stoop down and feel the ground with his hand as a doctor 'palps' a patient in order to discover the place where it hurts. Impatient voices would assail him: 'Come along!' 'Play up!' Standing up, however, he would demonstratively shake the water off his hand as a cat shakes its forefoot after having stepped in a puddle.

After a time the crowd made up its mind that, if inspecting the wicket was to be the only sport of the day, it would relieve the monotony for everybody to do it.

A number of the bolder spirits, having decided that the wicket could be passed as at least C3, then made their way towards the pavilion, and began to call loudly for the players to come out.

They were joined by a thousand or so other people who had come to see what was happening. They seemed to have got it into their heads that it was Armstrong who was responsible for holding up the game, and one youth went so far as to suggest that the Australians were afraid to face England.

Imitating the voice of a newsboy he yelled: 'Speshul; Orstrylia runs away!' Others contented themselves with bellowing: 'Come out of it!' 'Be sportsmen!' 'Play up!' One youth every now and then interjected a wonderful '*Coo*-ee!' like the cry of a shriek-owl prolonged and a hundred times magnified.

This subtle invitation to the Australians to come out dissolved the anger of the crowd into laughter, and the laughter became universal when a breath of wind lifted the canvas awning over the pavilion seats and upset a gallon of water that lay there in a pool, drenching the man who stood under it. That is always an excellent joke.

As the tumult continued, a policeman made his way to the pavilion and hurried up the steps, with the evident desire to get somebody to do something.

An instant later, Tennyson appeared on a balcony, holding up his hand for silence. But there was no silence—only worse pandemonium, with most people cheering, and the rest interrupting one another with a thousand indistinguishable remarks.

Tennyson beamed on them, like a fair-haired undergraduate about to make a speech amid the tumult of a 'rag.' His smile at length took effect. Amid what was as much like silence as could be expected, he bent forward and, in the voice of one not accustomed to open-air oratory, called out: 'If you people will get back to your places, Mr Armstrong and I will inspect the wicket.'

This simple speech, in spite of the charm with which it was delivered, merely served to inflame the crowd. They did not wish to see the wicket inspected. They wished to see the game resumed.

Instead of going back to their places they began to shout all the louder: 'Where's Armstrong?' and to chant in chorus: 'We—want—Armstrong! We—want—Armstrong! We—want—Armstrong!'

This naturally led to the wicket not being inspected, and this in turn led to increasing turbulence on the part of a section of the crowd. Tennyson at last could endure it no longer. He came down the pavilion steps and made his way through the surging crowd towards the wicket.

After Tennyson's return to the pavilion the clamorous section of the crowd still remained on the field calling for Armstrong, cheering Fender, cheering Tennyson, and then, one or two of them, booing Armstrong again.

Tennyson's report on the wicket was apparently, as they say, 'favourable,' for in a few minutes a boy was sent out into the crowd carrying a blackboard with the inscription chalked on it: 'If no more rain, play will take place at 5.15.'

That meant another half-hour's waiting, but it changed the temper of the crowd sufficiently to enable a score or so of policeman to shepherd the people slowly back to their places and off the field of play.

Once back in their places, the crowd waited patiently till a quarter past five, and shortly afterwards it was cheering the appearance of the umpires.

When Armstrong and his men tripped down the steps, however, bad temper broke out again, and there were volleys of boos mingled with the general cheering. Cries of 'Shame!' were raised by the more sportsman-like section of the crowd, and the cheering in the end entirely drowned the booing.

But all through the afternoon the malcontents showed that they had not forgiven Armstrong. They jeered when he tested the condition of the wicket with his foot, and one man called out: 'Roll on it! Roll on it!' They cheered him derisively every time he fielded the easiest ball. They shouted at him if he seemed to walk in too leisurely a manner to his place in the field.

In the end, it was as if Armstrong had resolved to amuse them out of their anger. He never moved but he ran. He would bolt even the shortest distance, like a fat man running desperately to catch a train that is just moving out of the station.

Great is the power of comedy. Gradually ill-temper faded, and men remembered that they had come to watch an entertainment and not to take part in a squalling match.

As I have said, the row itself was a comparatively small affair, and only a tiny minority made themselves hoarse joining in it. It was interesting because of its novelty rather than because of its seriousness. It was interesting, too, because it did express in a rude and unlovely way the boredom that nearly everybody felt.

The truth is, Saturday was no day for cricket as the game is now played. When I arrived in town at ten o'clock in the morning the rain was dripping down, and the sky in the east was discoloured and dark, like a black eye.

It was still raining when I reached the Oval just before eleven. There was no crowd assaulting the gates. The scene inside the ground was more depressing than a picnic in macintoshes. The Oval is a wonderful cricket ground, but its good qualities even at the best of times are those of usefulness rather than beauty.

As I sat watching the rain falling, I did my best to be interested in the gasometer by speculating on what would happen if a thunderstorm came on and the gasometer were struck by lightning. I saw myself, in my mind's eye, blown into surprisingly small bits, some of them travelling as far as Kew, others of them going in a northerly direction and reaching Willesden Junction. Then, just as my thoughts were beginning to get morbid, the rain stopped.

There was no sign of play beginning, however, when half-past eleven came round. Not until some time after twelve did the long preliminary ritual begin—the inspection of the wicket with prodding fingers (Armstrong still wearing the blue suit and grey hat of a private citizen), the rolling-away of the low pent-houses that covered the wicket, the arrival of the bag of sawdust, the spilling of the sawdust so as to make two little yellow hills, the arrival of the stumps, the arrival of a man with a bucket, who set up the stumps and whitewashed the crease, the arrival of the roller, the departure of the roller, the spinning of the coin at the gate of the pavilion, the inspection of the coin on the grass, and then the arrival of the umpires in long robes whiter than whited sepulchres.

Compared to the whiteness of the umpires, the flannelled Australians, as they poured out over the field, seemed figures of a faint and charming yellow, like that of evening primroses. And, indeed, on their appearance, it was as if the field had suddenly blossomed. There was a lingering gleam of summer in the air. It made the slates shine. It made Gregory's and Macdonald's hair shine.

It did not succeed, however, in making the cricket shine. Gregory, who bowled the first over from opposite the pavilion, did not find the slippery ground the springboard that he needs for his great feats.

Both Russell and Brown settled down to play him with confidence, if without violence. They both scored off his first over, but they seemed to do so in the spirit of men digging themselves in and making occasional small sallies rather than of men about to take a position by assault. The excitement of the play was not owing to any tremendousness in their hitting, but to their readiness to steal every slightest opportunity of a run. Brown, especially, was like a restive horse at the starting post— almost too ready for a forward plunge.

Russell batted with light ping-pong strokes, and looked as if he might have gone on doing so till he had made his century, when something happened, as he tried to sweep a ball of Macdonald's round to leg. It was impossible for a spectator to say whether he had struck the ball at all, but Oldfield, who had taken Carter's place as wicket-keeper, sprang after it as it bounded into the air, and Russell was out, for 13 without apparently believing that he had even touched the ball.

Tyldesley seemed a good deal less confident than he on taking his place. He frequently struck at the ball in the way in which one strikes at an insect that contrives just to keep out of one's way.

Brown played a more resolute game, the bat looking small as a child's bat in his hands as he crouched, a huge figure, over it and scooped the ball past the fielders. He was beginning to score fairly rapidly when Mailey was put on to bowl instead of Macdonald.

But at length Mailey lured him into the mood of a man who believes it is safe to hit out at anything, and sent up a suave little ball that just deceived his eye and took his wicket when his score was 32.

Woolley, who was received as an idol, also showed before long that a good batsman can play almost any sort of bowling, and he delighted the crowd by lifting a ball from Mailey into one of the stands.

It seemed at first to be a 6, but apparently the ball had bounded into the stand off the ground. He, too, looked capable of scoring a century—or, say 99—when he cut a ball in a way that ought to have sent it to the boundary. He attempted to score a second run off it, when Bardsley, who was fielding with the genius of a Pellew, threw the ball fiercely at the wicket from a long way off, and Woolley was run out for 23.

This did not happen, however, till after the rain, and after the interval, and after the second rain (that sent up five thousand umbrellas, giving the crowd on the other side of the ground the appearance of a field of gigantic purple mushrooms), and after the row, and all the rest of it.

Tyldesley was by this time playing more daringly, striking violently at the balls that Macdonald sent bounding round his head. One of these balls struck him on the neck, and play had to be stopped while he recovered. The crowd cheered him uproariously when he caught the next ball and swung it magnificently on its way to the boundary. He drove another ball to the boundary high over the fielders' heads. Then he became reckless, and sent another into the sky. Macartney leaped after it across the field, and Tyldesley was caught out with his score at 39—the highest score of the day.

Mead, who had been his partner for some time, played a game of skilful rather than of massive strokes. He has an amazingly keen eye, that seems both to take in the position of every fielder and to time the ball exactly.

He gives the impression of brilliant preparedness and, with a slight tap, he again and again sent the ball gently into an empty part of the field for a single. A sturdy, left-handed batsman, he does not wait for the ball (as most batsmen do) with his bat pulsing in the block-hole. He beats it against the ground once or twice, then droops his body into the exact position he wants, and awaits the bowling with the bat almost still in his alert hands.

He and Sandham, who had taken Tyldesley's place, were obviously thinking more of keeping the wicket safe for Monday than of performing miracles on Saturday. And, in the queer flow of varying light in which they batted, it was manifestly the only thing to do.

They were still batting defensively when stumps were drawn at half-past six, with the English score at 129 for four wickets.

It would be a false report, however, that suggested that either the cricket or the scene outside the pavilion was the chief feature of the day at the Oval. The chief feature of the day was the number of yawns during the long waits between shower and shower. There were never before so great a number of yawning faces seen at a cricket match. Everybody had been longing for rain, and, now that it had come, everybody resented it. Hence the scenes.

I think one result of these scenes ought to be to bring about an innovation in the game of cricket. Cricket ought to be a game capable of being played in all weathers. There should be a special wicket for wet days, and the players should be provided with oilskins and non-skid shoes. That would have saved the situation on Saturday.

Meanwhile, the customs of cricket being what they are, the disturbers at the Oval on Saturday should in fairness have directed their anger, not against the Australian captain, but against the English weather. They should have summoned, not Armstrong out of the pavilion, but the sun out of the clouds. It would have been equally effective.

From *The Sporting Life*, 1922.

The modern age had begun, and the technique of coming to the quiddity of cricketers by the route which Lynd takes, from the outside, as it were, was followed by many. An almost exact parallel to Lynd's coverage of the 1921 Tests is offered by the Liberal journalist A. G. Gardiner (1865–1946), who for a time edited The Daily News, *the paper on which Lynd served as literary editor. While Lynd sometimes masqueraded as a purveyor of literate persiflage called 'Y.Y.', so Gardiner contributed essays to* The Star *under the disguise of Alpha of the Plough. The player he chose to apostrophise in the following sketch, J. W. Hitch (1886–1965; Surrey and England), was one of several around whom a special significance must have gathered for observers like Gardiner. For Hitch, who played his first game for England against Australia in 1911 and his last against them ten years later, must have contributed considerably to the illusion that the war had after all not changed things very much.*

Billitch at Lord's

OF COURSE, there were others there besides Bill. There were twenty thousand people there. There was the whole Oval crowd there. I was there—I always try to put in a day at Lord's when the Oval crowd charges across the river with its jolly plebian war cries and swarms into the enclosure at St John's Wood like a crowd of happy children. It makes me feel young again to be caught in that tide of fresh enthusiasm. I know that is how I used to feel in the good old days of the eighties when I used to set out with my lunch to the Oval to see Walter Read and Lohmann and K. J. Key and M. P. Bowden and Abel and Lockwood and Tom Richardson and all the glorious company who filled the stage then. What heroes they were! What scenes we saw! What bowling, what batting, what fielding! I daresay the heroes of today are as heroic as those of whom I speak; but not for me.

Cricket, to the ageing mind, is never what it used to be; it is always looking back to some golden age when it flourished, like chivalry, in a pure and unsullied world. My father used to talk to me with fervour about the heroic deeds of Caffyn and Julius Caesar, and I talk to young people about the incomparable skill of Grace and Steel and Lohmann, and they no doubt will be eloquent to their children about Hobbs and Gregory. And so on. Francis Thompson explained the secret of the golden age when he sang:

Oh, my Hornby and my Barlow long ago.

That is it. It is that 'long ago' that makes our giants so giantesque. Cricketers, as the old gentleman said of the peaches, are not so fine as they were in our young days. How could they be? Why have we lived all these years if we are not allowed to have seen greater things than these youngsters who are shouldering us out of the way have ever seen? Of course, they don't believe in 'our Hornbys and our Barlows long ago' any more than I believed when a boy that Caffyn and Julius Caesar could hold a candle to W.G. or Walter Read, and they will find that their children will think lightly of Hobbs in comparison with some contemporary god of their idolatry.

But whatever change has taken place in cricket—or in me—I swear there is no change in the jolly Oval crowd. It is, as it has always been, the liveliest, most intense, most good-humoured mob that ever shouted itself hoarse at cricket. It is as different from the Lord's crowd as a country fair is from the Church Congress. At Lord's we take our cricket as solemnly as if we were at a prayer-meeting. We sit and smoke and knit our brows with portentous gravity. Sometimes we forget ourselves and say: 'Well run, sir', or 'Missed. By jove!' Then we turn round to see if anybody has heard us. We have even been known to clap; but these extravagances are rare. Generally we end up by falling asleep.

But we were done out of our sleep on Monday. There's no possibility of sleep when the Oval crowd is about and when they have brought Billitch with them. At Lord's we never have a popular hero or a comic figure. Cricket is far too serious a thing to turn to fun. If Little Tich came and played at Lord's, we should not smile. We should take him very seriously, and call him Mr William Tich if he came out of the front door of the pavilion, and Tich (W) if he came out of the side door. On Monday we had several bad shocks to our sense of the solemnities of cricket. For example, we saw Fender, the Surrey captain, lead the 'gentlemen' members of his team to the professionals' quarters and bring his team out to the field in a body, just for all the world as though they were all one flesh and blood. It was a painful sight, and many of us closed our eyes rather than look upon it. We felt that Bolshevism had invaded our sanctuary at last.

And then there was that unseemly enthusiasm for Billitch. I don't know what there is about Bill that makes him such an idol of the Oval crowd; but there it is. If Bill went on to bowl the ring shouted, 'Good ole Bill'; if he went off bowling it said that 'Ole Bill wants a rest'; if he hit a ball it said, 'That's one for ole Bill'; if he missed a ball it said, 'Ole Bill let that go by'; if he tapped the wicket with his bat it was confident that 'Ole Bill had found a narsty spot'; if he made a short run it shouted, 'Brayvo, ole Bill'. I think that if he had stopped to blow his nose the crowd would have blown its nose too, for the pleasure of keeping him company.

It is not that Billitch is a comic figure, as Johnny Briggs used to be. Nor an incomparable cricketer, as Lohmann used to be. Nor a home product from Mitcham Common, for I think he comes from Lancashire. But he has a certain liveliness, a sense of enjoying everything he does, and putting his whole heart into it, that gives a lusty spirit to the game and touches the affections of the Oval crowd, which always mixes up its affections with its cricket. And his name does the rest. It is an irresistible name. You can go on saying Billitch all day without growing weary. It will suit any circumstances and go to any rhythm. What jolly verses old Craig would weave about it if he could come back and hawk poems to us on sunny afternoons. But it needed the Oval crowd to discover the riches of that name. If Billitch had come to Lord's he would not have been Billitch at all. He would have been Hitch (W) and as solemn as all the rest of us. I wish we were as merry at Lord's as they are at the Oval.

From *Many Furrows*, 1924.

Another essayist who wrote this sort of thing at will was J. B. Priestley (b. 1894), although his ability in other areas has drawn attention away from the skill of some of his earlier essays. At one point, worried by the violent fluctuations in the public reputations of great cricketers, and drawn by sympathy to a fellow-Yorkshireman, Priestley wondered aloud what might happen to writers if they too were subject to the fickle nature of batting averages and bowling analyses. In savouring the tone of this essay, one is not surprised to see that the book from which it comes, Open House, *is dedicated by Priestley to Robert and Sylvia Lynd.*

Sutcliffe and I

HERBERT SUTCLIFFE has had such streams of printer's ink, frequently of the vilest quality, poured over him of late that I am sure he will not be offended at the little cupful I propose to add to the torrent. I will, however, offer my apologies to this fine cricketer and fellow Yorkshireman, if only because under cover of his name, which will probably lure so many honest cricketers to this page, I am about to write a very egotistical essay. I have chosen him as my stalking-horse because he and I have many things in common. We are about the same age, come from the same part of the world (though we are not acquainted, I regret to say), and have not entirely dissimilar biographies. Thus, we both served in France, first in the ranks and afterwards as officers, and then, when the war was over, we both became professional entertainers of a rather curious kind. He earned his bread by hitting a ball hard with a shaped piece of willow. I decided to earn mine by setting down on paper various odd fancies and thoughts about men and books. Oddly enough, there are several friends of mine who tell me that they dislike his profession, that a man should not play a game for money, though they do not object to my method of earning a living. They do not seem to see that if it is ridiculous that a man should play cricket for money, it is still more ridiculous that a man should air his feelings for money, that a professional batsman is less absurd than a professional sonneteer. The fact is, of course, that these friends of mine are unjust to Sutcliffe and his fellow professionals because they have not grasped the simple fact that sport and art are similar activities, that none of us, whether we are batsmen or poets, bowlers or essayists, work away in our fields or our studies for the money itself. We bat or write because we have a passion for batting or writing, and only take the money so that the butcher and baker may be paid while we are so happily engaged. 'Don't stop', the community says to us, and hands us a cheque now and then so that we have not to quit the cricket pitch or the writing desk in order to seek a livelihood. Indeed, it would not be difficult to turn the tables on these objectors to professional sport and to prove that it is the amateur who is in the weaker ethical position, for while he is playing cricket from May to September it is possible that he is neglecting the estate it is his duty to manage or the business house from which he draws a salary as director.

Both of us, then, have chosen these odd but by no means disreputable means of earning a living. On the score of money, I do not suppose there is much difference between us. But here the likeness ends. Millions bandy his name who have never heard of me. He himself has probably never seen my name, whereas I know all about him and read about him every day all through the summer. If he strains a muscle, the evening papers tell me all about it in great headlines, but if I should die, probably the tiny paragraph giving the news would never reach the eye of this contemporary and fellow countryman of mine. Do not misunderstand me, however; there is here no touch of bitterness. Not only is his work harder than mine, but he is a better performer. If I sit down, tired, dispirited, to fill these pages, it does not very much matter for I can muddle through somehow. No wickets are scattered in the middle of the second paragraph; no howl of disappointment goes from a vast crowd, to be echoed all over England the next morning; there is, for me, no melancholy walk back to the pavilion. If Sutcliffe were to fumble as badly at the wicket as I have fumbled many a time down a column of writing, his reputation would be sent flying with the bails. I can mistime my strokes and drop catches in page after page, but no one is any the wiser. I have only to tell myself that I will try to do better next time, and have not to show a shamed face to all England and half the Antipodes. Not only must he work under conditions far more trying to the nerves and temper, but he is, as I have said, the better performer. Not for long years, if ever at all, shall I achieve in this prose the grace, the lovely ease, that shines through innings after innings of his. I may pull off a little trick or two before I have done, but such mastery of the medium as he shows is to me only something gleaming on the far horizon, and long before I arrive there, before that distant gleam becomes a full flood of light, I shall probably be a crazy dodderer or dead and forgotten.

Yet these are facts with a double edge. There may be something nerve-racking in the conditions under which he works, but there is something heartening too. If I send a sentence flying to the boundary, no shout goes up to tell me that twenty thousand of my fellow men have followed the glorious stroke. When I take up my pen, there are for me no friendly slaps on the back, no cries of 'Good luck, old man'. I work alone, in silence, and often when all is done I cannot say whether it has been well or badly performed. It is true that no howl greets me if I fumble, but then no cheers come my way if I am on top of the bowling; nothing but silence, broken from time to time by little whispers of stilted praise or disapproval. How curious it would be if our conditions of work were changed about! Sutcliffe would have to go on batting, week after week, without a word, let alone a cheer, reaching his ears, until at last, after he had been slogging away for about two years, a little notice would appear in some newspaper saying: 'Undoubtedly Sutcliffe is proving himself to be one of the younger batsmen to be reckoned with', or 'With these 2500 runs, Sutcliffe is establishing himself as one of our younger cricketers'. And these, it must be understood, would be the complimentary notices, and there would be others. Already he probably imagines that nothing could be more nonsensical than some of the criticisms passed upon him, but if this change were brought about, he would soon realize that there are no limits to solemn nonsense. Thus, I remember once bringing out a book of strictly personal essays, in which it was avowedly my intention to write about myself, yet one newspaper chided me for being egotistical and having so many I's to the page. That newspaper would complain that Sutcliffe used a bat too much during his innings: 'We should like Mr Sutcliffe better as a batsman if he did not make such unnecessary use of the bat'. He would also find himself confronted by a crazy difference of opinion. One half the papers would tell him that he did not hit hard enough, the other half that he hits too hard, until at last, like the sensible fellow he is, he would decide to laugh at the whole crew of them.

Meanwhile my own position would be so much more exhilarating that it would be embarrassing. I should wake up one morning and find the country placarded with 'Priestley Disappoints' or 'Wonderful Essay by Priestley'. Now and then the evening papers would come out with special editions: 'Priestley's Essay Begun. Latest Reports. Some Good Phrases.' Retired essayists, writing long reports every other day or so, would analyse every paragraph, contrast this week's essay with that of a fortnight ago, and comment at length on every change of mood and style. If anything went wrong with me, all the country would be told about it, just as it was when Sutcliffe strained a muscle a short time ago. I can see the placards and headlines: 'Priestley Out of Humour. Says in No Mood for Work. May Not Write Essay this Week', and there would probably follow then a long interview with the local wine merchant, who would tell the reporters that I had just bought a bottle of Chambertin so that there was still some chance of my writing after all. There would be warm discussions all over the country, in newspapers, clubs, bar parlours, on the subject of my possible inclusion in the England Essay Team. Everybody would send in lists: Belloc, Lynd, Chesterton, Beerbohm, Lucas, Tomlinson and so forth. In the end I should probably be selected as twelfth man, to wait in the library. Messrs. Belloc and Lynd would probably be sent in first. But I have no intention of discussing the composition of this team: all that I wish to point out is that it would beat Australia in any kind of weather. This is a fact worth remembering, for after all there are other things in the world besides games, and England is not ruined just because sinewy brown men from a distant colony sometimes hit a ball further and oftener than our men do. And I am sure that Sutcliffe, to whom, after such a picture of a life passed in the full glare of public interest, I offer my sympathy, will agree with me, though I hope, for his sake and mine, he will go on gracefully stealing runs, hitting the manful boundary, with more and more power to his elbow.

From *Open House*, 1927.

Raymond C. Robertson-Glasgow (1901–1965; Oxford University and Somerset), was a bowler good enough to take over 300 first-class wickets and to play for the Gentlemen. His Somerset connections led him as a writer to the composition of several casual but brilliant fragments of portraiture, of men like the county captain John Daniell, the slow bowler Jack White, but especially Samuel Moses James Woods (1867–1931; Cambridge University, Somerset, Australia and England). Woods was one of the great natural athletes of his time, who played three times for Australia against England and three times for England against South Africa, besides representing England as a Rugby Union forward. Robertson-Glasgow's affectionate sketch of Woods closes with one of the most exquisite dying falls throughout the range of cricket literature.

IF YOU wanted to know Taunton, you walked round it with Sam Woods on a summer morning before the match. Sam was Somerset's godfather. He was a lover of life and of nearly all things living. On those walks, he would take you into the back-parlours of little shops and inquire after the youngest son's measles, and whether it had been decided to put Tom into the cornchandling trade. 'Much better let him be a farmer, Missis,' Sam would say, 'and marry a fat wife who can look after his money. For HE won't, no more than I could, my dear.'

Everyone loved Sam, for the whole world's manliness and generosity seemed to have gathered into his heart. He lived at the George Inn, Mr E. J. Lock, and when not there, might be found at the Club. I believe he decided to do some looking after of me, because he thought I needed it, and also because I opened the bowling sometimes, though not as Sam had opened, continued, and closed it, with speed and invincible hope.

I wish I had seen him in the prime of his bowling, but I only saw him trundling a few down, in waistcoat and watch-chain, at the Oxford nets, when he was fifty-two. He had tremendous shoulders, but was lame in walk owing to rheumatism in the hip. This he attributed to a fall off a camel in Egypt. 'I was in charge of a bunch of those sods,' he said, 'when they stampeded and made for a cactus forest; so off I rolled, and

97

fell a bit wrong.' C. B. Fry told me that Sam, when a young man, was the finest build of an athlete stripped that he ever saw.

Sam came over to Australia from Brighton College when he was fourteen. He was one of a family of thirteen, at Manley Beach, near Sydney. 'At least I THINK we were thirteen,' he would say. For Cambridge against Oxford, he took 36 wickets in four matches, at nine each, and, while still an undergraduate, he played in three Test matches against England for Australia. At rugger he played forward for England, and was a terror in the loose, for he weighed nearly fifteen stone and could run the hundred yards in under eleven seconds. He had neither the wish nor the aptitude for any settled profession. In early youth, he tried a little banking, but was so often absent at cricket when he should have been shovelling sovereigns that he, and his employers, both felt that he should try something else.

As a batsman, he was an attacker, and only G. L. Jessop excited more anticipation in the crowd. Many a time he pulled Somerset out of the ditch; especially at the Oval, when he would walk out, chin first, to tame the fury of Richardson and Lockwood. In technique, he always advised against deflections to leg. 'You're not Ranji,' he would say, 'so aim at mid-on's nut, and you'll find the ball will go to the square-leg boundary.' I was with him at the Oval when he met little Bobby Abel, who had gone nearly blind. Abel touched Sam on the arm, smiled, and said, 'Oh, Mr Woods, the times you've nearly knocked my head off out in the middle,' and Sam said, 'Ah, Bobby, but the times you carved me off your whiskers to the boundary.'

Sam would hear nothing against W. G. Grace, and loved to tell of the Old Man's hundredth century, 288, for Gloucestershire against Somerset in 1895. W. G. scored at 50 an hour, and gave no chance. 'I had him plumb leg before,' Sam said, 'when he'd made only three or four, and that was the only time I got one past him. I bowled him a shooter when he was in the nineties, and he didn't stop it; he hit it for four to square-leg.' My great-uncle A. P. Wickham was keeping wicket behind Grace, and he told me that W. G. only let five balls pass his bat throughout the innings.

After that match Gloucestershire supporters gave Grace a complimentary dinner. 'He drank something of everything,' Sam said, 'before and during dinner, and afterwards he sent for the whisky. You couldn't make the Old Man drunk. His nut was too large. About midnight, some of us thought we might start for home; but the Old Man said to me, "Shock'ead, get two others, and we'll play rubbers of whist till two in the morning." So we did.'

Sam had his learning from nature, not from books; but a strong memory and a vivid power of corroborative illustration made him a talker who never lacked for an audience. He was convivial; too convivial, some thought; but I could never see that it mattered. Drinking was just part of his life, and it made no difference to his kindness and his humour. He made the younger ones among us stick to beer and early hours—'Whisky and one o'clock in the morning won't suit you, my dear.'

Sam will never be forgotten in Somerset, and they still talk of him as if he were just around the next corner. Not long ago, I met an elderly lady on a railway journey near Taunton. Within five minutes our talk reached Sam. 'Ah,' she said, 'I last met him at a dance when I was eighteen. I had been told that I was not to dance with Sam. But I did.'

From *46 Not Out* in *Crusoe on Cricket* ed. Alan Ross, 1948.

A hero even more ancient than Woods was J. Maurice Read (Surrey and England), who played for his country thirteen times between 1884 and 1892. Read subsequently administered a private club ground, and it was in this capacity that the itinerant J. C. Squire occasionally encountered him. Taking careful note once again of the timescale, one begins to understand Squire's reverence with the realisation that when Read played his last games for England, Squire was just eight years old, the perfect age for hero-worship.

SUPPOSE, ABOUT 1906, a man now in his twenties were suddenly to encounter, in a remote Kentish huddle of cottages, with an ancient church and an ancestral park, a shy inn, thatched, dormered, covered with roses, benches in a little garden in front of it, a great heraldic signboard hanging over it, and written on the lintel, 'Frank Woolley, licensed to sell wines, spirits, beer and tobacco'. His impression would be much the same as that which was made upon men of my generation in the post-war years when they visited the exquisite and secluded village of Tichborne and found Maurice Read in charge both of the inn and of the cricket ground. One of the most polished bats—he was also a wily bowler—who ever played for Surrey, he played for England both here and in Australia, but retired early, in the 'nineties, when Sir Joseph Tichborne offered him the job of looking after his private ground. There, for more than thirty years, he was a kind of secondary king of the place and, after his old master died, a perfect host both on and off the field. The inn was a minor interest, though, in his quiet way, he loved seeing natives and visitors foregathering in bar and courtyard for beer and laughter in the evenings after matches were over. The ground was his passion; in the early morning and at twilight, whenever he could, he would steal up to it looking for the least blemish in wicket and outfield. And, to the last, he himself played in his peaceful corner, against local sides and men on holiday, a straight bat to the end and, in his late sixties, a beautiful judge of a run and a wary fielder.

On cricketing days and others I had often talked to him, in company and alone. The last time I had seen him was in Winchester Hospital, a few days before he died of a wasting internal disease. There he lay, tired, faintly smiling, uncomplaining. His face—he had a high head, candid blue eyes, a thin aquiline nose, hollow cheeks, fair-grey drooping moustache and brief cropped side-whiskers—a more humane version of the late Lord Lansdowne—was like parchment stretched over bone, and his hands, all knuckles and cords, drooped weakly over the coverlet. An English side was in Australia; he knew every man's form and abilities. 'Incidents' had occurred; he remembered tours of forty years before, and said that they would always occur because of differences in national character.

A nurse brought some minced chicken. He ate a little, then lay back again. He looked the great gentleman he was; there was still in his face the old beauty, modesty, intelligence, dignity, nothing of collapse extreme except leanness; and smiles came into his eyes (for he had never been one, even in health, to laugh aloud except very quietly) as he recalled games long over, and the lusty figures of the past— the bravery of Richardson, the pace of Spofforth, the cunning of 'W. G.', and the sheer impudence of E. M. Grace, 'the Coroner' who, he said, used on insist on a waiter bringing out a large whisky-and-soda as he reached each fifty, and who had once marched out on the field and stayed there in a county match when his name, because he was out of form, had been left out of the XI. We parted at last; he was still talking of 'next season' and playing again. . . .

From *The Honeysuckle and the Bee*, 1948.

As time advances, and yesterday gradually evolves into the distant past, so further generations of cricketers enter the pantheon. When players like Robertson-Glasgow were making their way in first-class cricket, Maurice Tate (1896–1956; Sussex and England) was a contemporary giant. By the time Jack Fingleton met him in 1948, Tate was very much a representative of a lost past.

THE STATION-MASTER at Leicester entertained the Press while we were waiting for our train to Bradford. He looked hard at Maurice Tate and said, very seriously, 'You remind me very much of a chap who used to play cricket for England, Maurice Tate.' Maurice looked at him hard, and said, 'Ummph.' 'Yes,' said the station-master, 'remarkably like him. I suppose a lot of people have told you that.' 'Well,' I said, 'he IS Maurice Tate.' The station-master collapsed, but recovered, put on his top-hat and walked down to put us on the train. The war has come and gone and the British Railways are nationalised, but the English station-masters still retain their top-hats, striped trousers and frock-coats. They always look to me, like the father of a bride.

Maurice Tate has two outstanding characteristics, apart from a sunny nature. He has the biggest feet I've seen (apart from Tiny, deckhand of the *Strathaird*, who has his size 15s specially made for him in Belfast) and he has the smallest voice ever. He barely whispers. Maurice was three pounds when he was born and was minus finger-nails and toe-nails. For every cricket season for twenty-five years he shed the nail of his big toes, so hard did he pound the turf in delivery. A room attendant said to him one day in Adelaide (when Tate was in terrible agony) that he could fix things for him. The attendant left for town with Tate's boot. He returned with the toe of the boot opened up and the stiffener removed. Tate played with his boot like that until the end of his cricketing days. The first ball he ever bowled in Australia, in Perth, threw him back. The hard pitch, unlike the soft English ones, would not take his weight. He was very worried and told Strudwick so, but 'Struddy' told him not to worry, that he would get used to it. He did. Used to shedding his nails!

I think Tate was very hurt when Bradman said that Bedser was the better bowler. Bedser, though I have never played against him, and that is the best way to judge a bowler, is a great trier and, I am told, has always to be watched for the one that does a little something extra off the pitch, but I have never found anybody to agree with Bradman regarding the two. Tate was undoubtedly one of the great bowlers of all time. He showed me a cutting in which Alan Melville, the South African skipper, who had played against and with Tate when at the University and Sussex, and against Bedser the preceeding season, plumped solidly for Tate. Maurice was proud of that cutting.

Tate told me one very interesting thing about his bowling. For the one he wanted to swing across from the leg, he did not put his front foot straight down the pitch, as most bowlers do, but it was thrown out to his right across his body. This meant that the ball was delivered more than side-on. It was delivered against his body. He held the ball with two fingers down the seam as if for a natural swinger but he did not deliver the ball with the seam full on to the batsman, as a swing bowler does. He rolled his two fingers over the ball towards the batsman . . . the opposite to an off-break . . . so that the ball was delivered with what we might call a leg-break roll. This with the positioning of his front foot, could well explain how he made the ball run away so well. He was a master in this. He never used the crease, he told me. He always delivered from the same place. The in-swinger, as it was becoming in 1938, is the fetish in English cricket today with its fieldsmen packed in on the on-side. I know which is the harder ball to play by miles. I think Jackson, of Derbyshire, was the only one we met, apart from Bedser, who ran the ball away. Tate's methods might repay study.

Pace of the pitch? Was there such a thing or was it merely an optical illusion? I have heard that one argued for hours on end, but Tate thought increased pace off the pitch was certainly possible. 'You know, Jack,' said Maurice, in a tremulous whisper, looking about and as if on the verge of imparting a secret about the atom bomb, 'I got pace off the pitch from these.' And he motioned down towards his feet. 'Maurice,' I said, 'say nothing more.'

From *Brightly Fades the Don*, 1949.

Exactly what degree of truth is there in any of this? To what extent do cricket writers succumb to the temptation of sacrificing the facts on the altar of professional expediency? After all, if there are schools of cricket reporting, if there are several approaches to the same end, is it not possible that some of these approaches may not lead to the end at all? Very possibly. A guide through the labyrinth of contemporary cricket journalism has been most thoughtfully provided by Ian Alexander Ross Peebles (1908–; Oxford University, Middlesex, Scotland and England), one of the great slow bowlers of his generation, who played thirteen times for England, took 875 wickets, and would perhaps have taken many more but for the Second World War and bad luck with injuries. Peebles subsequently became a quietly humorous commentator on cricketing affairs, of the kind too easy to underrate. The following essay may perhaps serve as a useful reminder of the spin bowler's art.

How to be a Cricket Writer

SOME YEARS ago I had the honour of introducing the late Charles Fry to my then newly acquired wife. He was dressed in a smock-like shirt of his own design with a neckband of somewhat clerical cut. This was surmounted by a terai, the double-brimmed hat favoured by the Boer farmer and other workers under the equatorial sun, with the resultant effect of a tropical mission of the Greek Orthodox Church.

He greeted her with his customary courtliness, and almost immediately was launched into a dissertation of great technical brilliance on the reasons why Hobbs, in playing back, retained the position to score past mid-on. My wife, being at that time completely unversed in the mysteries of the great game, was nigh overwhelmed, but much cheered when, to illustrate his point, he snatched a neighbouring stranger's umbrella, precipitating the owner, who happened to be leaning on it at that moment. The point of his address, if not altogether appreciated by the startled stranger, was that cricket was an art which could not be taught, but must needs be handed down by precept and example.

Whether Fry believed the same of cricket writing, in which he also excelled, I do not know, but I feel that it is an arguable point of view. In any case, having embarked under this ambitious chapter title, I am bound to say that, apart from a few rudimentary rules, obvious to all, I have no idea how in the heck you become a writer on any subject. It will therefore be convenient, nay imperative, in this case to regard cricket writing as art to be handed down by precept and example, and crib what we can from the works of the established. I am sorry if you were in any way misled by the title; but this is the best I can do for you.

First the rudimentary rules. In almost any press box you will want sweaters and woollies in the proportion of two to one to those worn on the field. If you are prosperous enough to own a pair of binoculars keep the strap round your neck fairly short. The press box is a matey, co-operative place and this will mean that, even if you cannot see through your own glasses, they cannot be further away than one neighbour due N., S., E. or W. If your spelling is anything like mine it is advisable to carry a pocket dictionary, as this will do something to diminish the kindly contempt with which telephonists, sub-editors, compositors, etc., must inevitably regard your masterly prose.

So much for the mechanics of your profession. Now a most important aspect—psychology. And this means the study of the Editor, at a distance, and the Sports Editor more intimately. Should they be producing something on the lines of *The Times* it is improbable that they will be looking for 'angles,' 'exclusives' or 'revelations'. On the other hand, the readers of *The Daily Splash* are unlikely to revere quotations from Horace. Having grasped these principles all that remains is a little guidance on how to word an expense sheet and you are off.

Here then is a simple practical exercise in the various methods of dealing with a day's play, summarised on the Television News as— 'The Test Match. England declared their second innings closed at 482 for seven wickets. Hogshead batted all day and was not out at the end, having scored 224.'

The first great school for your contemplation is the orthodox and traditionalist. This is a difficult one, for it entails not only a profound knowledge of the game itself but also of its history, manners, customs and traditions, for of these you are vigilant custodian and protector. Thus:

'Yesterday at Lord's, admittedly in chilly weather, a young batsman went to the wicket wearing a flannel balaclava helmet in the shade of blue appropriate to his university. It is not for an older generation to discourage progress and innovation; but, in a case where the innovator infringes the rules of decorum and taste, it may be appropriate to draw his attention to the somewhat rigid sartorial code established and enforced by W. T. (Bully) Pockleton in the early 'seventies. One of its less exacting clauses provided that any member of the XI wearing turn-ups on his trousers should be publicly flogged round the outfield with his own braces. Such restriction and penalty may seem totalitarian to modern eyes, but have we not travelled rather too far in the opposite direction?

'Despite this distraction it was a fine day's dricket, during which England increased their overnight score to 482 for seven wickets on a wicket which the early dew had rendered a treacherous surface on which to counter Flockerty's skilful manipulation of the seam. Later a slight superficial disintegration gave purchase for Moriarty's diagonally spun leg-breaks. The chief architect etc. . . .'

On the same level, but rather less technical, is the romanticist who sees the game through a cultured and visionary eye. It is seemingly a harrowing experience and its translation has the snag that it calls for a considerable degree of education on the part of both the author and reader. Still, if the reader is baffled from time to time so much the better. There is at the present time a great opportunity for a revival of this school.

'Umpire Boggins crouched over the wicket entrusted to his care, his white coat streaming behind him, a toga symbolic of the stern justice it was his to dispense. His face was a mask of pain as he strove to utter the pregnant syllable which would raise the curtain on the last act of this drama, so delicately poised between tragedy and farce. "Play!" In the oppressive silence there seemed to echo the rattle of some ethereal firing squad, mowing down our faint remaining hope in bloody disorder.

'But between the grim-visaged Flockerty, thundering Valkyrian to the crease, and final annihilation stood two champions so different they might be born of different planets. The buccolic effervescence of Hogshead threw into agonising relief the delicate tracery of Button's weaving wrists, searching vainly midst the perils of the off. The scene was set as surely as Snouton's production of Burkwasser's *Gheistein mit Phunffbach*. To the metaphysician . . .'

Never mind, England still declared, a fact you will have to present rather differently if your appointment is to one of the racier journals. The reader whose eye has fallen on the sports page fresh from 'Bigamous Burglar's Dramatic Outburst' will demand some stronger meat. As you will probably be presented to your public as 'The World's Greatest Cricket Writer' or 'The Man They'd Like to Strangle,' the first step is to put yourself in proper perspective in relation to the subject and the reader. A positive rather than objective attitude is called for, so don't just kick off by saying you have been to a press conference:

'Portly, parrot-faced Panton Festonhaugh de Vere Binks, third Baron Brum, President of the M.C.C., was waiting for me at the gate. "Thank goodness you're here, Blabberty," he boomed. "There is real trouble with the Australian captain." I brushed him impatiently aside and hastened to the ancient ivy-clad dressing room where the trouble was just as I had figured. The gangling, crew-cut cornstalk burst into tears when I told him he was holding the bat the wrong way round and the bulge should be *at the back*. "But they go better side-ways," he protested. "Get wise to yourself, Ned," I advised. "Take a look ahead—no fielders."

'As the day went he didn't get a break as the Gloamshire glamour boy, taking my advice about an early night once in a while, slammed his side to a sensational declaration.

'The President left the Committee room to see me into his sleek crested limousine. "Nice work, Snip," he chuckled as we slid through the armorial-bearing gates.'

That about covers the field of day-to-day commentary in this country, but in other parts of the world there is a really red-blooded school. The column is the ideal firing platform for this performance as it provides an all-round field, and it should have a subtly challenging title such as 'Want Your Teeth Kicked In?—Come On.' However, the style is readily applicable to straightforward description:

'Eleven shambling zombies hauled out of their simpering dotage by despairing, ham-handed selector Stiggins tottered on to the field at Lord's yesterday. Their scrawny necks could hardly support the Australian caps they had the cheek to wear. Bradman would have eaten the lot for breakfast and coughed them up again before lunch. They couldn't even get the ageing, decaying Gloamshire beauty queen out—not even before he got the gin and fog of El Paradiso out of his blood-shot eye. You're digging your own grave, Stiggins—go on, get in it before you dig one for Australian cricket.'

If you think this is your metier it is a good plan to have a few words with the legal department before introducing this particular style to this rather old-fashioned country.

Finally, a very different cup of tea. It is unlikely that you will be called upon immediately to record these mighty events for posterity, but it is just as well to be prepared. In this case, despite the rather damping prospect of complete anonymity, it is satisfactory to reflect that your words will likely be quoted by generations yet unborn. With this responsibility in view the style must of necessity be more in the White Paper tradition, but with a nice judicial flavour. In recent years the chroniclers have become almost brisk, but for my taste, as for millions of other fireside readers, the older school. Here we find a distinctly Teutonic flavour in that the main verb comes at the end of a lengthy and meaty sentence, so that the reader has all the delight of his first birthday cake, when he left the icing until the very last:

'Occupying the crease for a period of four and three-quarter hours, driving powerfully and excelling in the cut, although in early difficulty with Flockerty's express deliveries and missed at 92 and 151 in attempting to force the pace, despite a tendency to hit against the spin, Hogshead was undefeated when England declared their innings closed at half past four o'clock. During this prolonged episode there were times when the tactics of the Australian captain, apparently troubled by some indecision regarding his present method of gripping the bat were, not to put too fine a point upon it, adjacent to the confines of lunacy.'

P.S.—An eminent journalist who was kind enough to help me in correcting the proofs of this book points out that I have omitted one school of journalism which he jocularly calls 'The Weekly Woffle'. He has rectified this omission by sending me a sample devoted to a slightly different subject; one which he says gives this type of writer full scope. Personally, I do not recognise the school, but can appreciate that it is thoughtful, knowledgeable, readable, prescient and reliable. I therefore print this extract as being a rewarding study for the ambitious young journalist.

'When it comes to picking the bowlers for the M.C.C. tour of Australia the selectors, for all the wisdom and experience of Mr Allen and his subordinates, will be up against a task which your correspondent for one, with his canny Scots upbringing and—dare I say—having known, albeit in a humbler role as sometime Muddlesex captain, the divers factors, unappreciated by the uninitiated but ever-present in the minds of those whose job is to shoulder the responsibility, certainly does not envy them.

'If I may venture to say a word, it is that the choice of the right men is all-important. In the first place one must gauge the correct number—for it is as embarrasing to have too many quickies and tweakers aching to turn their arms as it is to have to take the field without a balanced attack equipped for all wickets and to suit all the range of conditions that the side may reasonably expect to encounter. Then comes the question of variety, and here is the nub. For though it was the quick who were the basis of success last time wickets are unpredictable things, and it may well be that the curators (to use the idiom of Down-Under), with the best will in the world, will find themselves nurturing, in the swiftly-changing climate that is apt to be encountered in the sub-continent, a very different sort of surface such as will draw the teeth of Statham, Tyson, Trueman, Bailey, and (if he should be chosen, and that is a matter which cannot be decided without due thought and consideration nearer the time) Loader, and may leave our alert and thoughtful captain sighing for a more crafty form of attack, or perhaps for a stock trundler of the type of Alec Bedser, who though possibly just past his peak . . . I will consider these in due course. . . .'

So now you know.

From *Batter's Castle*, 1959.

At the point where factual records become transmuted into art, there emerges the figure of Sir Neville Cardus (1889–1975), the most gifted writer on cricket in all its history, and a critic accused consistently of embellishing the truth to suit his own aesthetic ends. I once jokingly accused him of it myself, and he laughingly agreed even as he destroyed my argument as I desired him to. Briefly, his stance was identical to that of the incorrigible romancer Ford Madox Ford, who did for the Pre-Raphaelites what Cardus did for the various Lancashire elevens of his day: that although a man may sometimes stray a little from the paths of factual accuracy, he does so in hope of finding that higher honesty, poetic truth. If Cardus was a liar, then he was one whose lies are true to nature; so fine a prosodist was he that even in composing his apologia, he beguiles the reader utterly.

Guilty, m'lud, to fiction if it serves higher Truth

OF THE making of books about cricket there is no foreseeable end. Players compete with professional writers; players not accustomed to an intensive reading of books apparently find no difficulty about writing them. As far as I can gather, I am probably the only man in the profession who can't sit down at will and write a cricket book.

But an addition to the library, well worth while, has just come my way: *Sing all the Green Willow*, published by the Epworth Press at 25s. Don't let the title put you off, as easily it might. The book has truly been written by the author himself—Ronald Mason who, a year or two ago, produced a classic biography of the incomparable Walter Hammond. Ronald Mason, in this engaging book, writes on a variety of things, from Hornby and Barlow to P. G. Wodehouse and cricket. For purely personal reasons I was especially interested in the introductory chapter called 'The Truth about Cricket', because in it Mr Mason brings forward evidence that, long ago, while reporting a Lancashire v. Oxford University match for this newspaper, I wandered or floated from actual fact to the higher Truth.

I described how Lancashire batted throughout a bitterly cold May day at the Parks. The day was so cold that Parkin, Dick Tyldesley, and the other tail-enders, never left the warmth of a fire, never saw an Oxford bowler, until Dick went to the wicket half an hour before close of play, by which time Oxford's two really fast bowlers, Hewetson and Holmes, had spent their forces, so that Dick could lambast twenty or thirty runs off slow stuff. So much did Dick enjoy himself that, back to the warmth of the pavilion, not out, he said to me: 'Coom to ground early tomorrow, and Ah'll give thi summat to write about.'

Next morning, Hewetson, fresh and erratic, let fly at a terrific velocity, bang into Dick's bread-basket, then whizzing past his head. Dick, next ball, retreated to the square-leg umpire and watched the total wreckage of his stumps. When I asked him what about the grand strokes he had promised, he honestly replied: 'Eh, Mr Cardus, Ah didn't know them two young buggers was playin'.'

Mr Mason has taken the trouble to investigate, and has discovered that Holmes and Hewetson played together only once against Lancashire in the Parks; and that on that occasion Dick Tyldesley went in late on the second morning and was caught off J. L. Guise. Moreover, Holmes did not bowl at all! Mr Mason is charitable; he notes the distinction between 'Science' and 'Art'. The astronomer, he points out, can tell us about a sunset, but only a painter can tell us what it looks like. All very well; but in my mind's eye I can still, to this day, see Dick Tyldesley assaulted by Hewetson, see his vast rotundity shaken and toppled. And Mr Mason goes on to ask: 'Likewise with a number of other stories that, with the aid of this author's native genius' (meaning me) 'have passed into the language, about Barnes, or Brearley, or MacLaren. . . . Can we trust them, or him, at all?'

Before I plead guilty, m'lud, I'd like to point out that I have always tried to observe truth to character. And I was lucky, in my epoch, to have before me, every day, material for my work, a column every morning, wet or fine. One August holiday, completely wet and washed out at Old Trafford, I was welcomed by huge smiles by the 'MG's' chief sub-editor. 'Thank God,' he said, 'there's been no play—perhaps we can find some space for other events today.' But I had written an even longer piece than usual on what *might* have happened that day at Old Trafford had the weather kept fine for it.

Such cricketers as Parkin, Dick Tyldesley, Herbert Sutcliffe, Maurice Leyland, simply set the humorous or picturesque imagination free to go its way. Once, at Sheffield, Herbert Sutcliffe, glossy and immaculate, was fielding close to the bat. A terrific leg-hit struck him on the knee. Momentarily he winced, and bent down to rub the bruise. One or two of his Yorkshire colleagues solicitously approached him; but Sutcliffe waved them comprehensively away; as though saying 'I am quite all right. We Sutcliffes do not suffer pain.' True? How could I have invented something so penetrating to the quiddity, the essence, of the Sutcliffe presence and temperament? These 'natural' cricketers, pre-television and computer age, not yet standardised, simply prompted the reporter's sense of character.

It was, in respect of the inner and only truth, necessary for the writer to go beyond the potential to complete the ripe human implications. For example: in a match at Old Trafford, Dick Tyldesley apparently brought off a marvellous catch in the leg trap. (With all his assemblable bulk, he had alacrity.) But, as the batsman was departing pavilionwards, Dick called him back; the ball had just touched the grass. I congratulated Dick, in print, on this act of sportmanship. Also, next morning I congratulated him by word of mouth. 'Thanks, Mr Cardus,' he said: 'Westhaughton Sunday School, tha' knows.' Did he really say it? To fulfil and complete him, to realise the truth of his Lancashire nature and being, it simply *had* to be said. Whether he himself said it, or whether I put the words into his mouth for him, matters nothing as far as truth, as God knows it, is concerned.

I am myself often at a loss to remember if I am accurately reporting an event or a saying. My hand on my heart, I cannot be sure if Ted Wainwright, at Shrewsbury School, once said to me, after I had asked him how did Ranjitsinhji really bat—''E never made a Christian stroke in his life.' But I am able, on oath, to affirm that Wainwright's own words remain vivid in my memory, the identical words he used, to describe an event at Lord's: 'Year before, Albert Trott hit ball reight over pavilion. Next year he set 'isself to 'it ball reight out of ground t'other end, into Nursery. Ah were fieldin' near Nursery sight-screen. Suddenly Albert lets fly, and oop ball goes, 'igh as Blackpool Tower. Ah loses sight of 'er 'genst black pavilion—then Ah see 'er agen, high as Blackpool Tower, mind you. An' Ah sez to miself "Tha can catch it, Ted, tha can catch it." Then Ah 'ad another look at 'er, and Ah said, "Oh bugger 'er, and lets 'er go." And Lord Hawke 'e cooms racin' over field, and sez "Ted, why didn't you try to catch it?" and Ah sez, "Well, your Lordship, it were a bit 'igh, weren't it?" '

I vouch also for the factual accuracy of the remark made to me in the press box at Brisbane at the beginning of a Test match between Australia and England. Sydney Barnes, the superb Australian batsman, and a true Sydney-sider, had retired from actual playing, and was now reporting. He sat behind me in the press box, and, before a ball was bowled, moved over my shoulder, saying 'This is going to be an exciting rubber; and you and me, Neville, will have plenty to do—never mind these other blokes and their typewriters. Now, when *you* are hard pressed, I'll take on from you. And when I am hard-pressed, you can take on from *me*. Similar styles, you know. . . .'

A year or two ago, Mr P. G. H. Fender expressed the opinion that the public is discouraged from attending country matches by the press. Reporters, he argued, concentrated overmuch on statistics and technical fault-finding, and didn't write enough about the personality of the players, the scene and the atmosphere. By all means, a cricket writer should keep his eye on the ball, and give his readers the technical clues and explanations. But while he is describing how the ball 'moved off the seam', he should try to tell us what the bowler is thinking and saying, or what he is very likely to be thinking and saying, as he delivers the ball—especially if a catch is missed off it. . . .

From the *Guardian*, 20 October 1967.

Having been thus warned, posterity may read on at its peril. But it is worth pointing out that even the wildest romancer would hesitate to claim as part of his experience the sequence of events which happened to Cardus. Beginning as a waif at the turnstiles of a great county club in 1901, he ended up seventy years later its president. That much is certainly factually accurate. It is also the poetic truth.

An urchin at Old Trafford

WHEN THE recently elected President of the Lancashire County Cricket Club takes his seat to watch this year's Whitsuntide match, Lancashire v. Yorkshire, at Old Trafford, he will probably remember the small, frail urchin who, for the first time, pushed his way through the Old Trafford turnstiles. The admission fee was sixpence to the part of the ground occupied by what was then known as the 'working classes'.

The small schoolboy, aged ten, was, curiously enough, the President himself. He was not yet qualified to count among the 'working classes', but soon he would be, for the school-leaving age, at the turn of the century, was thirteen, with no 'O' level certificates and whatever was needed to get a job pushing a handcart from Oldham Street to the joiner's shop of E. Moss, in Upper Brook Street, Manchester.

I saw my first Lancashire and Yorkshire match at Old Trafford on Saturday, July 21, 1901. Yorkshire narrowly escaped defeat, salvaged by an obstinate innings from E. Wainwright, who, by another turn of the screw in my life, became head professional coach at Shrewsbury School, with myself his assistant. ('Tha'll never be a bowler,' he told me, 'till tha gets a few steaks in thee.') In this, my first baptism in 'Roses' matches, the players included J. T. Brown, Tunnicliffe, Denton, Hirst, Haigh, Lord Hawke, Rhodes, MacLaren, Ward, J. T. Tyldesley, Briggs, Wainwright—ten of them England cricketers.

Old Trafford was in those days the 'country', surrounded by fields; Stretford a village! No women or girls were to be seen in the crowd, except in the 'Ladies' pavilion, a black and white timbered seclusion. No motor cars in 1901; the telephone was a privilege of commerce;

no radios, of course; no television; no horse-driven trains, no Welfare State, but in the distance from Old Trafford, the Withington Workhouse was a somehow pervading presence for many folk. The amateurs came to the field through the Pavilion gate, the professionals from a side entrance, a sort of exit from the servants' quarters.

My earliest vivid recollection of Lancashire v. Yorkshire is from an Old Trafford encounter round about 1903. George Hirst was given out leg before wicket to Walter Brearley, fast bowler and 'gentleman-amateur,' a gale of a man from Bolton. He was wrong to appeal for this lbw against Hirst and knew it himself, for he cut off the 'H'zat?' even as he roared it out. But the umpire's finger went up and Hirst had to go.

Whereat A. C. MacLaren came to Brearley saying: 'You so-and-so fool Walter. George will make us suffer for this.' And when Lancashire's second innings began, Hirst rolled up the sleeve on his Yorkshire ham of a left arm and bowled Lancashire out for less than a hundred. Hirst sent down fastish left-arm swingers. C. B. Fry maintained that a late in-swing from Hirst came to the batsman like a ferocious throw-in from mid-off. In those years only one ball was available to bowlers throughout the longest of a team's innings. Hirst began the Yorkshire attack (a slow bowler, Rhodes, at the other end), and he placed two or three short-legs in the field. Nothing new under the sun.

I was terrified when R. H. Spooner flicked Hirst, with his wrists, through this leg-trap. Spooner, if my memory is not faltering, once scored 200 in a day at Old Trafford against Yorkshire. The 'Roses' match, during the reigns of A. C. MacLaren and Lord Hawke, was not the dour humorous feud of later summers; it was almost a North Country tournament: batsmen in Lancashire and Yorkshire matches of the early 1900s were actually caught in the long field.

None the less, this great match was at its characteristic best when Harry Makepeace, Rhodes and Emmett Robinson were the planners and powers behind the throne. If Lancashire should win the toss, Harry Makepeace would say in the professionals' dressing room: 'Now, lads, we've won the toss and it's a good wicket. No fours before lunch.'

The comedy of 'slow' batting in Lancashire and Yorkshire matches between the wars is that the batsmen didn't hit boundaries plentifully *on principle*. They could have scored more quickly had they wished; the great thing was to *annoy* the other side. County grounds in Yorkshire were packed for the 'Roses' match; gates were closed at noon at

Old Trafford. The multitudes did not pay to see 'bright' cricket; they were there to witness and enjoy Lancashire frustrating the old enemy.

In 1926, at Old Trafford, 78,617 paid at the turnstiles to watch Lancashire v. Yorkshire. The Old Trafford wicket was so much a batsman's heaven, stuffed with runs, that every Lancashire and Yorkshire batsman's determination was not to get out. We would all see the gorgeous humour of Rhodes, bringing to bear all his subtlety, all his experience, to the end of keeping Makepeace 'quiet'—Makepeace, who before lunch, would not have risked a violent stroke if the ball had been put before him on a plate surrounded by parsley.

Lancashire, in the 1920s, amassed 500 against Yorkshire at Old Trafford. Lancashire's captain, Leonard Green, was batting when the score was 499. To himself he said: 'Never again will Lancashire score 500 against Yorkshire. If it kills me I'll get this 500th run.' So he pushed a ball from Rhodes towards mid-off, and ran for his life. The ball was savagely fielded, savagely thrown-in, hitting Rhodes on the wrist. And Rhodes 'chuntered' or mumbled: 'There's somebody runnin' up and down this wicket. Ah don't know who it is, but there's somebody runnin' up and down this wicket.' The operative words in that sublime remark are: 'Ah don't know who it is.'

There is still a certain free-masonry about a Lancashire and Yorkshire match. There are still splendid cricketers to settle the ancient argument, some as skilful and as 'county' as the immortals—Boycott, Jack Bond, Pilling, Sharpe, Padgett, Shuttleworth—though I'm not sure that Emmett Robinson would have approved of the presence in the Lancashire eleven of Clive Lloyd—not on racial or apartheid grounds, but simply because Lloyd was not born in Lancashire.

Emmett even objected, to me, by word of mouth, to the presence in the Lancashire team of the glorious E. A. Macdonald. 'Can't tha find good enough cricketers in Lancashire?' he asked. 'Hast thi to bring in a Tas-may-nian?' The way he pronounced Tasmanian conjured up Macdonald with a ring through his nose.

I am reminded of the occasion at Lord's last summer, when Lever took six wickets for 37 against Middlesex. I went into the Lancashire players' dressing-room to congratulate Lever. 'Aren't you proud,' I asked him, 'to be a Lancastrian?' And charmingly he replied: 'Thank you, sir—but, you know, I wasn't really born in Lancashire, but on border, in Todmorden.' Farokh Engineer, Lancashire's wicket-keeper, was with us as Lever confessed his not quite Lancastrian origins. 'These bloody foreigners,' said Engineer, with a smile as heart-warming as sunshine.

The present President of the Lancashire County Cricket Club will certainly be a proud man to watch his county, this Whitsuntide, playing yet again against his next favourite county. And he will be as proud to be in the company of Clive Lloyd and Engineer as in the company of Boycott, Pilling and the rest. And all the North country crowd, not forgetting small Lancastrian boys, who have paid at the gates and pushed through the turnstiles.

From the *Guardian*, 29 May 1971.

When Cardus began his lifelong odyssey in search of the quiddity of cricketing character, the game, as well as the world at large, was still divided into Gentlemen and Players, and it is hardly surprising that the one professional with an amateur's vocabulary, Albert Knight, should have depicted in glowing terms one of the great vanished glories of cricketing past, the Country-House game.

COUNTRY-HOUSE cricket must be the most delightful of social and sporting experiences. The mere professional often wishes that cricket could be confined to his own backyard, and he is apt to muse upon the wisdom of men who might playfully wrestle with rustics on the green, or with prettier nymphs dance upon the lawn, but who yet prefer to wrestle with giants in the grim arena of a harsher competition. In country-house play, cricket is the salt and savour of the day, not its stuff and staff, nor is the game of that too dangerous or too serious a character to which to its participants in more strenuous fields it inevitably inclines. The vision of sylph-like figures distributing tea and strawberries at four o'clock to tired players reclining in wicker chairs of ample dimensions, contrasts so vividly and painfully with that of the scanty tea interval in a midsummer county match. A few moments, snatched from scowling spectators who desire a better value for their sixpence, and who are full of lamentation over the decadence of the modern player, sum up the iniquity of the quite modern 'tea-interval', which includes Messrs A. B. and C. to suggest legislative removal. Country-house cricket reminds one of days spent in eating apples under an old tree, reading the 'Earthly Paradise' of William Morris. It is the cricket of an Eden future when we shall saunter through the fields, 'without tomorrow, without yesterday', nor scent laziness in ease, nor distrust good-humoured chaff as incompatible with seriousness.

From *The Complete Cricketer*, 1906.

The world which Knight is describing hardly sounds real, yet it must once have existed. In the opinion of at least one romantic, E. R. Eddison (1882–1945), it exists still, and may be savoured easily enough, provided only that we can slip through one of those gaps in the Space-Time continuum with which existence is supposed to be peppered. Eddison was a retired civil servant who wrote four bizarre novels which drift between medieval romance and science fiction. In A Fish Dinner in Memison *(1941), the dual time-scale shuttles between some other existence at some other time, and the world of Edwardian privilege. However outlandish Eddison's imagination, there is at least one point in his saga where both the action and the characters not only come down to earth, but have the good sense to alight on a cricket field.*

A Match and Some Lookers on

'TIME, YOU know, is a curious business', said Lord Anmering, tilting his head forward a little to let the brim of his panama hat shade his eyes; for it was teatime, and the afternoon sun, from beyond the cricket field below, blazed out of cloudless blue in their faces. 'Love of money, we're told,—root of all evil. Gad! I think otherwise. I think Time strikes deeper.'

Lady Southmere replenished the vacuum with one of the more long-drawn, contemplative, and non-committal varieties of the inimitable transatlantic 'Aha'.

'Look at Mary', he said. 'Look at me. If I wasn't her father: wasn't thirty-two years her senior. Wouldn't I know what to do with her?'

'Well, I dare say you would.'

'Easy enough when they're not your own,' he said, as they walked on slowly, coming to a halt at the top of two flights of shallow steps that led down to the field from the gardens. 'But when they are,—By Jove, that's the style!' The ball, from a magnificent forward drive, sailed clean over the far fence, amid shouts of applause, for six. 'If you let your boy go and smash my melon-houses, knocking the bowling about like that, I'll tell you, I'll have no more to do with him. We musn't forget,' he said, lower again: 'she's very young. Never force the pace.'

'O but don't I just agree? And the very dearest, sweetest,—'

'You know her, well as I do. No, you don't, though. Look there,' putting up his eye-glass to examine the telegraph board: 'eighty. Eighty: a hundred and sixty-three: that's eighty-four to win. Not so bad, with only three wickets down. It's that boy of yours is doing it: wonderful steady play: nice style too: like to see him make his century. You know our two best bats, Chedisford and the young Macnaghten, didn't add up to double figures between 'em: Hugh's got his work cut out for him. Look at that! pretty warm bowling. A strong team old Playter's brought us over this time from Hyrnbastwick: Jove, I'd like to give 'em a whacking for a change. Well, Hugh and Jim seem settled to it. Would you like to come down over there: get a bit of shade?'

'I would like to do anything anybody tells me to. This is just too perfect.' She turned, before coming down the steps, to look back for a minute to the great west front of Anmering Blunds, where it ranged beyond green lawns and flower-beds and trim deep-hued hedges of clipped box and barberry and yew: long rows of mullioned windows taking the sun, whose beams seemed to have fired the very substance of the ancient brickwork to some cool-burning airy essence of gold. This wing, by Inigo Jones, was the newest part, masking from this side the original flint-built house that had been old Sir Robert Scarnside's, whom Henry VIII made first Earl of Anmering. Round to the right, in the home park, stood up, square and grey, Anmering church tower. A sheltering wood of oak, ash, beech and sycamore was a screen for hall and church and garden against the east; and all the midsummer leafage of these trees seemed, at this hour, impregnate with that golden light. Northwards, all lay open, the ground falling sharply to the creek, salt marshes and sand-dunes and thence-away, to the North Pole, the sea. Southwards and landwards, park and wood and meadow and arable rose gently to the heaths and commons: Bestarton, Sprows-wood, Toftrising. Lady Southmere, waiting on the silence a minute, might hear as under-tones to the voices of the cricket field (of players and lookers on, click of wood against leather as the batsman played) the faint far-off rumour of tide-washed shingle, and, from trees, the wood-pigeon's rustic, slumbrous, suddenly started and suddenly checked, discourse: *Two coos, tak' two coos, Taffy, tak' two coos, Taffy tak'*—. From golden rose to larkspur a swallowtail butterfly fluttered in the heat. 'Just too perfect for words,' she said, turning at last.

They came down the steps and began walking, first north, and so round by the top end of the cricket field towards the tents. 'I'll make a clean breast of it,' she said: 'twenty-six years now I have been English and lived in the Shires; and yet, Blunds in summer, well, it gets me here: sends me downright home-sick.' Just as, underneath all immediate sounds or voices, those distant sea-sounds were there for the listening, so in Lady Southmere's speech there survived some pleasant native intonations of the southern States.

'Home-sick?' said Lord Anmering. 'Virginia?'

'No, no, no: just for Norfolk. Aren't I English? and isn't your Norfolk pure England as England ought to be?'

'Better get Southmere to do an exchange: give me the place in Leicestershire and you take Blunds.'

'Well and would you consent to that? Can you break the entail?'

'My dear lady,' he said, 'there are many things I would do for you,—'

'But hardly that?'

'I'm afraid, not that.'

'O isn't that just too bad!' she said, as Jim Scarnside, playing forward to a yorker, was bowled middle stump.

Fifty or sixty people, may be, watched the game from this western side where the tents were and garden chairs and benches, all in a cool shade of beech and chestnut and lime and sycamore that began to throw shadows far out upon the cricket field: a pleasant summer scene as any could wish, of mingled sound and silence, stir and repose: white hats and white flannels and coloured caps and blazers contrasting here and there with more formal or darker clothes: a gaiety of muslin frocks, coloured silks, gauzes and ribbons, silken parasols and picture hats: the young, the old, the middle-aged: girls, boys, men, women: some being of the house-party; some, the belongings of the eleven that had driven over with Colonel Playter from Hyrnbastwick; some, neighbours and acquaintance from the countryside: wives, friends, parents, sisters, cousins, aunts. Among these their host, with Lady Southmere, now threaded his way, having for each, as he passed, the just greeting, were it word, smile, formal salutation or private joke: the Playter girls, Norah and Sybil, fresh from school: old Lady Dilstead, Sir Oliver's mother, and his sister Lucy (engaged to Nigel Howard): young Mrs Margesson, a niece of Lord Anmering's by marriage: Romer, the bursar of Trinity: Limpenfield of All Souls': General Macnaghten and his wife and son: Trowsley of the Life Guards: Tom and Fanny Chedisford: Mr and Mrs Dagworth from Semmering: Sir Roderick Bailey, the Admiral, whose unpredictable son Jack had made top score (fifty) for the visiting eleven that morning: the Rector and his wife: the Denmore-Benthams: Mr and

Mrs Everard Scarnside (Jim's parents) and Princess Mitzmesczinsky (his sister): the Bremmerdales from Taverford: the Sterramores from Burnham Overy: Janet Rustham and her two little boys: Captain Feveringhay; and dozens besides.

'Sorry, uncle,' said Jim Scarnside, as their paths met: he on his way to the pavilion. 'Ingloriously out for three.'

'I was always told,' Lady Southmere said, 'you ought to block a yorker.'

'My dear Lady Southmere, don't I know it? But, (I know you won't believe this), it was all your fault.'

'That's very very interesting.'

'It was.'

'And please, why?'

'Well. Just as that chap Howard was walking back, the way he does to get properly wound up for one of those charging-buffalo runs that terrify the life out of a poor little batsman like me,'—

'Poor little six foot two!' she said.

'Just at that instant, there, on the horizon, your black and white parasol! And I remembered: Heavens! didn't Mary make me promise that Lady Southmere should have the first brew of strawberries and cream, because they're so much the best? and isn't it long past tea-time, and here she comes, so late, and they'll all be gone? So there: and Nigel Howard sends down his beastly yorker. Is it fair? Really, Uncle Robert, you ought not to allow ladies to look on at serious cricket like ours. All very well at Lord's and places like that; but here, it's too much of a distraction.

'But dreadfully awkward,' said she, laughing up at him, 'not to have us to put the blame on? Jim!' she called after him as they parted: he turned. 'It was real noble and kind of you to think about the strawberries.'

'I'm off to rescue them.' And, using his bat like a walking-stick, he disappeared with long galloping strides in the direction of the tea-tent.

St. John, next man in, was out first ball. This made an excitement, in expectation that Howard should do the hat-trick; but Denmore-Bentham, who followed, batted with extreme circumspection and entire success (in keeping his wicket up, though not indeed in scoring).

'Who's this young fellow that's been putting up all the runs? Radford? Bradford? I couldn't catch the name?' said an old gentleman with white whiskers, white waistcoat, and that guinea-gold complexion that comes of long living east of Suez. His wife answered:

'Lord Glanford, Lord Southmere's son. They're staying here at the house, I think. And that's his sister: the pretty girl in pink, with brown hair, talking now to Lady Mary.'

His glance, following where hers gave him the direction, suddenly came to rest; but not upon Lady Rosamund Kirstead. For Mary, chancing at that instant to rise and, in her going, look back with some laughing rejoinder to her friends, stood, for that instant, singled; as if, sudden in a vista between trees, a white sail drawing to the wind should lean, pause, and so righting itself pass on its airy way. A most strange and singular look there was, for any perceiving eye to have to read, in the eyes of that old colonial governor: as though, through these ordinary haphazard eyes, generations of men crowded to look forth as from a window.

Glanford, with a new partner, seemed to settle down now to win the match by cautious steady play, never taking a risk, never giving a chance. When, after a solid half hour of this, a hundred at last went up on the board, the more cavalierly minded among the onlookers began to give rein to their feelings. 'Darling Anne,' Fanny Chedisford said, arm in arm with Lady Bremmerdale, 'I simply can't stick it any longer: poke, poke, poke: as soon look on at a game of draughts. For heaven's sake, let's go and drown our sorrows in croquet.'

'Croquet? I thought you agreed with Mary—'

'I always do. But when?'

'When she said it was only fit for curates and dowagers, and then only if they'd first done a course in a criminal lunatic asylum.'

'O we're all qualified after this. Try a foursome: here's Jim and Mr Margesson: ask them to join in.'

'Did I hear someone pronounce my name disrespectfully?' said Jim Scarnside. Fanny laughed beneath her white parasol. 'Ah, it was my much esteemed and never sufficiently to be redoubted Miss Chedisford. You know,' he said to Cuthbert Margesson, 'Miss Chedisford hasn't forgiven us for not making it a mixed match.'

'Broom-sticks for the men?' said Margesson.

'Not at all,' said Fanny.

Jim said, 'I should think not! Come on: Margesson's in next wicket down. It does seem rather cheek, when he's captain, but after all it's his demon bowling made him that, and his noted diplomacy. Let's take him on and coach him a bit: teach him to slog.'

Anne Bremmerdale smiled: 'Better than croquet.' They moved off towards the nets.

'Are you a bat, Miss Chedisford? or a bowler?' said Margesson.

'Well, I can bat more amusingly than this': Fanny cast a disparaging glance at the game. 'My brothers taught me.'

'All the same,' Margesson said, 'Glanford's playing a fine game. We shall beat you yet, Lady Bremmerdale. How is it you didn't bring your brother over to play for Hyrnbastwick?'

'Which one? I've five.'

'I've only met one. The youngest. Your brother Edward, isn't it?'

'She couldn't bring him because she hasn't got him.'

Fanny said, 'I thought he was staying with you now at Taverford?'

'Not since early May.'

'He's the kind of man,' said Jim, 'you never know where he is.'

Fanny looked surprised. 'I'd have sworn,' she said, 'it was Edward Lessingham I saw this morning. Must have been his double.'

'Antipholus of Ephesus,' said Jim: 'Antipholus of Syracuse.'

'About eight o'clock,' said Fanny. 'It was such a dream of a morning, all sopping with dew, I'd got up with the lark and walked the dogs right up onto Kelling Heath before breakfast. I'd swear no one in these parts had that marvellous seat on a horse that he has. So careless. My dear, I'll bet you anything you like it was he: galloping south, towards Holt!'

'Really, Fanny, it couldn't have been,' said Anne.

'There are not many young men you'd mistake for him,' said Fanny.

Jim said to them, 'Talking of Kelling Heath, I'll tell you an idea of mine; why can't we get up a point-to-point there this autumn? What do you say, Cuthbert?'

'I'm all for it.'

'I tackled Colonel Playter about it to-day at lunch: very important to get him, as M.F.H., to bless it: in fact, he really ought to take it over himself, if it's to be a real good show. He likes the idea. Did you sound Charles, Anne?'

'Yes I did: he's awfully keen on it, and means to get a word with you this evening. Of course you could have a magnificent run right over from Weybourne Heath to Salthouse Common, and back the other way; pretty rough and steep, though, in places.'

Fanny accepted the change of subject. May be she thought the more.

Bentham was out: caught at the wicket: six wickets down for a hundred and nine, of which Glanford had made sixty off his own bat. Margesson now went in, and, (not because of any eggings on of impatient young ladies—unless, indeed, telepathy was at work—for Glanford it was who did the scoring), the play began to be brisk. Major Rustham, the Hyrnbastwick captain, now took Howard off and tried Sir Charles Bremmerdale, whose delivery, slowish, erratic, deceptively easy in appearance, yet concealed (as dangerous currents in the body of smooth-seeming water) a puzzling variety of pace and length and now and again an unexpected and most disconcerting check or spin. But Glanford had plainly got his eye in: Margesson too. 'We're winning, Nell,' said Lord Anmering to his niece, Mrs Margesson. 'A dashed fine stand!' said Sybil Playter. 'Shut up swearing,' said her sister. 'Shut up yourself: I'm not.' People clapped and cheered Glanford's strokes. Charles Bremmerdale now could do nothing with him: to mid-off, two: to mid-on, two: a wide: a strong drive, over cover's head, to the boundary, four: to long-leg in the deep field, two—no—three, while Jack Bailey bungles it with a long shot at the wicket: point runs after it: 'Come on!'—four: the fieldsman is on it, turns to throw in: 'No!' says Margesson, but Glanford, 'Yes! come on!' They run: Bremmerdale is crouched at the wicket: a fine throw, into his hands, bails off and Glanford run out. 'Bad luck!' said Jim Scarnside, standing with Tom and Fanny Chedisford at the scoring table: Glanford had made ninety-one. 'But why the devil will he always try and bag the bowling?'

Glanford walked from the field, bat under his arm, shaking his head mournfully as he undid his batting-gloves. He went straight to the pavilion to put on his blazer, and thence, with little deviation from the direct road, to Mary. 'I am most frightfully sorry,' he said, sitting down by her. 'I did so want to bring you a century for a birthday present.'

'But it was a marvellous innings,' she said. 'Good heavens, "What's centuries to me or me to centuries?" It was splendid.'

'Jolly decent of you to say so. I was an ass, though, to get run out.'

Mary's answering smile was one to smoothe the worst-ruffled feathers; then she resumed her conversation with Lucy Dilstead: 'You can read them over and over again, just as you can Jane Austen. I suppose it's because there's no padding.'

'I've only read *Shagpat*, so far,' said Lucy.

'O that's different from the rest. But isn't it delicious? So serious. Comedy's always ruined, don't you think, when it's buffooned? You want to live in it: something you can laugh with, not laugh at.'

'Mary has gone completely and irretrievably cracked over George Meredith,' Jim said, joining them.

'And who's to blame for that?' said she. 'Who put what book into whose hand? and bet what, that who would not be able to understand what-the-what it was all driving at until she had read the first how many chapters how many times over?'

Jim clutched his temples, histrionically distraught. Hugh was not amused. The match proceeded, the score creeping up now very slowly with Margesson's careful play. General Macnaghten was saying to Mr Romer, 'No, no, she's only twenty. It is: yes: quite extraordinary; but being only daughter, you see, and no mother, she's been doing hostess and so on for her father two years now, here and in London: two London seasons. Makes a lot of difference.'

Down went another wicket; score, a hundred and fifty-three. 'Now for some fun,' people said as Tom Appleyard came on the field; but Margesson spoke a wingèd word in his ear: 'Look here, old chap: none of the Jessop business. It's too damned serious now.' 'Ay, ay, sir.' Margesson, in perfect style, sent back the last ball of the over. Appleyard obediently blocked and blocked. But in vain. For one of Bremmerdale's master-creations of innocent outward show and inward guile sneaked round Margesson's defence and took his leg stump. Nine wickets down: total a hundred and fifty-seven: last man, nine. Hyrnbastwick, in some elation, were throwing high catches round the field while Dilstead, Anmering's next (and last) man in, walked to the wicket. Margesson said to Tom Appleyard, 'It's up to you now, my lad. Let 'em have it, damn slam and all if you like. But, by Jingo, we must pull it off now. Only seven to win.' Appleyard laughed and rubbed his hands.

There was no more desultory talk: all tense expectancy. 'If Sir Oliver gets the bowling, that puts the lid on it: never hit a ball yet.' 'Why do they play him then?' 'Why, you silly ass, because he's such a thundering good wicket-keeper.' George Chedisford, about sixteen, home from Winchester because of the measles, maintained a mature self-possession at Lord Anmering's elbow: 'I wish my frater—wish my brother was in again, sir. He'd do the trick.' 'You watch Mr. Appleyard: he's a hitter.' By good luck, that ball that had beaten Margesson was last of the over, so that Appleyard, not Dilstead, faced the bowling: Howard once more, a Polyphemus refreshed. His first ball was a yorker, but Appleyard stopped it. The second, Appleyard, all prudent checks abandoned, stepped out and swiped. Boundary: four. Great applaudings: the parson's children and the two little Rustham boys, with the frenzy of Guelph and Ghibelline, jumped up and down jostling each other. The next ball, a very fierce one, pitched short and

126

rose at the batsman's head. Appleyard smashed it with a terrific over-hand stroke: four again—'Done it!' 'Match!'

Then, at the fourth ball, Appleyard slogged, missed, and was caught in the slips. And so amid great merriment, chaff and mutual congratulations, the game came to an end.

From *A Fish Dinner in Memison*, 1941.

In such a game, who would be the visitors? And what protocol would they follow that night at dinner? In which subtle ways would they indicate, with a patrician blend of modesty and arrogance, their affiliations? The social game such gladiators played was of such a complexity as to terrify a more plebeian age. The fancy-dress aspects of the old Country-House game are often overlooked, and so, for those who manage to follow Mr Eddison through the bolthole into the past, here are a few guidelines provided by E. H. D. Sewell (1872–1947).

AT DINNER on tour, or at country houses, all members of I Zingari wear a broad ribbon of the club's famous black, yellow and red colours diagonally across the chest like the Order of the Garter.

There are also in existence some buttons of the IZ colours for wear with the white dress waistcoat, but these are very unusual.

The well-known Kentish club, the Band of Brothers, have a special tail-coat for great occasions. Those who have not this coat wear a bow with the pale blue and black stripe of the B.B.'s when in dress clothes.

I have heard from an Old Etonian himself how proud he felt when, though not a member of I Zingari, he was informed by Lord George Scott, who had obtained the necessary permission from Sir Spencer Ponsonby, that he, the O.E. who had only just left Eton, might wear the IZ sash at dinner, when playing at Viceregal Lodge, Dublin. In IZ rules sash is always spelt with long 's', thus 'fafh'.

One of my pleasantest recollections was hearing the I Zingari team singing the IZ song, with Charles Carlos Clarke as their captain, after a dinner at Ascot during one of Anthony de Rothschild's delightful Weeks.

Pleasant memories only sleep, they never die; but when we reach a certain age, however softly Time shall trot, his footfall surely awakens many such well-liked echoes as the above, of far-off days at Ascot.

From *Overthrows*, 1944.

The breed of Gentleman-amateur who played such games is virtually extinct. In his Cricket: A History of its Growth and Development throughout the World, *published in 1970, Roland Bowen lists only six houses left in England still capable of sustaining an authentic Country-House match and then accommodating the sides after Close of Play. One of the paragons of the world of white dress waistcoats and sashes at dinner was Charles Inglis Thornton (1850–1929), captain of Eton, 1868; captain of Cambridge University, 1872; player for Kent and Middlesex, creator of the Scarborough Festival, and one of the biggest hitters of all time. For the likes of Thornton, cricket was a lark; Thornton's genius lay in his success in reconciling the larkiness with prodigious ability. Across the gulf of a century his good-natured laughter can still be heard.*

WITH REGARD to my reminiscences of over fifty years of cricket life, I am afraid I should weary my readers if I gave more than a limited quantity of them, and should certainly take up more than my share of your paper. Suffice it to say that I was born at Llanwarne, Herefordshire, on March 20, 1850, my father being parson of Llanwarne and Rural Dean of Hereford. My father and mother both dying when I was five years old, I was adopted, together with my brother Henry, by Archdeacon and Mrs Harrison, of Canterbury, and that was really the commencement of my cricket life, as we began playing in the garden, and also on its bowling green belonging to my uncle, at a very early age, and I used to take on all the neighbouring boys at single wicket.

I think my first regular cricket match—ie; with bails on and a marked-out crease—was about 1861, when I played at Great Mongeham, near Ramsgate. I got 22 not out, and caught their best man out at long slip; and my good friend and tutor, Mr Malden, congratulated me, and told me he thought I should gain fame as a cricketer. I went to Eton in 1861, but, as far as I remember, didn't do much cricket during my first three years; but in 1864 I began to take an interest in it, and in 1865 some of the Upper Club boys noticed my hitting propensities, and I was summoned to Upper Club to practise with Fred Bell, the professional engaged to coach the boys. Our ideas did not coincide, as I hit all his best balls into the trees, and, as he had to fetch them, he did not care much about it. I think I might have been in the Eton XI in 1865 if it had not been for him; but as it was about the worst eleven Eton ever had I did not miss much. Anyhow I got in next year, and obtained about 50 in my first match against Christ Church, Oxford. We were well beaten by Harrow; Frank Cobden bowling us out. I got 46, I remember. I never was on the winning side in Eton v Harrow matches, though I made over 50 runs, each year. I went on to Cambridge in October, 1868, and had four glorious years of cricket, winning three matches out of four against Oxford. My cousin, P. M. Thornton, and I then took lodgings at Cambridge for the two following seasons, and we had a lot of cricket, running up to town for Lord's and Oval matches. The following year, 1874, we took a hunting-box at Luffenham, near Oakham and Uppingham, and had a splendid time hunting three days a week. We had a capital cricket pitch in the stableyard, the floor being of bricks. I made the grooms play, and it was fine exercise. We also in the summer made a pitch ourselves on a ridge and furrow field of grass, and played the villages around. One day when alone, I went over to Oakham Grammar School ground, and had a good bit of fun. The school were playing against the Rev. Munro's XI, and Munro, being a man short, asked me to make up the eleven. No one knew me, and I played as C. Inglis, Esq. Curiously enough, this is the same alias adopted by Carl Lodz, the first German spy shot here during the war. I made 35 not out, going in eighth, and when the time came for our second innings I claimed the right to go in first, having been not out in the first innings. I went in and got 188 out of 210 runs from the bat, hitting thirteen times out of the ground. Munro and I became great friends afterwards. This is slightly better than the Winchester boy Guise, who got 278 out of 343.

I think I have had more fun out of cricket than most people. I never recollect losing my temper, or dashing the bat down when getting a duck, and I always thought, 'Well, it is but a game, and there are many more serious things in life after all, so "*aequam memento rebus in arduis servare mentem*".' I was very lucky in my cricket career, notably happening to hit the ball over Lord's pavilion in the Eton v Harrow match at the age of nineteen, and having a lot to do with winning the match for Cambridge next year, getting 50 and 36 on a very dirty wicket, with A. F. Walter bowling for Oxford. The innings I most enjoyed was at Scarborough (in 1887, I think) when I hit A. G. Steel over the houses into Trafalgar Square, and, to the best of my recollection, I got eight 6's in that innings. A curious episode occurred in connection with this hit. I was returning last year in a crowded compartment from Bradford to Harrogate, having been over to the Middlesex and Yorkshire match there, and a man in the compartment called out to me and said, 'Ain't you the gent, what hit the ball into Trafalgar Square some years ago?' I said 'Yes,' and he said, 'Very glad to see you again.' The next day someone who had heard of it asked me if it was true that I had hit a ball into Trafalgar Square, and was it hit from Lord's or the Oval? When I said it was Trafalgar Square, Scarborough, just outside the ground, he wasn't so much impressed. In the old days—ie; fifty years ago—when we played on the Castle Hill the wind was sometimes awful, and we frequently had to use iron bails, which were kept for the purpose, as they couldn't be blown off. People used to say they were dangerous for the wicket-keeper, but I never heard of any accident from their use.

We played the old Yorkshire XI there in 1871. We were the Scarborough visitors, and we had a good side—R. D. and I. D. Walker, Dale, Arthur Smith, and A. J. Wilkinson—and we should probably have won had it been finished, as Yorkshire had about 28 to get and two very moderate wickets to go down. Lord Londesborough paid for the whole show, and let everyone in free, which rather annoyed the Scarborough Cricket Club. Old Roger Iddison described him well, saying, 'He hangs his purse on the gate and lets everyone help themselves as likes to.' And very true. For many years I have enjoyed his princely hospitality at Scarborough, and many other places. Scarborough cricket week has now, and for many years past, been quite an important affair, and twenty years ago the club presented me with a splendid silver cup, with a most complimentary inscription, and now, in my fiftieth year there, the Corporation of Scarborough are presenting me with the Freedom of the City and my portrait. Of course, the cricket week has brought thousands of people every year into the town, and it has always been my great desire to have the best cricketers in the world playing. I think every Australian XI has visited there and played against my team, and I think practically every first-class professional and amateur cricketer has taken part in the Week. Where, fifty years ago, we had perhaps 200 people on the ground, we now have 5000 or 6000. Of course, I could never have done what I have had it not been for the loyal co-operation of Yorkshire, headed by that splendid captain, Lord Hawke; and the MCC have always backed me up by letting me have their best bowlers, Shaw, Morley, Barnes, &c. For the last twenty years I have been greatly helped in getting up the sides by H. D. G. Leveson-Gower, who, being an active player and much younger than myself, knows all the later generations of cricketers.

There is one thing in cricket where my opinion, I expect, is not shared by good judges of the game, and that is in the coaching of young players.

I was never coached, or perhaps I might have done better; but my firm belief is that cricketers are born, and not made. I do not mean to say that many fine batsmen have not been greatly helped by coaching, such as G. H. Longman, A. P. Lucas, F. E. R. Fryer; but take a few well-known names, A. J. Webbe and W. H. Hadow, if they had been coached, would they have been taught to stand with their legs a yard apart? What about Jessop or Hendren and their magnificent unorthodox methods? E. M. Grace again, who played with a horizontal bat, and A. N. Hornby, who stood with his bat behind his legs. The present H. Lee, who stoops almost onto his bat handle, and recently made 235 runs not out. Coaches nearly always teach the boys to stand tight-footed to slow bowling, whereas, in my opinion, they ought to be ready to jump out and hit the slows. I wish some of them had done this to W. W. Armstrong, the great Australian bowler. They would have done much better than fiddling about in their ground, and either getting bowled out or lbw.

I have often been asked as to my longest hit. It was at Brighton, on the present ground, and went far over the entrance gate, and pitched in the road close to where Mr Pycroft was passing. He made a mark there and then, and we measured it with a chain—160 yards. They say Mr Fellowes hit one farther; but I do not know if it was actually measured. I have made many more sensational hits, over buildings and pavilions, but a real long hit must not be too high. At Canterbury I hit W. M. Rose (a slow bowler) over Lord Harris's tent into the hop garden. That was measured 152 yards; while the one off A. G. Steel, over the houses at Scarborough, was measured 136 yards. At Ranelagh I hit one 156 yards, and old Bonner was dining with us there after, and said he'd heard I'd made a long hit, and said that he had a sister who could hit as hard as I could, so I said, 'Bring her over here, and marry her to Barlow or Louis Hall, and there would be some fine future cricketers.'

Curiously enough, when on the Melbourne cricket ground, about 1891, I was asked by a stranger if that story was true, and I was able to say it was. I always say that Spofforth was the best all-round bowler I ever saw, and certainly one of the most amusing chaps to play a club cricket match with. The questions the country bowlers and batsmen used to ask him! How he held the ball for a slow break-back ball, or a fast one with leg break, and he would describe the whole thing. One man he told that he learnt to catch sharp short slip catches by when a boy he used to walk along a hedge and get someone to throw stones into the hedge, and he caught the sparrows as they darted out. E. M. Grace was almost as amusing.

Talking of bowlers, I think it is a great pity that something cannot be done to stop the absurdly long run that many of our fast bowlers here and in Australia take. I would limit it to ten yards. In my early days I do not remember anything like a run of over twenty yards. Take our best bowlers of the 'seventies—Freeman, Hill, Tarrant, for instance, three of the finest and fastest bowlers of that time. They all took about seven or eight yards. With regard to the pernicious habit of getting in front of the wicket, as many of our best batsmen do, when playing a straight ball, there is only one way to stop that, and that is by prohibiting pads, except little shin guards as worn at football. Batsmen would soon give up playing the ball with their legs, like Shrewsbury, Gunn and Co used to in the old days, and I think it would shorten the scores, too. I do not think I shall have many to agree with me in this matter of lbw.

I have had so many funny episodes at cricket that I cannot remember half of them. I recollect one evening, coming out of the Scarborough ground with Tom Emmett, one of the best and most amusing chaps I ever played with, and one or two others, and he met his wife and boy just outside. He introduced her to me, and I said to Tom, 'And is this your little boy?' Tom replied, 'Well, leastways I pay for him under that apprehension.' We all laughed, including Mrs Emmett. Once, in Canterbury week, all the pros were at lunch with me in my tent as usual. Amongst other delicacies was some horse-radish sauce, and Tom was having some cold tart, and took what he thought was cream (ie the horse-radish sauce). He enjoyed it so much that he had two goes at it. Flowers reached across for it, and Tom handed it to him, and said, 'You have 'oggish manners, Wilfrid; don't reach over.'

Tom never minded being hit, and used to pitch them up to me. I made a long hit off him at Scarborough Castle Hill, and he called out, 'By gad, it's gone into the sea!' I hit one off him once—a very high one —to Louis Hall, in the deep field, who ran forward, and then back, finally not touching it. I once played for the United North v Eighteen of Bingley and District, a pretty but very small ground, and a very sticky wicket. I think he got about eighteen wickets in the two innings for 25 runs. It was simply a procession. I remember hitting one over cover-point's head, and he ran back, and went backwards into the sandy edge of the river, which was fortunately low at the time.

Some of the best games I ever had were at the Orleans Club, Twickenham, from 1878 to 1880. We played the Australians there twice, and very successfully. I remember the first ball I received from Frank Allen—I played forward at it, and it hit me right on the shin bone. I never saw any bowler curl in the air as he did. He, however, never did much in England—he couldn't stand the climate. I. D. Walker and I got a good many runs, and I hit Boyle 150 yards, measured by Rylott and Barratt. Against the Green Jackets there one day, we got 180 in the first hour, of which I got 138, and a week or two after I got 104 in thirty-eight minutes, including seven sixers.

Rickling Green was one of the best run-getting grounds I ever saw. The famous 920 score we got there, I fancy, is a record now, but I am not sure. We had a wonderful match there in 1883. We had 250 runs to get in two hours, and, having been bowled out first innings by B. A. F. Grieve, the Harrow fast under-hand bowler, for nothing, I determined to have a go for the runs. We got them in 100 minutes, my share being 170 not out. Appleby and Jack Dale stayed in with me. I lost £5 over it, as I laid my cousin, J. C. Partridge, 10 to 1 we didn't get them. Sir W. Gilbey and the brothers Jim and Henry Blythe entertained us all right royally.

The following week was Canterbury, and I went down to Canterbury with W.G., Steel, Studd, Barnes, Flowers, Morley, Alf Shaw, etc to play against Kent. The train was behind time, it being Bank Holiday and Lord Harris was very annoyed at our late appearance. Old W.G. replied, 'If we win the toss you will wish we had been a bit later still,' which, fortunately, turned out to be the case. Dear old W.G., he was always ready with an apt reply. We had some good fun in those Canterbury weeks. I played there about fifteen years, I should think. My old uncle, Archdeacon Harrison, and Mrs Harrison, were always delighted to put up a dozen of us, and I think I may say the most celebrated cricketers of the day were entertained by them. One day, after dinner, A. J. Webbe put on my uncle's archidiaconal hat, with its very broad brim, and little laces. It went nearly over A.J.'s ears, but he solemnly walked into the club in it about 10.30 pm. Those who saw him —and they are many—will never forget the episode.

Kent were a good side, and splendidly captained by George Harris. We used to have capital fun there in mid-September, when my eleven played the two schools and St Augustine's College one-day matches. We began at 10 am sharp, and played till it was dark. Webbe and I. D. Walker usually came, and we used to fill up with the servants, lamp-lighter, superintendent of police, and others, and we had some splendid matches. The schools played masters, too, one of whom, the Rev. R. G. Hodgson, was quite a good player, and, I think, played for Kent once or twice.

The Orleans Club used to have some rare keen matches, notably with Esher, headed by the indefatigable Charley Clarke. I remember one match specially. I got 91 out of 100 first innings, and 49 out of fifty in the second. Another Esher match we had was most amusing. Miss K. Clarke asked me in July if I would bring a team to Esher and play them after Scarborough, say, September 12 or so. I said, 'Yes, if you will give us first innings, as otherwise I may find it difficult to get a side up.' She agreed, so we duly arrived. C.C.C. wanted to toss. I said, 'No; your sister arranged the match and agreed to my terms.' So in we went, and I got 140. Charley Clarke has never forgotten that match. It was a real pleasure to play with him, as he was so keen, and worked hard all the time.

Another good match we used to play was against the Merchant Taylors' School in Charterhouse Square, E.C. It was a tiny ground, surrounded by warehouses, and only two to the boundary. One match there we got 300 in two hours, of which I got 183, and Harry Paravicini 107. The captain came to me at the end of the day and said 'Thank you, sir, for the great treat you have given us.' He was a good sport, that chap!

We used to have some fine games at Southgate in the seventies. I believe I got the largest score made on the ground, *viz*, 180. E. Rutter tried to catch me in that innings 130 yards off, and injured his thumb badly. Old David Buchanan was the bowler, and got very angry. I got 124 runs off 100 consecutive balls, and when I got out he said to point, 'Now we will have some cricket'. When at Cambridge, I had hit him for 24 in one over of five balls, but we were always great friends.

I got up a good many teams v the different Australian XIs, and was very successful altogether. I had rather a set-back at Scarborough when we played Turner and Ferris on a sticky wicket. I got a pair—bowled off my legs first time, and caught at wicket second innings. In the evening, when dining at Lord Londesborough's (about twenty of us) the butler brought in a parcel which he gave to me. I somehow smelt a rat, and I just said, 'Oh, leave it in the hall; I will take it to the Grand when I go.' That didn't suit the conspirators, and Lady L said, 'Oh, don't mind us; open the parcel.' Well, it contained a pair of spectacles, each eye-part about a foot wide. Old W.G. and George Harris had worked it with the town optician. That wasn't all, for at the circus after, where Lord L took about a quarter of the seats for us cricketers, including all the pros and their wives, etc., Whimsical Walker walked into the arena in a light blue cap (mine, I fancy) and a sweater like mine, and carrying a bat. He then began fumbling in his pockets, and the ringmaster said, 'Now, Walker, what are you looking for?' Walker replied, 'I got a couple of duck's eggs on the cricket ground today, and I am looking for them.' Everyone roared and cheered, including myself.

W.G. came up next morning at breakfast and said he hoped I didn't mind. I said, 'Certainly not, I didn't know I was so popular.'

Shortly afterwards I got a bit of my own back with W.G. Farrands, the umpire, gave him out lbw, a decision W.G. disagreed with (not for the first time), and told him so. O'Brien and I concocted a letter from Farrands, saying how surprised he was at Dr W. G. impugning his decision, and speaking to him, as umpire, in the way he had done, etc. and I got the butler to give this note into W.G.'s hand at dinner. The Old Man took it all in, and was in a rare stew over it, as in our letter Farrands was going to bring it before the MCC. Of course, we let him know later on, and he said, 'Well, Chairly (as he called me) you took me in this time, proper.'

We had a funny match at Beeston, near Nottingham, in the seventies —Gents of North v Gents of South, a very heavy scoring game. We got over 500 runs, I think, and I used to say, 'Wonderful thing to get 500 runs in an innings, and only one double figure' (W.G.'s 78) 'on the side'. People couldn't make it out, but as I. D. Walker made 170, and Fred Grace 150, or so, it was quite true.

We used to have some good fun with the old Surrey pros at the Oval —old Ben Griffiths, Mortlock, Caesar, and Co. Some played in pot-hats, and usually spotted red shirts, with little collars and black ties—rather different from the present smart chaps who walk in and out. Jupp and Humphrey were two capital cricketers, and took a lot of shifting. They didn't like my fast under-hand.

In one Gents v Players match I began the bowling, and was successful. When the Players went into the field H. H. Stephenson commenced with fast under-hand, and W.G. and Cooper hit him all over the place. At Canterbury, once, v Surrey, I got 130 or so, and hit Southerton twelve times into one tree on the on-side—there was a bit of a cross wind. In that match I hit a big skyer, and Jupp and Street both went for it, and between them it came to the ground. Jupp was furious, and said to Street, 'Why didn't you let me 'ave it, you old carthorse?' Street was rather heavy and slow.

We were playing at Malton, Yorkshire, some years ago—Scarborough Visitors v Malton, and Roger Iddison bet five shillings I couldn't hit right out of the ground. Reynolds, the old Lancashire bowler, began, and I heard Roger tell him to keep 'em short, so I dashed out at the first ball and landed it in the station. There was a pond in one corner of the ground, and E. S. Carter put a man beyond the pond to catch me out. I hit one just right; the fieldsman forgot the pond, and went clean into it. It was shallow, so no harm resulted.

I have had some funny experiences with umpires. At Wycombe one Saturday I got 105 runs. The following Saturday I played there again, and when I had got 70, a ball hit the outside of my trouser, and the wicket-keeper took it and appealed. 'Out', said the umpire. I said, 'Why? I never even played at it.' 'No,' he said, 'but I gave you "not out" last Saturday when you was out, so this makes it equal,' and I had to go. Another umpire, when we were playing at Sir Theodore Brinkman's place near Cambridge, gave Tim O'Brien out off his shoulder. I was in the other end. Tim walked up to the umpire, and said, with a soupçon of adjectives, 'You must either be a rogue or a fool.' All the umpire replied was, 'I guess I'm a bit of both, sir.' An umpire in Colombo once n-balled me for knocking the wicket down when bowling, and the game was stopped while a book of rules was fetched and examined, without much result, I remember.

From *Cricket*, 1921.

In the light of Thornton's colossal hitting powers, one wonders what country-house teacups were smashed by his towering on-drives, what conservatory windows were blasted by his cheerful excesses, whether indeed hostesses expecting Mr Thornton for the weekend took the precaution of summoning the estate's glazier to stand by, and whether the local insurance agents began licking the ends of their pencils in anticipation of handsome commissions. In view of the lethal aspects of a cricket ball descending from a great height, it is astonishing that so little damage, comparatively speaking, has been wrought. Gerald Brodribb (b. 1915) has summarised the details of this undeclared war between batsmen and the rest of the world.

Danger and Damage

A CRICKET ball is a shining miracle of leather, cork and twine, but when dispatched by a bat swung by a Bonner or a Dexter it becomes a missile of enormous power and speed. It is amazing to consider how few fielders have been seriously damaged by a hit from a cricket ball —even those who have fielded almost within hand-shaking distance of the batsman. Such daring close-in fielding may be *magnifique*, but it sometimes places the batsman in an embarrassing position.

There have been some batsmen who have kept fielders in all positions well on their toes, and sometimes their hits have kept the spectators equally alert. If people go to watch the cricket they must be aware that occasionally a ball will be landed in their midst. It is a good sight when it does; the crowded lines of spectators divide like the Red Sea, 'Oohs!' and 'Ahs!' arise from beaming faces, and some lucky one throws the ball self-consciously back on to the field. But there have been times when some powerful skimming drive has hit somebody, and the injury may be serious. That most genial of cricketers, Keith Miller, twice put spectators into hospital during the Australian tour of 1948, but they were young ones who possibly enjoyed the attendant kudos, and the link with the great man. Escapes from serious injury have been legion: in 1930, at the Parks, N. M. Ford of Oxford University, in scoring 155 v. Kent, hit a ball over the ropes and it landed almost on the toes of a baby in its pram, but scarcely wakened the child. Long years ago Lewis Carroll deplored the use of the Parks for the playing of cricket:

> 'Sunk are thy mounds in shapeless level all,
> Lest aught impede the swiftly rolling ball;
> And trembling, shrinking from the fatal blow,
> Far, far away thy hapless children go.'

One would like to have heard his comment on N. M. Ford's hit.

E. W. Swanton tells how, at Worcester in 1953, he witnessed a near-tragedy when one of the New Zealanders hit a ball which landed in a lunch basket carried by a mother whose small boy was 'allowing himself to be dragged alongside'. The ball missed the boy's head by inches, and broke an empty bottle in the basket. At Lord's once a child seemed likely to be hit, when one of the crowd moved swiftly to extend a hand and hold the ball most brilliantly. The catcher was none other than a great cricketer of the past, but his age and altered appearance caused few of the bystanders to realise who it was; it was a catch worthy of his greatest days.

Even if he is not actually hit, the spectator may suffer a certain amount of shock. When J. H. Parsons hit one of his 4 consecutive sixes off the West Indies at Edgbaston in 1928, one of them sailed into the lunch room in the pavilion and landed in a cup of tea held by a lady; as she was about to drink it, the cup was smashed to fragments, but left its handle—nipped off with almost surgical neatness—in the startled owner's fingers.

Sometimes a spectator has thus been taken unawares, unwitting yet blameless; to others a dull moment of play and a comfortable deck-chair have induced a spell of sleep, and the spectator then becomes a sitting bird. W. E. Phillipson, the Lancashire bowler, tells how he hit a six at Bournemouth in 1946 which landed on the middle of a gentle-man sitting (or rather sleeping) near the sight-screen. The ball landed with a hideous thump, but the victim was miraculously unhurt though, to quote Phillipson, 'the ball straightened him right out.' On another occasion a spectator went to buy a score-card, and when he came back found that one of Frank Woolley's most powerful drives had put the ball right through the canvas of the deck-chair he had just been sitting in. At the best of times it cannot be easy to make a deep-field catch when seated in a deck-chair, so this watcher must be regarded as lucky. Another fortunate one was the mother of the great Kent bats-man K. L. Hutchings; she was once seated at the top of the pavilion at Canterbury—a safe enough place at most times—when her son made a colossal straight drive which landed on her but fortunately did no greater damage than smashing the fob-watch which she was wearing pinned to her dress.

When some batsmen are on the warpath a spectator with imagination can feel that he is almost under fire; the whizzing, leaping ball can quicken the pulse, and D. V. Smith, in one great innings at Hove in 1957, in scoring 166 v. Gloucester, filled the pavilion with real panic. The wickets were pitched at a distance of only 53 yards from the pavilion fence, and Smith decided that this was an opportunity not to be missed. At tea-time on the last day it seemed that Sussex had little chance of knocking off the runs, but after the interval Smith launched an all-out offensive on the spinners before they could make use of the now dusty wicket, and he swept them fiercely over or towards the pavilion. Here is his own account of the hitting:

'Fortunately the first ball after tea pitched in just the right place, and was duly lapped or swept over the pavilion. From that point things happened so quickly that I was being applauded for my hundred without realising for a while what the clapping was about. I played only two shots to the off-spinners: the "lap" or sweep if the ball was pitched up, or the pull, when, as was bound to happen, they pitched short to avoid the then inevitable lap.'

By the time Smith was out, and Sussex had only 16 runs to win, he had hit no fewer than 9 sixes, 6 of them right over the pavilion and the other 3 into it. These lofty hits caused considerable apprehension, but, as Smith himself says, more real damage came from the hits which failed to carry for six and went first bounce among the seats. One such hit struck a spectator a glancing—but not serious—blow upon the side of the face, and while he was being carried off, another spectator walked on to the field and requested the umpires to suspend play while the ambulance men were seeing to the casualty. Many members leapt metaphorically for their tin hats or retired to a safer viewpoint, while other Sussex supporters, sniffing victory and seated out of the danger area, urged play to continue:

'But those behind cried "Forward!"
And those before cried "Back!" '

It is one thing to be hit by a ball inside a ground which one is deliberately visiting, and another to be struck by a ball when going on one's lawful business outside the ground. Every time a ball flies over the confines of the ground it may hit some unheeding passer-by. It was one such carefree stroke which gave W. G. Grace a most unpleasant experience. Here is his account of the incident:

'I was staying with a friend at a hospital at Leicester, and one afternoon we went out on the grounds for a little cricket practice. After I had been batting a little while I hit a ball out of the hospital grounds into an adjacent street. We thought it was useless to go after the ball, so we abandoned play.

'A few minutes later the casualty-ward bell rang, and word was brought to us that a child had been struck on the head with a cricket ball and was lying unconscious in the ward. We jumped to the conclusion that our ball had done the damage, and with feelings easier imagined than described we hurried to attend the little patient. The injury was a severe one, and the case looked hopeless. I was greatly distressed, and felt very miserable, until someone inquired where the child had met with the accident. It then transpired that the injuries had been inflicted on a cricket ground a mile and a half away from the hospital.'

There must have been several occasions in a first-class match when passers-by have been damaged by a ball flying out of the cricket ground, but there seems to be little record of any repercussions except for the time in 1901 when J. H. Sinclair made a drive at Harrogate which dislodged from his perch a cabby who was watching the game from outside the ground. It is said that a solicitor's letter was sent, but 'nothing happened'.

It was not in fact until quite recent times that the legal responsibility for damage from such a hit has been defined and a celebrated case drew attention to the whole problem. In August 1947, Miss Bessie Stone, of Beckenham Road, Cheetham, Lancashire, was standing at her garden gate when she was hit on the head by a ball struck by a batsman playing in a match on the nearby Cheetham Cricket Ground. The distance from the wicket concerned to a 7-foot fence surrounding the ground was 78 yards, and Miss Stone was standing another 20 yards distant across the road. Though 98 yards is not really a very long hit, it was stated that it was very rare for the ball to be hit over the fence. Miss Stone sued the club for the injury caused to her, and in the hearing of the case at Manchester Assizes in 1948 Mr Justice Oliver found in favour of the club, who were not held responsible for the injury. Miss Stone appealed against this, and by a decision at the Court of Appeal the original verdict was reversed, and Miss Stone was awarded damages of £104 19s 6d. as well as costs, which amounted to £449. The Cheetham Club found difficulty in raising such a sum of money and, after consultation with the National Cricket Club Assocation and the M.C.C., it was decided to take the matter further and to make the ultimate appeal to the House of Lords. There, in May 1951, the Court of Appeal decision was reversed and the case was decided in the club's favour; costs amounting to £2,000 were awarded against Miss Stone. Much dismayed at this, she was heard to remark that if cricketers were really sportsmen they would themselves pay the costs involved. In July the National Cricket Club Association debated the matter, and then advised the Cheetham Club not to claim the full costs against Miss Stone. The chairman of the N.C.C.A. stated: 'We regard the case as being conducted on behalf of cricket generally rather than on behalf of the Cheetham Club only, and so we feel it is only right that cricket should pay for it.' A fund was created to pay for the costs; M.C.C. guaranteed a three-figure sum, and the remainder was raised by club cricketers all over the country. Since then almost every club insures itself against doing damage to person or property. All cricketers (and club secretaries) owe a debt of gratitude to the unfortunate Miss Stone for bringing a case which proved not only very interesting, but beneficial to the interests of cricket.

So long as he does not do hurt to anyone, the big hitter can get vast enjoyment out of the damage his strokes can produce. The crash of broken glass or splitting wood, the satisfactory thump as the ball lands on some car, can provide all the fun of a long-distance coker-nut shy. The Surrey hitter, G. J. Whittaker, says that the one regret of his career was that he was never able to put a ball through one of the huge plate-glass windows of the Oval pavilion. In 1885, S. W. Scott, of Middlesex, hit a ball from W. G. Grace right to the Tavern at Lord's 'scaring the barmaid nearly out of her wits'; the ball bounced back off the wall of the bar on to the grass. Soon after, in the very same innings, 'W.G.' was again hit through the same door into the bar, this time by Sir Timothy O'Brien, whose hit smashed some claret glasses. It is not known what the barmaid said about the second hit. S. W. Scott, who told this story, says he never saw a ball hit into the Tavern before or since. In 1865, E. M. Grace, with one of his famous pulls, had hit a ball most gleefully through the window of an upper room of the Tavern, and it was humorously suggested that the landlord should frame the broken pane and keep it as an heirloom. Strangely enough, when Hammond made his famous hit through a window of the power station at Newport, the groundsman *did* keep the shattered round window-frame as a relic, but it was lost during the war.

There is something infinitely satisfying about a glass-smashing hit; and the boy who hits a ball through the neighbour's cucumber frame may well feel that, whatever the cost and penalty, it was worth it. A broken window at Lord's would seem especially awe-ful. W. G. Grace once drove a ball through the Committee Room window, and I believe windows in the Long Room have in comparatively recent times been smashed by both Jim Smith and Trueman, who no doubt enjoyed it immensely. Hammond, with a more precise straight drive, once put a ball through the open door of the Long Room, but the ball bounced right against one of the show-cases without damaging it.

Score-boxes and Press boxes are often situated in a direction tempting to the batsman, and several county scorers have had at times to dive for safety. One of the oddest of such incidents was in a match at Taunton in 1926, when G. F. Earle of Somerset and E. Tyldesley of Lancashire in turn put a ball through the same window of the score-box.

Perhaps the most attractive target for a batsman is some clock on the pavilion or elsewhere. There are numerous legends of so-and-so hitting the clock, but few seem authentic. At Bradford, however, in 1914, J. B. Hobbs, who hit 8 sixes during the match, drove a ball from Drake, of Yorkshire, which landed on the face of the clock on the football stand. Hobbs obviously relished the hit, and waved to his fellow players sitting in the pavilion. The time was 4 o'clock, and the minute-hand struggled on for ten minutes, and then fell with a flop to 4.30, and stayed like that until the clock was repaired after the war. The somewhat disgruntled bowler, who felt that he had seen enough of Hobbs, said that it was a pity that the hands had not been knocked on to 6.30 as then 'we'd have been finished with this mucking about for t'day'. In 1948, K. Cranston, of Lancashire, made a glorious straight drive off Hollies at Edgbaston which shattered the pavilion clock. Cranston offered to pay the cost of the repairs, but the Warwickshire Committee refused the offer, and regarded his hit as a remarkable one well worth the cost it may have incurred.

Though, at Blackpool in 1958, P. Marner, also of Lancashire, once hit 7 balls in an innings into the car park without damaging a single car, cars parked beside the boundary frequently suffer. At Gravesend in 1959, R. L. Hollands, a newspaper correspondent, had interesting copy provided for him when a Middlesex batsman shattered his windscreen. W. H. Sutcliffe once made a huge drive which dented the car of his illustrious father, who, no doubt, readily forgave his son. P. A. Whitcombe, playing for Oxford University against the Australians in 1948 on the Christ Church Ground, landed a ball on the bonnet of a car and then scratched his name by the spot to tell the owner who had done the deed. Perhaps the best of all car-damage tales is that of the Hon. Charles Lyttelton (now Lord Cobham), in a club match at Canterbury, driving a ball clean over the huge concrete stand next door to the pavilion—a very rare feat. Soon after the ball had vanished over the top there were horrible sounds of shattered glass. His lordship seemed uproariously amused at his vast hit and the damage it had wrought, only to discover later that the ball had landed on his own car.

Sometimes as a result of such adventurous hits the ball has itself been so damaged that it has had to be replaced; and it has at times been returned to the field prickly with splinters of glass. F. T. Mann possesses the relics of a ball almost cut in half when he once hit it to a remote corner of Old Trafford. He has also a sliver of one of the seats on the top tier of the Lord's pavilion, the result of his famous onslaught on Rhodes in 1924; a spectator sitting uncomfortably near the scene of the damage sent the chip of wood to Mann to add to his trophies.

Some balls have vanished out of the ground and never been seen again; others have been lost and then found again much later. The winter after Cameron's great hitting off Verity at Sheffield in 1935, a blocked drain on the pavilion roof led to the discovery of a saturated ball that had last been seen leaving Cameron's bat. The ball from Col. A. C. Watson's famous drive at Canterbury in 1925 which made such havoc among the tea-cups was found months later in a bush on the edge of the road with fragments of china still embedded in it.

Other balls have no doubt been casually found by a passer-by and made good use of; one of Alletson's hits at Hove is said to have bounced its way down one of the seaward roads, and a doubtful legend reports that a small boy was found playing with it on the beach. A more reliable report suggests that at one time during that historic innings of 189 some four or five balls were posted as missing, and when D. V. Smith in 1957 was sweeping balls into the gardens behind the pavilion fresh supplies were constantly in demand. Though it is not a particularly small ground, Hove provides a good history of lost balls. In 1955 Marlar there bowled three consecutive deliveries in one over with three different balls, after R. G. Broadbent, of Worcester, had driven the first two out of the ground and lost them.

Sometimes a ball can easily be retrieved; sometimes not. The River Tone which runs past the ground at Taunton must be full of balls which have landed in it, and in the days of G. F. Earle it was customary to launch the salvage boat as soon as he came in to bat. Several other grounds, such as Tonbridge, Chelmsford, Worksop, Ebbw Vale, have nearby rivers into which a ball can easily be sploshed; but with cricket balls at a price over £2 a time this can become a very expensive pastime.

It would be interesting to know what legal right there is to claim the return of a ball hit into private property, especially when it has caused damage. Back-garden cricket has constantly provided a request to the neighbours of 'Can we have our ball back, please?', and the same situation must have arisen in first-class cricket. At Hastings, where Jessop broke many a window, one of his longest hits landed in an upper-storey room, and the old lady who lived there refused to return the ball until she was given something to pay for the broken window. At Scarborough an old gentleman similarly disturbed (but not to the extent of a broken window) flatly refused to return a ball hit into his room, and humorously assumed it to have been a present for him. At Swansea one of the flat-dwellers returned home to find one of her windows smashed and, thinking that burglars had broken in, she rang for the police. After a search a cricket ball was found lurking under the sofa.

Of all the many big-hitting stories, none have been so frequent as the tale of balls hit into passing trains and carried on to distant destinations. Every ground which has a railway passing by has some such legend. It has been difficult to discover how much, if any, truth lies in these stories. Old Trafford, with its Warwick Road Station, provides several tales of transported balls, and I am assured by the groundsman there that Paynter once really did put a ball into a moving goods wagon, which took it on to Chester. Desmond Eagar also tells me that he saw E. R. T. Holmes drive a ball out of the Guildford ground into an open charabanc which drove serenely on; and I have been sent a picture of a lorry destined for Newcastle into which H. A. Peach, of Surrey, in 1924 landed a ball when making one of his out-of-the-Oval hits.

All such stories could be true, but unfortunately few are proven. I am inclined to discount the tale that C. B. Fry hit the first ball he ever received from K. S. Ranjitsinhji into a train with such Fryish cleverness and precision that after a skittish bounce or two on the boiler it popped neatly down the funnel.

From *Hit for Six*, 1960.

The student of such affairs knows, however, that sometimes a cricket match in which the ball is hit consistently for great distances and at prodigious heights, may be surpassed for sheer melodrama by the match in which nobody manages to hit the ball at all. This anecdote comes from Edward Verrall Lucas (1868–1938), biographer of Charles Lamb and prolific anthologist.

I HEARD the other day, between the innings of a village match, the best single wicket story of recent times that has come my way. Two octogenarians, A. and B., both old Blues, were so carried away by enthusiasm at the last University match, that they arranged a single wicket contest. On the day appointed they met, among a number of sympathetic friends. B. won the toss, and went in and had made 12 before he was bowled; but when the time came for A. to take the bat he was unable to do so. *Anno Domini* asserted itself: his weariness and weakness were too serious; he could only lie on a sofa and cry for his lost strength. It was therefore decided that B. should go out to bowl the absent man's wicket down. Off he went, with the crowd, while A. groaned indoors in an agony of disappointment and feebleness. Suddenly, however, his friends came running back, all excitement and satisfaction. 'Bravo! well played, old man!' they cried. 'You've won the match—he's bowled 13 wides!'

From *Fireside and Sunshine*, 1906.

As Cardus and Ford Madox Ford would have said, if such a story isn't strictly true, then it ought to be. How many seasons of cellarage such a tale requires for its final consummation, is unknown. But in cricket the ghosts of the past are never quite laid. In 1900, a profound technical revolution changed the face of cricket, the revolutionary being Bernard James Tindal Bosanquet (1877–1936; Eton, Oxford University, Middlesex and England). Bosanquet, an attractive all-rounder who played seven times for England, scored twenty-one centuries and took over 600 wickets, introduced the diabolonian device of an apparent leg-break which turns from the off, 'The Googly'. Sixty-three years later, the correspondence columns of The Times *were still clamorous with the implications of Bosanquet's invention. The protagonists included the distinguished English novelist, Nigel Dennis, and an equally distinguished theologian, Canon Alan Richardson, who was later to be Dean of York.*

Sir,

Do you want to be torn to pieces by nettled Bosanquets? That family claims two major innovations: (1) the introduction into Oxford of Hegel and 'German idealism'. (2) the introduction into cricket of the googly. It is obvious that (2) was merely the sporting consequence of (1): But just as Bradley must be granted to have helped with the philosophical juggle, so must my mother, dear mother (née Louise Bosanquet) be allowed her share in the bowling one.

As a little girl she hero-worshipped her cousin, BJT, and paid for it in the 1890s by being made to stand at one end of a lawn for hours, retrieving his experimental googlies. A tennis ball was always used— 'Not a *billiard* ball, a *tennis* ball' were among my mother's last words to me. As she knew nothing about German idealism, I must append the following highly significant dates off my own bat:

1886. Publication of B. Bosanquet's *The Introduction to Hegel's Philosophy of Fine Art.*

1890. The googly ideal conceived by B. J. T. Bosanquet.

1893. Publication of Bradley's *Appearance and Reality.*

1893–1900. Intensive work, helped by my mother, to hide the reality behind the googly's appearance.

1903. The Ashes regained by the googly—German idealism's first and last sporting victory.

Yours faithfully,
Nigel Dennis.

From *The Times*, 13 May 1963.

Sir,

Nigel Dennis rightly points out the connexion between Hegelian Idealism and the philosophy of cricket at the turn of the century. It was well understood that the game was a necessary incident in the evolution of the Absolute Idea, in which all differences are reconciled, and that in every cricket match the Absolute was achieving self-realization. You will recall the lines of Andrew Lang, which indicate the ultimate reality behind the invention of the googly:

> If the wild bowler thinks he bowls,
> Or if the batsman thinks he's bowled.
> They know not, poor misguided souls,
> They too shall perish unconsoled.
> I am the batsman and the bat,
> I am the bowler and the ball,
> The umpire, the pavilion cat,
> The roller, pitch, and stumps and all.

Yours faithfully,
Alan Richardson.

From *The Times*, 18 May 1963.

The quotation from Andrew Lang (1844–1912), is a reminder that Lang, who translated The Odyssey, *published several volumes of poetry, and wrote copiously on historical and literary subjects, also wrote a history of Scotland, from which he omitted the most interesting chapter. This subsequently appeared in the volume on cricket in the* Badminton Library of Sports and Pastimes *(1904) under the title* Border Cricket, *and is a prime example of the sentimental approach to cricket as the gateway to a vanished past.*

A BORDER player, in his declining age, may be allowed to make a few remarks on the game as it used to be played in 'pleasant Teviotdale', and generally from Berwick all along the Tweed. The first time I ever saw bat and ball must have been about 1850. The gardener's boy and his friends were playing with home-made bats, made out of firwood with the bark on, and with a gutta-percha ball. The game instantly fascinated me, and when I once understood why the players ran after making a hit, the essential difficulties of comprehension were overcome. Already the border towns, Hawick, Kelso, Selkirk, Galashiels, had their elevens. To a small boy the spectacle of the various red and blue caps and shirts was very delightful. The grounds were, as a rule, very rough and bad. Generally the play was on *haughs*, level pieces of town-land beside the rivers. Then the manufacturers would encroach on the cricket-field, and build a mill on it, and cricket would have to seek new settlements. This was not the case at Hawick, where the Duke of Buccleuch gave the town a capital ground, which is kept in very good order.

In these early days, when one was only a small spectator, ay, and in later days too, the great difficulty of cricket was that excellent thing in itself, too much patriotism. Almost the whole population of a town would come to the ground and take such a keen interest in the fortunes of their side, that the other side, if it won, was in some danger of rough handling. Probably no one was ever much hurt; indeed, the squabbles were rather a sham fight than otherwise; but still, bad feeling was caused by umpires' decisions. Then relations would be broken off between the clubs of different towns, and sometimes this tedious hostility endured for years. The causes were the excess of local feeling, and perhaps the too great patriotism of umpires. 'Not out', one of them said, when a member of the Oxford eleven, playing for his town-club, was most emphatically infringing some rule. 'I can *not* give Maister Tom out first ball', the umpire added, and his case was common enough. Professional umpires, if they could be got, might be expected to prove more satisfactory than excited amateurs who forgot to look after no balls, or to count the number of balls in an over. But even professionals, if they were attached to the club or school, were not always the embodiment of justice.

The most exciting match, I think, in which I ever took part was for Loretto against another school. When our last man went in, second innings, we were still four runs behind our opponent's first score. This last man was extremely short-sighted, and the game seemed over. But his partner, a very steady player, kept the bowling, and put on some thirty-eight more. We put our adversaries in to get this, and had lowered eight wickets for twenty-eight. I was bowling, and appealed to the umpire of our opponents for a palpable catch at wicket. 'Not out!'. Next ball the batsman was caught at long-stop, and a fielder triumphantly shouted, 'Well, how's *that*?'.

'Not out', replied the professional again, and we lost the match by two wickets.

If this had happened on the Border, there would have been trouble, and perhaps the two clubs would not have met again for years. I have no doubt that a more equable feeling has come in among those clubs which retained a good deal of the sentiments of rival clans. The Borderers played too much as if we were still in the days of Scotts and Carrs and as if it were still our purpose

> To tame the Unicorn's pride,
> Exalt the Crescent and the Star.

Sir Walter Scott encouraged this ardour at football when he caused to be unfurled, for the first time since 1633, the ancient banner of Buccleuch, with its broidered motto 'Bellendaine'. The dalesmen, the people from the waters of Yarrow, Ettrick, and Teviot, played against the souters from Selkirk, all across country, the goals being Ettrick and Yarrow. The townsmen scored the first goal, when the Galashiels folk came in as allies of the shepherds, and helped them to win a goal. 'Then began a murder grim and great', and Scott himself was mobbed in the evening. But he knew how to turn wrath into laughter.

''Tis sixty years since', and more, but this perfervid ardour, while it makes Border cricket very exciting, is perhaps even now a trifle too warm. The great idea, perhaps, in all country cricket is not so much to have a pleasant day's sport, win or lose, but to win merely. Men play for victory, as Dr Johnson talked, rather than for cricket. This has its advantages; it conduces to earnestness. But it does not invariably promote the friendliness of a friendly game.

Border cricket is very pleasant, because it is played in such a pleasant country. You see the angler going to Tweedside, or Teviot, and pausing to watch the game as he strolls by the cricket-ground. The hills lie all around, these old, unmoved, unchangeable spectators of man's tragedy and sport. The broken towers of Melrose or Jedburgh or Kelso look down on you. They used to 'look down', as well they might, on very bad wickets. Thanks to this circumstance, the present writer, for the first and only time in his existence, once did the 'hat-trick' at Jedburgh, and took three wickets with three consecutive balls. Now the grounds are better, and the scores longer, but not too long. You seldom hear of 300 in one innings on the Border.

In my time the bowling was roundhand, and pretty straight and to a length, as a general rule. Perhaps, or rather certainly, the proudest day of my existence was when I was at home for the holidays, and was chosen to play, and bowl, for the town eleven against Hawick. I have the score still, and it appears that I made havoc among Elliots, Leydens, and Drydens. But they were too strong for our Scotts, Johnstons, and Douglasses: it is a pleasure to write the old names of the Border clans in connection with cricket. The batting was not nearly so good then as it is now; professional instruction was almost unknown. Men blocked timidly, and we had only one great hitter, Mr John Douglas; but how gallantly he lifted the soaring ball by the banks of Ettrick! At that time we had a kind of family team, composed of brothers and other boys, so small that we called ourselves Les Enfants Pred Perdus. The name was appropriate enough. I think we only once won a match, and that victory was achieved over Melrose. But we kept the game going on and played in all weathers, and on any kind of wickets. Very small children would occasionally toddle up and bowl when the elder members of the family were knocked off. Finally, as they grew in stature, the team developed into 'The Eccentric Flamingoes', then the only wandering Border club. We wore black and red curiously disposed, and had a good many Oxford members. The Flamingoes, coming down from Oxford, full of pride, had once a dreadful day on the Edinburgh Academy Ground. We were playing the School, which made a portentous score, and I particularly remember that Mr T. R. Marshall, probably the best Scotch bat who ever played, and then a boy, hit two sixes and a five off consecutive balls.

It is a very great pity that this Border bat is so seldom seen at Lord's; his average for MCC in 1886 was 85. The Flamingoes lasted for some years, and played all Teviotdale and Tweedside.

In those days we heard little of Dumfries and Galloway cricket, into which Steels, Tylecotes, and Srudds have lately infused much life. In recent years Lord Dalkeith, Lord George Scott, and Mr Maxwell Scott, of Abbotsford, have contributed very much to the growth of Border cricket. Money has never been very plentiful north of Tweed, and when scarcely any but artisans played, the clubs could not afford good grounds, or much professional instruction. In these respects there has been improvement. Perhaps the boys' cricket was not sufficiently watched and encouraged. Veterans used to linger in the stage with a mythical halo round them of their great deeds in the Sixties. Perhaps the rising generation is now more quickly promoted, and better coached than of old. I feel a hesitation in offering any criticism because I had only one quality of a cricketer, enthusiasm, combined for a year or two with some twist from leg. But, if I never was anything of an expert, my heart hath always been with those old happy scenes and happy days of struggling cricket. What jolly journeys we had, driving under the triple crest of Eildon to Kelso, or down Tweed to Galashiels, or over the windy moor to Hawick! How keen we were, and how carried beyond ourselves with joy in the success of a sturdy slogger, or a brilliant field! There were sudden and astonishing developments of genius. Does J. A. A., among his savages on the other side of the globe, remember how he once took to witching the world by making incredible and almost impossible catches? *Audisne, Amphiarae?* Michael Russell Wyer, I am sure, among Parsee cricketers, has not forgotten his swashing blow. But one of whom the poet declared that he would

> Push into Indus, into Ganges' flood,
> While all Calcutta sings the praise of Budd
>   (the maker of a formidable bat)

will no more 'push leg balls among the slips'

> No longer make a wild and wondrous score,
> And poke where never mortal poked before.

This is the melancholy of mortal things.
As Mr Prowse sang

> The game we have not strength to play
> Seems somehow better than before.

Our wickets keep falling in this life. One after the other goes down. They are becoming few who joined in those Border matches where there was but one lazy spectator, when we made such infrequent runs, and often dropped a catch, but never lost heart, never lost pleasure in the game. Some of them may read this, and remember old friends gone, old games played, old pewters drained, old pipes smoked, old stories told, remember the leg-hitting of Jack Grey, the bowling of Bill Dryden and of Clement Glassford, the sturdy defence of William Forman. And he who writes, recalling that simple delight and good fellowship, recalling those kind faces and merry days in the old land of Walter Scott, may make his confession, and may say that such years were worth living for, and that neither study, nor praise, nor any other pleasure has equalled, or can equal, the joy of having been young and a cricketer, where

> The oak, and the ash, and the bonny ivy tree,
> They flourish best at home in the North Countrie.

From *Border Cricket*, 1904.

Poets are by no means the only group of artists clamouring for entry into the pavilion. Thespians too have demonstrated an admirable weakness for the game, and have in fact far greater claims to fame than the likes of Lang, Barrie and Squire. An all-time Actors' eleven would inevitably be captained by the same man who once led Sussex and England. Sir C. Aubrey Smith (1863–1948), Hollywood's epitome of the patrician English gentleman, made valiant attempts to bring civilisation to California by running a side of expatriot actors. The degree to which he succeeded is described by the Yorkshire writer A. A. Thomson.

YOU WILL remember Sir C. Aubrey Smith, the tall, handsome Englishman who went into films and, late in life, became the uncrowned king of Hollywood. Even Hollywood is not wrong about everything, and when it came to regard Sir Aubrey as the ideal of a fine old English gentleman, it showed more than usual intelligence. Long before that time, though few can recall it now, he had been C. A. Smith, of Cambridge University, Sussex and England, and captain of the MCC's first touring side in South Africa. He was a slow bowler—slow to the point of slow motion—who used to start his run about mid-off and then, as though by an afterthought, bowled round the wicket. That is why they called him 'Round-the-Corner' Smith and his house in Hollywood was christened 'Round the Corner'. In the film colony he ran his own cricket team, and he ran it as strictly as Lord Hawke or Lord Harris would have done. He was a stickler, as you may imagine, for etiquette and insisted on the correct interpretation of cricket's laws, both social and sporting, on all occasions. As he grew older, he grew stricter; as he grew older, too, his eyesight grew sketchier and one day in the field he committed the enormity, so hard to forgive in others, of dropping a slip catch. Instantly he stopped the game and signalled for his butler, who walked ceremoniously across the ground and bowed low.

'Bring me my spectacles', ordered Sir Aubrey.

Slowly the butler returned to the outer world and once more appeared, bearing a pair of spectacles (in case) on a silver salver. Sir Aubrey put on his spectacles and signalled to the umpires permission to resume action. The bowler bowled, the batsman snicked, the ball shot into Sir Aubrey's hands and shot out again. There was an almost interminable pause. Finally a loud complaint arose to heaven: 'Egad,' exclaimed Sir Aubrey, 'the dam' fool brought my reading glasses.'

One day Sir Aubrey's team were scheduled to meet a side from a visiting British cruiser and an acquaintance of mine had his name put down to play for the home side. Unhappily, just before the game was due to start he slipped and twisted his ankle. This was no riotous studio party; it happened on a slippery polished floor at a peaceful story conference, but the consequences and complications were just the same. He was so utterly scared of Sir Aubrey, who could be a merciless martinet, that he simply dared not confess to him what had happened. His only hope, he felt, was at all costs to produce a substitute. He therefore hobbled round Hollywood on the arm of a girl friend in a desperate search for some guy who could play this English game of cricket. Try as they might, the only man they could get hold of was the actor, William Boyd, the creator of Hopalong Cassidy, ten-gallon hat, top boots, cowboy's pony and all. Or so my friend told me.

Hopalong disclaimed the faintest notion of how to play cricket, but they assured him that it was a simple game, closely resembling baseball, only not so complicated, and at last they persuaded him to put on flannels, though, now I come to think of it, it may well have been a mistake not to suggest that he should take his spurs off first. Fortunately, when they reached the cricket ground, Sir Aubrey had already won the toss and decided to bat, so nobody had especially observed either the absence of the injured man or the identity of the substitute. My friend being a bowler, Hopalong was kept back to No. 9 in the batting order, and when he went rolling out to the wicket, all six feet three of him, he presented an imposing spectacle. There he stood at the crease, swinging his bat in one hand as though it were a policeman's truncheon. The umpire politely asked if he wanted centre.

'Start pitchin' ', commanded Hopalong.

The first ball he missed; the second he missed; the third was a nice slow full toss on the leg side and from it he hit a towering skier away in the broad direction of long-on, possibly into Beverly Hills, and even, for all I know, into the Pacific Ocean. Suddenly, to the horror of all the Englishmen present, Hopalong went mad. Without a word he dashed across to point, from point to cover, from cover to mid-off, from mid-off round the astonished umpire to mid-on, from mid-on to square leg and then, without reflecting on his latter end, slid like a toboggan into his own wicket. There was as breathless a hush as ever fell on Newbolt's Close. Every true born Englishman waited in panic-stricken silence to

155

hear what the outraged Sir Aubrey would say. Finally he exclaimed, 'Well, I declare!'

And, on reflection, that was the most useful thing he could have said.

From *Odd Men In*, 1958.

By all accounts C. Aubrey Smith kept his cricket and his acting apart. This may have been a mistake. It becomes apparent that by his diligence Sir Aubrey shattered the balance of many a harmless game between mere amateur enthusiasts.

Greyhounds in the Slips, 1908

WANTED: ACTOR to play Laertes and Lysander, preferably a slow left-arm bowler—Apply Benson Company.

On July 16, 1908, rain stopped play at Lord's and *The Stage* commented gravely on the pity of it all. If we seek another reason why the above advertisement (or some variation) excited not the ridicule it would today but an alert and knowing interest, we have only to consult *Wisden*.

During the third week of July sixty years ago, Fry and Ranji between them scored 568 in a couple of county innings, yet *Wisden* alluded to their performance as being akin to that of opera stars—'one which did not greatly benefit the ensemble.' Clearly the Edwardians were less specialised than ourselves, and if the young Henry Ainley was billed to appear at Lord's and the Haymarket on the same day, then that merely demonstrated the efficiency of the hansom cab service between NW8 and SW1.

And let it not be thought that cricketing Thespians were restricted to the capital. On the contrary, *The Stage* each week devoted the best part of a page to the summer game, so many matches being included that sometimes the absence of detail encourages speculation. That the East-bourne Hippodrome XI was enjoying a triumphant season, that in Suffolk a side raised by the local vicar trounced the cast of a touring melodrama, is information I shall always cherish. But what of the strange fate which befell the Jarrow Police? That staunch body of men were beaten by 'The Way of the World XI', as I surmise a concert party. Or could it be that the cast of Congreve's comedy had pushed north into Durham, confounding the local constabulary with Mirabell's leg-breaks while some Edith Evans surveyed the scene from a deck-chair and fluttered forth phrases about dwindling by degrees into a wife?

But to return to that week in July, 1908, when Woolley was a great bowler and Jessop took on Nottinghamshire almost single-handed, batting in the match for a couple of hours and scoring 153 out of 166. At Lord's the Actors reached 25 for three against the Authors before rain stopped play. Not that the Authors felt elated, for their rivals invariably started as feverishly as the West Indies do now. The Authors knew that when number six emerged, as it were, from the Playhouse where he was appearing with Cyril Maude and Lilian Braithwaite in *The Flag Lieutenant*, the game would slip from their grasp. For the Actors Sobers was none other than C. Aubrey Smith, a former captain of England.

Why Smith relinquished first-class cricket for the stage—at about the same age E. R. Dexter later relinquished it for business, when quite obviously his bearing would have carried him to Berlin as our Ambassador by the time he was forty, will remain a mystery. Still, relinquish it he did, to the gain of London, Broadway and Hollywood. Had it not rained on July 16, 1908, he would most surely have put the Authors' attack to the sword, unless he had been baffled by the sheer badness of one bowler. I assume, perhaps unjustly, that this bowler must have been bad, for no bowler who was good could later have created the character of Bertie Wooster.* However, it may be that Mr Wodehouse was included in the Authors XI merely to offset the presence of that most serious literary cricketer, Sir Arthur Conan Doyle.

However, I must confess that apart from Aubrey Smith, Henry Ainley, whose golden voice must have echoed as far as 221B, Baker Street, Conan Doyle and Mr Wodehouse, those two sides of sixty years ago were comprised of names now wholly forgotten. It was much the same a week later at The Oval when the London Actors (C. A. Smith not out 40) overwhelmed the Provincial Actors (C. A. Smith six for 26), although on this occasion the ladies present wore Merry Widow hats in honour of B. S. Foster. One of the famous Worcestershire cricketing family, Basil Foster had batted brilliantly at Malvern and, if not in the same class as brothers R. E. and H. K., promised much. Alas, Worcestershire had to do without him in 1908 as he was appearing in Lehar's masterpiece at Daly's.

But if only the selectors had gone about their task with imagination, what immortal names they might have chosen. True with so many actor-managers available, captaincy would have presented problems. All we can say for certain is that Tree was not the man, for if his definition of the ideal cricket team had coincided with his definition of the ideal

---

*A most unjust assumption. A very good cricketer at Dulwich College at the turn of the century, Wodehouse later immortalised a Warwickshire fast bowler (killed in the Great War), Percy Jeaves.

committee, then the Actors XI must have been ten men at home—and Tree. Anyway, I can visualise Lewis Waller as the Keith Miller of the side, with Forbes Robertson and Ainley opening so nobly that Hobbs and Trumper must have slunk away in shame. Benson, who in old age still liked to perform stage acrobatics, was the wicketkeeper, and A. E. Matthews the most inconsequentially talkative of slips.

Yet against a truly representative Authors XI, the Actors must surely have succumbed, Smith or no Smith. Imagine the scene in the Long Room with Hardy brooding, imagine Henry James drafting an appeal for lbw: 'How—and what I say is well as far as it goes; but it is only, after all, that, having struck the limb, I dare ask if the question which follows, may, possibly, conclude—is that?'

Meanwhile Shaw would have drafted *The Revolutionary's Handbook to Wisden*, Belloc and Chesterton engaged in polemics in front of, or more likely inside, the Tavern, Bennett far outstripped Conan Doyle in diary entries, and Barrie begun to explain the game to Conrad. All we know for certain is that after Max Beerbohm had sketched Kipling, one fielded at the Pavilion end, and the other in the Nursery—never the twain to meet.

After the First War literary cricketers were not the same again. Who nowadays, apart from Alan Badel, could achieve an iambic pentameter follow through of the bat and suggest butterflies going into the flame? Why, I can see even Albert Finney bowling short of a length medium-pace. So with the authors: Mr Rattigan once opened the innings for Harrow, and the editor of *Punch* did the same for Staffordshire. Mr Tynan may qualify on the grounds that he onced dragged Ranji's leg-glance into a review, perhaps to prove (Brecht-wise) that truth is concrete. But do these names inspire absolute confidence? Michael Meyer's may after appearing on the same card as Compton, Miller and Lindwall. Yet as an authority on Ibsen, Mr Meyer is doubtless at his best prodding grimly forward in a fiord, with Mrs Alving moping between the pavilion curtains.

Never again shall we encounter an advertisement for a Laertes and Lysander, never again will a former captain of England provide Hollywood with its epitome of our generals, dukes and chief constables. Of course what I regret more than anything is that Hardy was not really brooding in the Long Room on July 16, 1908, or he may have foreseen that exactly six week later in distant Cootamundra, a certain Mrs Bradman would give birth to a son which should be called Donald. An additional comment for the Spirit of the Pities.

From the *Guardian*, 24 June 1968.

The ghosts of most of those actors may be found on any weekday, non-matinee afternoon in front of the site of the old Tavern at Lord's; the Tavern itself was desecrated by improvements some seasons ago, but presumably ghosts remain unaffected by developments of that kind. In any case, Lord's has been in a state of ruination for much longer than the modern age realises. The storms of the 1970s over new techniques of advertising have their echo in the days of the Victorians. On 7 July 1900 there appeared the following apoplectic outburst from the famous artist Harry Furniss.

Sir,

I am not surprised to read your cricket correspondent's complaint in today's issue regarding the unsportsmanlike treatment the Press have received at the hands of the officials at Lord's.

Your reader will recollect how the Empire was nearly shaken to its foundation when the members of Lord's had to decide who was to be the new secretary of the playground in St John's Wood! The Queen's Hall was filled with swelled heads, and, judging from your correspondent's note, the swelled heads elected one of their own body. After all, Lord's is to cricket what St Andrews is to golf; but at St Andrews golf is the one thing considered; at Lord's cricket is a mere detail. At St Andrews golfers, lovers of the game, and even mere sightseers, and, I may add, members of the Press, are given every facility to enjoy the game. But alas! Lord's is fast degenerating from a club of gentlemen cricketers into a show run for the sake of profit.

Under the old management, for many years, Lord's was an ideal retreat for the tired worker and the cricket lover. Then the stranger felt that by paying at the gate he was free to sit in peace, and with the aid of a good cigar it was the ideal place in which to spend a happy day. Not so now, to those seated on the paying stands. Boys, heavily laden with open baskets containing merchandise one sees on Hampstead Heath on Bank Holiday or on a third-rate racecourse, but surely of little attraction to the frequenters of Lord's, trample continually on your toes and screech everlastingly in your ears, 'Cigarettes, cigars, chocolates—Cigarettes, cigars, chocolates', 'Correct card—Correct card', 'Cigarettes, cigars, chocolates', 'Correct card', ' 'Speshul 'dition latest cricket scores',

'Cigarettes, cigars, chocolates', ' 'Speshul 'dition, latest cricket scores', 'Correct card', 'Cigarettes, cigars, chocolates'. And to offend the ear still further these calls of screeching boys are sandwiched by 'Any seat, Sir, but the first four rows', 'Any seat, Sir, but the first four rows'.

Why, in the name of reason and peace, cannot the fact that, after paying extra, you can occupy certain seats be written on a placard, or, better still, on the tickets? In fact, we may soon expect swings erected in the practice-ground, shooting booths under that atrocious erection, the big stand, and knock-me-downs in and out of the many drinking booths now disfiguring the club—a club, once a quiet gentlemanly retreat, now a huge conglomeration of various monstrosities of masonry. In fact, I frankly confess, were I to see the buildings at Lord's, some winter's night, on fire, although I would not be guilty of incendiarism I would certainly not hurry to give the alarm, for, as an artist, I consider even the outside of Lord's Cricket Ground an outrage upon taste and an offence to the eye.

It is not enough that the committee of Lord's should offend the eye by having turned the pretty pitch of old into an ugly mass of sheds and patches of erractic architecture, but they must also offend the ear by turning it into a pandemonium as well. Many use Lord's Club as a fashionable picnic ground for five days in the year—genuine cricket lovers are absent then and look to the Press to read in detail the doings of the colts—but now it appears that, during the paying-picnic days, the Press is turned out of the stand and relegated to the tool shed, or, perhaps, to the roller horse's stable.

Nearly every sport in this country is being ruined by the 'gate' question—can we not save cricket, and particularly Lord's, before it is too late?

I am, Sir, yours obediently,

Harry Furniss.

From *The Times*, 7 July 1900.

If affection suffuses Cardus's recollection of great cricketers, something like idolatry colours the ruminations of Albert Knight on the theme of the great Australian batting genius Victor Trumper (1877–1915). To provide the statistics of Trumper's career would be as tactless as giving the measurements of the Mona Lisa; this, however, is one solecism which Knight is never in the faintest danger of committing.

IN VICTOR TRUMPER we have seen the very poetry and heard the deep and wonderful music of batsmanship. Not the structures of a great mentality, not the argument of logic, but a sweet and simple strain of beauty, the gift of the gods alone. Stylish in the highest sense, orthodox, yet breaking all canons of style, Trumper is just himself. On the occasion of a great Test Match at Sydney, the Englishmen had built up a colossal score after a relative Australian failure in the first innings, Mr R. E. Foster playing the record innings of his life and of these great contests. The Star of Australia seemed fast setting, but a couple of tail-end batsmen played out the last hour of the day with a quite heroic barndoor performance of exasperating correctness. The morrow dawned, and faint hopes glimmered in forty thousand minds, when, with the dismissal of one of these monuments of scientific patience, the young Australian champion emerged on the green.

A slender figure, wan and drawn of face, cadaverous, but spiritualised with the delicacy of ill health, glides to the wicket. Nor ornament nor colour marked his featureless attire, the personality was all-dominating. He took guard quickly, more quickly took a glance around the field, and received his first ball. 'Dreams of summer dawn in night of rain' presented no fresher vision than this boy's play to that black sea which hid the blistered grass of the Sydney hill. Not in his fascinating collection of strokes, nor in their frank and open execution merely, lay the charm; it was a man playing away a power which was himself rather than in him. With luxuriant masterfulness, yet with the unlaboured easy naturalness of a falling tear, or rather of showers from the sunny lips of summer, he diverted the ball in every conceivable direction which his genius willed. Not violently nor recklessly, like his comrade Duff the revolutionary slashing with his pike, not with the careworn, anxious deliberation of Noble, does he reach the heights, but, insensibly and unconsciously, lifts us with him to where winds blow cool and the outlook is infinite. Can the force of consolidated mass, a record of two hundred centuries, convey the power of high elevation? Perhaps so, at least we glorify the former more. Aglow with instinctive inspiration, this young prophet played with the world's greatest bowlers, played as men play when 'time and the hour' bring out the man and persuade us he is as the gods.

With bat whipping like a flail, he drove the fastest swervers of Hirst, and jumped in with fearless precision to the tempting slows of Rhodes, hooked the dropping googlies of Bosanquet, and alternatively late cut or pushed to square leg the pace-making deliveries of Arnold. One by one his colleagues fail and pass before an attack of magnificent precision and persistence. 'Our Vic' remains, and when a partner's lazy incompetence rendered his last effort to secure the bowling futile, with his colleague's loss, he left the field still undefeated. He had given to his country at least an outside chance of victory, and the glow of hope once seemingly impossible. Nothing akin to jugglery or contemptuous languor mars the incomparable grace and simplicity of this perfect batsman. His greatness is of that high kind which appeals to the technical no less than to the more human critic. His simplicity has no faintest touch of *simplesse*, he convinces the onlooker and the bowler that the stroke he executes is precisely what should be done. There is no subtlety, no show miracle, but the perfect openness and the direct simplicity of a master.

Like Ranjitsinhji, if apparently in doubt, his celerity is such, mind and action following judgment so directly, that jumping out to drive on a fast pitch to a fast-medium bowler he seems to have ample time to return to his crease and late cut the same ball. His wonderful eye, his great reach, so remarkable in one not over tall, and the quickness of foot which enables him to reach or cover the ball so often skimming away to third man when less skilfully dealt with, are the outer causes which one would assign as essential features in the mere mechanism and outer semblances of this great genius. He is all compounded, so to speak, of wrist and eye, full of faith in the latter. His execution of every stroke is superb, as powerful as it is graceful. Scarcely has the ball left the bowler's hand ere he has determined its length and moved his feet accordingly. Balls which many are happy enough if they can merely play, oblivious of scoring, are forced by him with wristy swing to the boundary. Such is the power of his strokes, that the race of the fieldsman whom the ball passes is hopeless. Trumper does not seem to have to watch the ball from the pitch, and then to flick it away by wrist and body turn, as does Ranjitsinhji. He divines what the ball will do and where it will be while it is still in the air, and can consequently put the whole force and swing of his body into his strokes. Such an one is scarcely to be written about, however, with a recipe book in hand, or with a bundle of statistics at one's elbow. The really highest manifestations of an art so emotional as well as technical as batting, have little relation to time or to quantity. Perchance the statistical expert will yet have many pages to fill with the first-class records of Victor Trumper. Probably not, for such eye and wrist, such lightning celerity, such risk, is for youth alone. Perchance the cold winds of ill-health have already swept across the stream on whose surface lies the glory and the gleam. Howsoever transient his career, none who have been privileged to see him play a great innings will ever forget that spirit, so self-forgetful, so manly, and so true. More than many a long summer of consistent scoring shall we revere this Sydney light which revealed magnificent possibilities of batsmanship, never before incarnate.

Nasty things, far more nasty than true, have been written of the Sydney larrikins who lounge away the sunny hours on that splendid ground. Sarcastic and severe maybe, but delightfully impartial are the Sydney larrikins. Not of them shall it be written 'rough to common men but honeying at the whisper of a lord', and they are far too cynical to be intensely bigoted, or, what is much the same thing, intensely patriotic. Trumper they may have misunderstood, but him they loved with that great love to which much is forgiven. Saint and savage and critic alike 'wondered with a foolish face of praise'. It was a rare and moving sight to look upon that crowd as it rose en masse to watch the ball strike the fence; to see those people standing in hushed expectation ere breaking into unrestrained delight. Never was the 'glow and glory of the game with the beautiful name' more freely scattered than by the charm of this incomparable master batsman.

From *The Complete Cricketer*, 1906.

164

But the history of cricket is not one long uninterrupted roseate glow. Some-
times the rules are stretched almost to breaking point; once or twice they
may be said to have snapped completely, and in the winter of 1932–33 the
noise of the snapping could be heard all the way from Canberra to West-
minster. The Bodyline Tour, in which English fast bowlers adopted tactics
which appeared to their opponents to be rather tactless, remains a puzzle to
posterity, because after digesting all the circumstances, it simply does not
seem possible that any such sequence of events was remotely within the
bounds of possibility. The events, however, did take place, and the fairest,
the shrewdest, the most technically informed description of them was achieved
by John Henry Webb Fingleton (b. 1908), who was there at the time. A New
South Wales opening batsman who played eighteen times for Australia
between 1931–38 and reached his test century five times, Fingleton had a
retirement more brilliant still, becoming one of the most distinguished
writers on the game in all its history. Characteristically, he tells us more
about the Bodyline War in a single chapter on the captain who declared it,
than most other writers have managed in whole volumes.

Introducing Mr Jardine

IN THE English season of 1921 an Oxford undergraduate made a slow
but decisive way towards the first century of the season against Armstrong's invincible team of Australians. English cricket had not then
recovered from the paralysis of the first European war and Collins's
A.I.F. team. Douglas's M.C.C. visit to Australia in 1920 had not
re-established the English standard, and against this Australia, with its
grand stiffening from the A.I.F. team, had moved from strength to
strength.

That 1921 tour was the most dismal for England in all its long history.
In addition to the paucity of talent, accidents befell leading English
players and the selectors called an inordinate number of men to the
colours. It was in vain. To the time of which I write, Armstrong's team
had walked rough-shod over English cricket and feelings, and not a
single home man had topped the century against them.

Enter the Oxford undergraduate! By precise batsmanship and with a
straight blade which never wavered a point from the perpendicular, he

passed his half-century and moved cautiously through the difficult seventies and eighties to the apprehensive nineties. That most distinguished century, of all the 1921 season, was only a stroke or two from him when he was beaten by time and a concession for which the Australians had fought vigorously—a day of rest before a Test match.

The three-day game against Oxford became a two-day game. The undergraduate who did not get his century and was left not out at 94 was (Yes, you've guessed it!) Douglas R. Jardine.

That was Jardine's introductory bow to Australians, and one might well wonder whether the memory lingered. None could blame the Australians for seeking a playless day before a Test. In their homeland they knew only six, or even less, first-class games in an average season and, in addition, played cricket only in their club games of a Saturday afternoon. Many an Australian found that the grind of playing cricket for ceaseless day after day in England turned a pleasurable game into a dull duty. As Oxford, however, had met the Australians half-way in depriving themselves of a day from their fixture, the Australians might well have exerted themselves to play an extra over or two to see whether Jardine could make his century.

When the Australian team captained by Victor Richardson was dealing harshly with South African cricket in 1935–36, the South African teams often agreed to play extra time on a second day so that a game could be finished. Bradman made a gesture to Edrich on the last day of May, 1938, when that player wanted a few runs at Lord's to complete his thousand for the month. Bradman did not present Edrich with his thousand. In declaring the Australian innings closed he merely gave Edrich a chance which he accepted.

I do not know the full circumstances of this Oxford game in 1921, and of those I have asked who were there, none could tell me. I do think, however, that extra time should have been made in some manner. Instead, there was talk of a train to catch, there was a hurried finish and, human nature being so, an undergraduate was left behind to ponder and doubtless regret that the signal honour had so narrowly eluded him.

At that impressionable age, when the first-class sphere was just unfolding to him, Jardine possibly felt resentful in some degree towards Australians. It was only human—though many Australians often wondered whether Jardine was blessed with such a quality—and it is not beyond belief that Jardine always remembered this first meeting with Australians, and was never afterwards prepared to show them any mercy or consideration.

Jardine, born of Scottish parents in India, made his first trip to

Australia in 1928–29 with Chapman, and his flannels had barely emerged from their first laundering before he had made up his mind that he liked neither Australia nor the average Australian. Even at this early stage feelings were reciprocated.

Jardine was not a good mixer. He was not the hail-fellow-well-met type like Chapman and Gilligan, whom Australians love to meet from the old country. An Australian likes to make a quick decision about the person he meets. He does not stand upon ceremony himself and, especially in sport, wants to be on a friendly basis with a visitor as soon as he shakes his hand.

Jardine was not responsive. He did not proffer his hand more than was necessary. He was aloof and discerning with a cold, judicial mind in gauging people and events before committing himself. He did not want to be rushed with friendship and gusto—he preferred to do his own picking and choosing. He was of that proverbial English type which shares a railway compartment on a journey and never enters into conversation. Their Australian prototypes, in comparison, would be playing poker together and possibly addressing each other by Christian names by the time the first station flashed past.

Nothing could better serve to illustrate the difference in disposition between Jardine and Chapman, his predecessor as captain in Australia, than an incident on a New South Wales railway station. At a train halt on their way north to the first Test in 1928 the three amateurs of the English side—Chapman, Jardine and the bowler who commanded respect and popularity wherever he went, J. C. White—strolled along the platform to stretch their legs.

A stranger accosted them with a cheery greeting. His garb was of the country, but he was a prominent identity of the district and a fairly accomplished sportsman. Jardine's reply was a supercilious stare and complete ignorance of the proffered hand.

I am neither blaming nor criticising Jardine for his attitude. To him the strange gentleman's approach, perhaps, was not *comme il faut*. The correct introduction was lacking. It was, however, in accord with Australian manners, for such men of the bush, who live a lonely life of solitude for month after month on their outback stations, readily and happily grasp their few chances of conversation and friendliness with passing strangers. Chapman and White warmly shook hands with the countryman, for they, like most amateurs who have visited the Commonwealth with English sides, invariably thought it proper to show some appreciation of the manners of the country of which they were highly honoured guests.

There is no better prey for many Australians than the overseas man on his first visit. Possibly because of its youth or remoteness from older centres of civilisation, the Australian feels he must publicise his country, and in no time the visitor is told that Australia has the best this and the best that in the world. The thing to do is to profess belief in such tales, and the Australian, cautiously wondering whether you are pulling his leg in turn, is delighted to know you and to do anything for you.

But Jardine was not amused by such understandable insularity. He was bored immeasurably, and that, in turn, nettled Australians, who abhor bored and critical visitors. The Australian wants to like his visitor; just as important, he wants his visitor to like him.

Had Jardine come to Australia in the late 18th century and been vested with the authority of that time, his coldness and indifference would have been in keeping with that grim period. Australia was founded in 1788; Marylebone Cricket Club a year later. That was the period when London was known as the City of the Gallows with rope-twisted bodies swaying in the breeze on Finchley Hill, on Tyburn, at Execution Dock on the Thames, at Wapping, below Purfleet and at Woolwich.

Dr. Johnson deplored the suggestion that public hangings should be abolished and 160 crimes were punishable by death. Women and children were burned, flogged and hanged. In 1810 Sir Samuel Romilly was heavily defeated in the House of Commons when he moved that transportation to Australia be introduced in lieu of death in cases of stealing from dwellings. The stealing of articles of 2/- and over in value was punishable by death and humane juries often defeated this law by finding victims guilty of 'stealing a diamond tiara, valued at 1/11'.

Had Jardine come to Australia in that 18th century and been cloaked in authority, he would have strutted the stage with the early Governors. Coming when he did, an Englishman needed a new approach, and many Australians considered that Jardine did not have that approach. He was incapable of unbending and his attitude to Australian newspaper men travelling with the M.C.C. team was always one of icy aloofness and frequently of downright rudeness. For a time in 1932 he was inaccessible to Australian journalists, while still ready to discuss team news with the Fleet Street men who accompanied the side.

When Australian reporters once asked him for the names of the English players selected for one of the Tests his reply was: 'We are here to win the Ashes, not to make stories for your newspapers.' His rare Press conferences took on something of the atmosphere of a Press interview with Winston Churchill. Rather than have to parry awkward questions on bodyline from Australian reporters, he used 'Gubby' Allen as a sort of liaison officer to meet Australian cricket writers.

Canon Hughes, a kindly old man of wide culture, who was president of the Victorian Cricket Association in that turbulent period, was very upset by Jardine. It was not the Canon's nature to speak strong words, but of Jardine he said this in an interview: 'I saw more of Jardine than most people did, and I do not like the gentleman. He does not like me and publicly insulted me in Sydney.'

What was there about Jardine that irked so many Australians? Was it that he was the leader of a successful side and the Australians did not like being beaten? That accusation was made, but it appears untenable. Only four years previously Chapman had led a more successful English side through Australia and Chapman was an Australian idol. Did Jardine lack tact? Was he a snob? Did he make obvious his hate of Australians?

For a beginning, and in Australia it was a particularly bad start, he first presented himself for analysis in 1928–29 in a Harlequin cap. Let that facet of his history not be underwritten, for in the loud and resplendent colours of that cap was woven much trouble for Jardine.

The Harlequins comprise Oxford University players, Blues and a few who have narrowly missed being Blues. Their counterpart at Cambridge is the Quidnuncs, and amateur traditions allow a Harlequin or a Quidnunc to bat in that cap when playing for any other team. When fielding, however, it is not amateur etiquette to wear any cap other than that of the team with which the man is playing.

An Australian who has toured England and the many Australians who have, themselves, been either Harlequin or Quidnunc know of these traditions; but the average Australian does not comprehend such privileged niceties nor does he countenance flaring caps or startling ties that announce, so he considers, that this player or that went to some particular Varsity. In effect, the Australian says this: If it is a school or a Varsity match, wear your caps by all means; if you are representing your country, represent it from the head down, for no cap should take precedence over that of a man's country.

Australians will not tolerate class distinction in sport. They could never understand why, in England, amateurs came out of one gate and professionals another. Members of the last Australian Eleven in England deeply resented a Lord's article written by Charles Fry, an Oxonian, a Harlequin, a Test player, a Royal Navy officer and therefore a gentleman who might have been more charitable, in which he described the second

Test and used the occupations of the Australians in ordinary life to preface their names.

'In all this Australian team,' wrote Fry, 'there are barely one or two who would be accepted as public school men . . . and while I am writing this, curator —— has just bowled another maiden over.'

Australians do not accept people at cap or public school value. They come to the face and work underneath, and though I have no wish to prick the susceptibilities of people whose modes and standards differ from ours, my point is that we must try and understand the Australian outlook on such matters in analysing Jardine's first trip in 1928–29.

His first public action was to gather exclusively the Varsity men of the South Australian team and wine and dine them. His second was to wear his Harlequin cap, and though other Englishmen had worn such caps in Australia before him, there was something about Jardine in a Harlequin cap which nettled Australians.

As he strode out to bat, a tall, angular acidulated and seemingly aloof Englishman, with a gaudy cap rampant and a silk handkerchief knotted around his throat, he walked into the vision of many Australians as the very personification of the old school tie. Perhaps, like most batsmen, Jardine was superstitious and wore such a cap for luck, but as he strode along with that stiff-legged walk so characteristic of him many Australians resented him, because they thought he was putting on 'side' in his Harlequin cap.

The Hill of Sydney and the Outer of Melbourne, always quick and eager to judge a new man on the flimsiest of impressions, welcomed him with open mouths, and ragged him.

'Eh, eh, Mr Jardine,' roared a barracker, 'where's the butler to carry your bat for you?'

They considered him a barracking gift from the gods, but Jardine could have won them to his side at that very moment had he doffed his cap and gaily waved it to them. A Churchill would have done that and added a victory sign for good measure. Any crowd likes to be recognised and acknowledged. One such act from Jardine and the barrackers would have accepted him—gait, cap, 'kerchief and all.

But who, even with the imagination of a Shakespeare, could imagine Jardine making the concession with such a cap to an Australian crowd? His face set more sternly, his walk became stiffer, he froze more antarctically beneath his cap of many colours—and the barrackers became more voluble, and less respectful.

In such manner did Jardine walk into Australian cricket. It was not that he hadn't been warned of the temperament of the crowds and of the many ways and means a man of tact had of winning them to his side. Every amateur who left England knew that the Australian barracker democratically leaned to the professionals and that an amateur was always a ready mark for criticism. Johnny Douglas (reverence to his memory!), Chapman and Arthur Gilligan knew well that all that was needed was a grin to the Hill or a cheery wave to the Outer when they were being barracked . . . just this to show the common touch . . . and they were the barrackers' friend for evermore. No crowd is quicker to condemn, no crowd quicker to applaud, than the Australian, and none is more easily won over.

It is necessary that something should be known of the Australian barracker, for the red-herring of barracking was drawn across the body-line trail by the M.C.C. as the crisis developed.

Barrackers are much the same the whole world over, and no country can afford to point the bone at another. It is all a matter of partisanship, and that partisanship, naturally, is noticed most by the visiting team. I heard a demonstration at Cape Town on New Year's Day, 1936, when Richardson and Wade said the wicket was unfit for play, that would have taken the honours in any land. I was the central figure at Trent Bridge in 1938 in what was as bright a barracking show as any I have heard or seen in any land. Even Sydney's renowned Yabba, with all his foghorn hoarseness and sarcasm, was no better barracker than that renowned woman who used to sit near the scoring board at Surrey's Oval.

Barrackers also differ in their home countries. Those of Adelaide are much more subdued than their brethren in Sydney and Melbourne; the people in the north of England are chirpier and more critical than in the south, although in 1938 I noticed that members of the Oval had much to say—and abusively at that—when Bradman refused to work his few bowlers into the ground before a Test and batted instead of making Surrey follow on.

Any Australian of the last trips home has no two opinions of the Trent Bridge gentry when they are in full voice, which means when an Australian pokes his nose on to the Notts ground.

It can be said, and no Australian will gainsay it, that the Trent Bridge crowd had patriotic reason to feel bitter against Australians. The bravest action seen on any cricket ground was that of a diminutive parson in 1934, when he walked through a hissing and booing crowd and clapped the Australians on to the field. The concerted clap-clap-clap of thousands all round Trent Bridge in 1938* was as crude a piece of barracking

*This was the occasion when I light-heartedly and momentarily sat down on the field, all else having failed to humour the Trent Bridge gentry. Australia was

as that seen on any sporting ground. Yet the Australians could understand the underlying feelings of the Nottingham crowd. Their loyalty to Larwood and Voce, their townsmen and the principal actors in the bodyline drama, came uppermost, though a country which had such essentially unsporting barracking in its midst could ill afford to accuse other countries.

From Thomas Wood's 'Cobbers' can be quoted a very interesting deduction on the toughs of Sydney.

'Sydney,' Wood writes, 'has more than its fair share of toughs. They are larrikins, deadbeats, grass-chewers, louts, gangs of youths and young men who live how they can and where they can and take their fun as they find it. Their steadiest interest is spotting a winner.

'They watch games, though they neither play them nor understand them, and they speak their minds. They, principally, are the barrackers, whose jeers and horseplay spoil many a good match. They get more publicity than they deserve.'

The opinion is good, but the point is that it could have been written of many lands, and, furthermore, that type did not comprise principally the barrackers in 1932–33. We have far too many horse races in Australia. I am always amused when I see a press photograph of some corpulent gentleman at the races, cigar in mouth and glasses over his shoulder, with the caption beneath running—'that well-known sportsman'. Why,

---

fighting a losing battle and our only chance was a draw. Brown and myself set about playing for time. The batting, naturally, was dull, but everybody knew it was our only game. Then came that concerted clap-clap-clap as the bowler was running up, which increased in intensity. I might mention that many of the grounds in England have no sight board at one end, and it is regarded as very bad form if anybody should move in his seat behind the wicket while the bowler is running to the wicket. The batsman will immediately withdraw from the wicket and the bowler starts his run again. That is accepted, and so also should be the principle that there is comparative quiet while the bowler is running up. What the barrackers do after that is of no consequence. Bradman sent out a message that if this clapping continued while the bowler was running up we were to withdraw from the wicket. I told the messenger that they were not worrying me. They weren't. He said: 'Those are the skipper's orders.' I told Hammond and he agreed with the orders. I therefore drew away. Next time I drew away and stopped Verity in his run-up, Verity squatted on his haunches and I went one further and sat on the turf. As I said, the barracking did not worry me, but I carried out orders. The Editor of Wisden's said: 'The barracking was never more than mild, certainly not hostile, and from only a small proportion of onlookers.' He and I must have been at different grounds that day, and, if what he claims was the case, Bradman would hardly have sent out orders. It came from around the ground, was continuous and loud, and, if I may say so, in execrable taste. Bradman, himself, later drew away from the wicket when these tactics were directed at him.

he'd have a stroke if he tried to run ten yards! One of the curses of Australia is over-gambling. It obtrudes itself at the slightest chance, and there are, at a Test match, quite a number of bad losers who 'can't take it' if their side is losing, and turn their tongues to abuse.

Dr. Wood has given a good description of such a type, but they would form a minute minority of an Australian Test crowd. By far the greater number of people at an ordinary Test match in Australia never utter a word, and those who do can be divided into several classes.

First there is the 'blah' type, whose loud voice speaks his vacant mind. He utters the same old parrot-cries that have come over the fence for years, and they are as boring to everybody as they are unoriginal.

'Get a bag' or 'Get the fire brigade to put him out,' he roars and he expects people to laugh at him. That barracker should have been drowned at birth.

The next is as much part and parcel of the game as the bat and ball. He is the real man of humour.* He does not spoil himself with continual chatter, but breaks out occasionally with the flash of humour and genius that sums up a situation and causes people to rock with merriment. He is an ornament to the game and, I might add, an essential, who helps many to sit through a grim Test.

Another type peculiar to Australia is the 'baiter'. He will join in to make a chorus with anybody to rag a person susceptible to barracking. I can best describe him by a little story of my experience at Randwick (Sydney) races. Just before an event I met a friend who intended backing a certain horse. That horse won, and as many punters thought his previous form had been inconsistent and that he was, in fact, a 'roughie', they formed a ring adjacent to the weighing enclosure and loudly boo-ed the horse's connections. To my surprise, I saw my friend there.

'You've only got yourself to blame for this,' I said to him—and he was boo-ing louder than anybody. 'You did intend to back him, you know.'

'Oh,' he replied, 'I backed him all right.'

I was surprised.

*Here are instances which come to mind. Jardine was fielding on the fence one day in broiling heat. The flies were worrying him and he made vicious passes at them. From a voice at his back came this cry in offended terms: 'Hey, Jardine, you leave our flies alone.' Clarrie Grimmett, who had just written a book entitled *How to Get Wickets*, was toiling away in Sydney, and though the score was mounting he hadn't taken a wicket. At the end of one of his overs a voice from the Hill called out to him: 'Hey, Clarrie, go home and read your book again.' Phil Mead had made no runs in twenty minutes. 'What's wrong with you, Mead?' boomed a big voice. 'Have you got white ants in the legs?' Herbert Sutcliffe's meticulous scraping and patting of the wicket was met with the stentorian advice: 'Hey, bring him out a b—— pick and shovel.'

'Then why are you boo-ing?' I asked.

'Oh, well,' he answered, 'I wouldn't miss a bit of fun like this.'

In dealing with Australian barrackers the only thing to do is humour or ignore them. The fatal mistake is to show resentment, for then the barracking is intensified. I know players who have come through turbulent games and do not know that there has been barracking, so intent have they been on their job. I know others who have kept a sensitive ear cocked for anything coming over the ropes and their play has suffered accordingly.

Barracking in Australia, as in other countries, has put many a player off his game. A case in point is that very capable all-rounder from Oxford, R. H. Bettington. He returned to his home in Australia at a time when it seemed he would win a place in a Test team against Chapman's M.C.C. side, but in one of his very first games in Sydney Bettington had the misfortune to drop several catches in slips. The best fieldsman in the world could have done so, but Bettington had the added handicap of having just returned from England with publicity surrounding his name.

Each succeeding time Bettington played on the Sydney ground the barrackers reminded him volubly of the catches he had dropped. They never allowed him to forget it, and I think Bettington tired somewhat of his home crowds. He did not make the Test side, but he won the amateur golf championship of Australia a few years later. He finished with cricket prematurely.

Fairfax was another Australian of recent years whom barrackers upset. The Australian barracker by no means confines his voice to visitors; and Fairfax was one of many Australians who incurred the crowd's ire. He dropped a catch one day, or was slow to move to the ball, and the barrackers trained their voices at him.

Fairfax had his own way of dealing with them.

'I've had enough of this, Kip,' he called across to his captain, Kippax, and he walked off the ground in the middle of an innings, accepted an offer to go to England from Sir Julian Cahn, and never again appeared on an Australian first-class cricketing ground.

The whole subject of barracking can be summed up this wise. It is harmful or harmless, depending upon the temperament of the man barracked, and when a player has won his way to Test ranks his temperament should be such that he does not care a fig about it.

Hendren knew how to handle Australian barracking. He had a jovial chat with them on the fence and no cricketer stands higher in Australian esteem. He had a sense of humour, too, which the barrackers loved.

'Eh, Patsy,' he was asked once on the Sydney fence, 'why isn't so-and-so in this English team?'

'Ah,' replied Patsy as he turned that incorrigible Irish face of his to the questioner, 'they'd only pick good-looking blokes in this side.'

Patsy belonged to the Hill evermore, and so did the Nawab of Pataudi when a Hill-ite asked him once whether he wanted the barrackers to address him as Your Highness.

'Just plain Pat to you boys,' replied Pataudi with a grin, and he also was considered a good fellow.

Like Hendren, Pataudi also had a quick sense of humour which won him immediate Australian friends. There was the occasion of his first Melbourne appearance, when a beery barracker offered him the deadliest of all insults by yelling out—'Hey, Gandhi, where's your goat?' Pataudi, instead of behaving like one or two other people who could be mentioned, turned around with a smiling flash of teeth, pretended to identify the man in the dense crowd and said, 'Ah, so there you are; would anybody lend me a piece of rope?'

King George VI (when Duke of York) and the Prince of Wales revealed in Australia the democratic touch that made them, like their father, such firm favourites with Australians; but Jardine, unhappy fellow, was of that English type which just did not know how to unbend, how to relax. When they called to him from the Hill, he remained with his back to them, a Gibraltar-like figure of bleak immutability.

Had he turned about and swapped an occasional remark with them, it would have tickled their fancy, their importance, and broken down the barracking he received. They would have gone home that evening and proudly told their families they were on speaking terms with Jardine, and, moreover, he was not 'stuck up', as people said, but a decent sort of a bloke.

Jardine, however, did not make friends easily, even among his own team. It was rumoured, when he left the 1928-29 team in Melbourne to make an early return to England, that he bade farewell to only a few in the side. It was not necessary, because of the barracking he always received, for him to analyse his thoughts on the 1928-29 homeward boat and decide that he did not like Australians.

Four years later, when a certain plan of campaign had been decided upon by somebody in England, the powers-that-be looked about for a captain who would carry that plan through. He had to be a captain above the ordinary. He had to be dogged, tenacious, remorseless, and who better in the whole of England, they told themselves, than the Cromwellian Jardine? He was the man to carry through the job. No task would be too big for Jardine. Indeed, with his temperament, with his inexorable sense of duty, he would have been the ideal type to have sent to the Ruhr Valley at that time to see that the Germans never rose an inch above themselves. It was a pity, both in a cricket and a worldly sense, that Jardine did not go to the Ruhr instead of returning to Australia!

Not for one minute do I think Jardine was directly responsible for bodyline. He was not a selector, and I mention again that those selectors chose four fast bowlers.

'Jardine came to me,' wrote F. R. Foster, the fast left-hander who bowled leg-theory in Australia when Warner was captain in 1911–12, 'and he asked me for my leg-side placings. I gave them to him, but had I known to what purpose they would be put in Australia, I would never have given them.'

That is interesting, but does not the evidence suggest that Jardine was a bodyline accessory after the selection act? The first bodyline exhibition in Australia was given under Wyatt's captaincy. At that, Jardine was the only English present-day cricketer I met whom I could have conceived as a bodyline captain. I never met A. W. Carr.

'You bowl another over like that,' Chapman threatened Voce at Folkestone just before the 1932 M.C.C. team left for Australia, 'and I will take you off.'

Voce was bowling his bumpers. He bowled another such over and Chapman, who was deputising for Jardine, whisked him off. Gilligan was another English captain who would not have stood bodyline for half an over.

Jardine struck immediate Press trouble at Perth in 1932. It is a wise Prime Minister, actress or sporting captain, on a quid pro quo basis, who makes the path easier for the average working pressman; but Jardine, so the flock of eastern pressmen said who met the team, was most autocratic. He would not play 'ball' with them in announcing his team to suit publication purposes, and, with other things added, he made quick enemies. Pressmen soon debunked the advance propaganda from England that Jardine was a changed character.

When he reached the Eastern States he was the same aloof Jardine. He was still unbending and he had the ground closed to the public in Adelaide before the third Test because a number of onlookers had chirruped at him at practice the preceding day.

Poor, unfortunate Jardine! Troubles never ceased to dive-bomb him all the time he was in Australia. Some of it emanated from his own team, incidentally, for a side which came so overloaded with bowlers was asking for internecine strife. Never once, however, did Jardine deviate from what he considered to be his path of duty. He was convinced he had been given a certain task to carry out. That task came within the laws of the game, and, by the beard of Grace, he would carry out that job and all the barracking in and out of Australia would not deter him.

Enter, now, the new crop of Australian barrackers. When you visualise those huge crowds of 90,000 and 80,000 which sometimes daily saw those Tests, imagine there thousands upon thousands of Australian grade, pennant and junior players, whose knowledge of the game was not elementary, but, indeed, very practical.

'I was sitting one day in Adelaide,' the Right Hon. R. G. Menzies, later Prime Minister of Australia, once told me, 'and it was before play had commenced. I was chatting to the man next to me, whom I didn't know. He was quietly-spoken, cultured and most interesting. We spoke of many things before the game started. That was the day Woodfull was struck by Larwood. I looked at that man again and he was a changed person. He was on his feet and his face was choleric. He shouted, he raved, and he flung imprecations at Larwood and Jardine because of what his eyes had seen.'

The noisy barracker is always with us in Australia, but this was a new type. This was the one who sat in his thousands for Test day after day and never uttered a syllable because of his cricket self-respect and his love of the game; this was the one in 1932–33 who, knowing the game and appreciating what was going on in the middle, deeply resented his countrymen being hit and turned into Aunt Sallies.

Larwood was bowling to an orthodox field that day in Adelaide when Woodfull was hit. Woodfull moved across rather awkwardly to the bumper, which appeared to be about the off stump. There was a great uproar, but this was intensified when, Woodfull having recovered sufficiently to take strike again, Jardine swung the field across immediately to the leg side and Larwood proceeded to bowl a succession of bumpers. Jardine's action at the best was a terrible error of judgment. I thought that the crowd would split the skies. If it had not been that the match was in Adelaide, the 'City of Churches', many of us felt that the crowd would have come over the fence and the match would have broken up in disorder.

The hitting of Woodfull could be discounted to a certain extent. It was the immediate swinging across to the leg field while he was still groggy and sick on his feet that created the real ill-will, even among onlookers who up to that time had taken a fairly detached view of the matter.

I have good reason to believe that Jardine himself very speedily regretted the decision he made on that occasion, but on the field he was cold and impersonal, oblivious of the near-rioting crowd.

Not even a rioting crowd on the field about him, however, would have deterred Jardine, that apostle of faith in the Englishman's power to do no wrong. From his dominating height he would have surveyed the milling crowd and probably called up the wicket, 'We appear to have some extra men, Larwood. Would you like a few more across on the leg side?'

The M.C.C. case against Australian barracking fell flat to the ground on this count. The unusual and intense barracking of that bodyline season was directly caused by bodyline. He was blind who could not see where bodyline was heading after the first Melbourne and Sydney games, before a Test was played, and the Englishmen could not expect to have it both ways—such tactics by them and not an outcry of protest by the Australian crowds.

A wise man, a tactful man, would have looked for a path out of the maze after the first few games of bodyline, but Jardine's nature never admitted that a maze even existed. In the middle of the season he laconically observed from Launceston that leg-theory appeared to have had its birth in Australian newspapers.

'We knew nothing about it when we came here, but we have learnt a lot since,' he said. 'The practice is not new and there is nothing danger-ous in it. I hope it goes on being successful.'

Cardus wrote that Jardine had no moonshine in his make-up; that he was a Scot who was in the habit of counting his change in any match, whether against Australia, Lancashire, Yorkshire or the blue blood of Middlesex at Lord's.

'He is armed with common sense and irony,' wrote Cardus. 'His batting lets you know what his conception of cricket is like. He takes nothing for granted, not even a long hop. None but a man of remarkable character could have stuck to his guns with Jardine's cool purpose in the face of a whole country's rage and indignation. It is easy to court popularity nowadays, so much so that we have come to the stage where the worst we can say of anybody is that he is popular. The sure sign of greatness is an ability to stand alone and to accept as inevitable the feeling that people are saying behind your back what they would not dream of saying to your face.'

Jardine certainly stood alone at the end of the tour so far as the Australian public was concerned, but they said nothing behind his back that they did not say to his face. He was the most hated sportsman ever to visit this country, yet there was something indefinably magnificent

178

and courageous in the resolute manner in which he stuck to his bodyline guns. They shouted, they raved, they stormed at Jardine in Australia and they cabled, but he remained calm. He remained coldly indifferent to the point of seeming boredom as he marshalled his fielding forces and kept them pegged all the season within picking distance of a batsman's pocket.

We never saw his captaincy under its greatest strain, more the pity. I would like to have seen his reactions had the Australians, too, employed bodyline, and whether he could have kept at a distance those elements in his team who would certainly have implored and beseeched him to stop Larwood and his tactics (as happened in England later). Jardine, the disciplinarian, would probably have been too strong for them. He would have fought them, pointing out that he was not going to forsake the taming of Bradman to save them a bruise or two, but, whatever happened, Jardine himself could have been battered black and blue and never cried 'enough'. He was chockful of courage.

Jardine was a magnificent captain in his knowledge of the game and his analysis of those he played against. To those who condemned him because he played cricket as if it were a war, he might have replied, had he so deigned, in the clipped, cryptic voice common to him, 'Have not the Australians always played Test cricket in such a manner?'

I saw much in Jardine to admire. I am not prepared to put the whole bodyline blame on his wide, courageous shoulders and leave it there, nor on those of Larwood, either. Each did a job, and the great pity of it, in the final analysis, is that two such eminent and gifted cricketers should have departed from the game under such an unmistakable cloud.

Larwood was a professional cricketer, and it is a fair deduction that he bowled as he was ordered. He was greatly upset when Oldfield was injured in Adelaide. He had no great personal liking for Bradman, whom he considered conceited; but Larwood, in his nature, in his outlook on life, was rather a meek soul. There was his quiet reply at Ballarat when an irate busybody crossed Larwood's name off a list which had just been posted at the Englishman's hotel showing the team for the morrow.

'I hope,' said this foolhardy soul to Larwood, 'that you never play cricket again.'

Larwood did not break out into a fury. 'You say that,' he said quietly to this fellow, 'when cricket is my life, my means of livelihood.'

From *Cricket Crisis*, 1946.

Perhaps the most striking aspect of this analysis of an enigmatic cricketer is its lack of asperity. Candour without rancour appears to be Fingleton's rule as a writer. Sometimes that approach mellows into honesty with affection. If Douglas Jardine declared the war, it was Harold Larwood (b. 1904; Notts and England) who was commanded to fire the guns. Larwood, who took over 1,400 wickets in his career, including 78 in twenty-one appearances for England, was one of the greatest fast bowlers of all time. After the Bodyline scandal, he was allowed to drift, first from the Test arena, and soon after from first-class cricket generally. The matchless irony of his retirement is that it was eventually spent in Australia. Before Larwood took the plunge, however, Fingleton, an old adversary, sought him out during the 1948 England–Australia Test series.

Retreat from Bowling Glory

It was in a side street in Blackpool that we found him. George Duckworth, one of his best friends in his playing days, knew the way. 'It is a neat little mixed shop,' said George, 'but you won't find his name on it.' And we didn't, which was strange, because in his day his name was possibly as famous as Bradman's, but he had not only finished with all that. He had not the slightest wish to be reminded of it.

His eldest daughter saw us first. She recognised George and gave him a great welcome, smiling broadly and motioning towards the back of the house. And there in a homely room, its walls festooned with photographs of some of the most stirring times known to the game of cricket, he gave me a quiet but a warm welcome. He recognised me immediately though I was the first Australian cricketer he had met since those stormy days of 1932–33 when his name was sprawled across the columns of newspapers in much the same manner as he sprawled his victims across the cricket field, but in 1948 he was much thinner. Walking behind him, one would never guess that here was the greatest fast bowler of the modern age; the possessor, in his time, of as lovely a bowling action as the game has ever known. But his face, though thinner, had not changed much. He was still the same Harold Larwood.

The conversation, for a time, was circumspect. Not only was I one of the 'enemy' of 1932–33 but I was a newspaperman, and Larwood had memories of how he had been publicised over the years by the stunting gentry of my profession. Then, in addition, he wanted to bury the dead. You saw that, clearly, in his refusal to have his name shown in the slightest manner over his shop. Dozens of former cricketers throughout the world, whose claim to fame could not compare with his, have capitalised their glory by having their names over balls or bats, by having it in books, by having it up in big letters outside their places of business, but not in the slightest manner, and certainly not by having his name blazoned to the outside world, did Harold Larwood wish to recapture the past. He wanted only to forget it and so his business, to all appearance, was no different to thousands of similar businesses throughout England that are run by the Joneses, the Browns, Williams and Smiths.

It was a pinch of snuff, so to speak, that broke the ice. He took his box out and offered it to me. I declined. Not so George Duckworth. 'Aay, laad,' said George, taking a copious pinch. He placed it on the back of his hand, slapped it with the other, sniffed simultaneously and forthwith began to sneeze so vigorously that tears ran from his eyes. Larwood smiled and took his with the air of a man long accustomed to the art.

'You know,' he said to me, 'I always had snuff in my pocket when I was bowling. I often used to take a pinch of it on the field in Australia. It used to freshen me up. And it's much better for you than cigarettes.'

An eminent medical authority in the last century, Dr. Gordon Hake, would have approved of that. 'Snuff,' wrote Dr. Hake to a critic of his habit, 'not only wakes up that torpor so prevalent between the nose and the brain, making the wings of an idea uncurl like those of a new-born butterfly, but while others sneeze and run at the eyes my schneiderian membrane is impervious to the weather or, to be explicit, I never take a cold in the head.' Soon after the introduction of snuff into Britain in the eighteenth century, the *Gentlewoman's Companion*, noble production, was advising its gentle readers whose sight was failing to use the right sort of Portugal snuff 'whereby many eminent people had cured themselves so that they could read without spectacles after having used them for many years.'

As Larwood was snuffing, I thought his Australian opponents might have been a little better off in 1932–33 had somebody got his box away from him. He might not have sighted his target or his victim so readily, but here at Blackpool, in 1948, it cleared also the atmosphere and when, at long last, George had got his schneiderian membrane to behave, the three of us fell to discussing the old days in a reminiscent manner. There was no bitterness. I had taken many on the ribs from Larwood and Voce in those bodyline days, but all that was forgotten as we recalled the players of those days and the many incidents—for incidents happened in the bodyline series every other minute.

One has not to talk long with Larwood to realise that he is still embittered over those days. I don't think it is with the Australians, but rather with those English officials who were glad to have him and use him before bodyline became ostracised, and then, conveniently, put him aside. He finds that impossible to forgive. Like the prodigal son, he would have been welcomed home by the M.C.C. in 1935 and had all forgiven, but Larwood is a man of strong beliefs. To satisfy all and sundry, the M.C.C. wished Larwood to apologise to them. Had he done that, like Voce, he would have been chosen again for the Australian tour of 1936–1937, but Larwood could not see that he had anything to apologise over and so he remained adamant and went out of the game under a cloud.

He did not say so, but I gathered that he considered himself badly treated, and many who know the story of those bodyline days will agree with him. With us, he recalled only the happy memories of the most distressing tour in cricket history, though when we talked of Bradman I detected again the same old glint of battle I had seen in his eye when I had faced up to him as a batsman.

'When I bowled against Bradman,' he said, 'I always thought he was out to show me up as the worst fast bowler in the world. Well, I took the view that I should try and show him up as the worst batsman. But, laad, he was a good 'un.'

We fell to looking through his photographic albums and the reminiscences among the three of us came thick and fast. His eldest daughter (and Larwood has five beautiful daughters, the youngest between our legs on the floor) had just begun to take an interest in cricket, and only a few days before Larwood had got out his souvenirs to show her, and they included innumerable balls with silver rings about them describing how in many places he had performed grand bowling feats.

Larwood made some pretty shrewd observations about batsmen. He reeled off the names of famous batsmen who, he considered, couldn't play the hook stroke and were thus at a disadvantage against him. The cricket world would be amazed if I repeated the men he named but, like Keith Miller, the Australian, he considered himself fully entitled to prove their weaknesses with bouncers. But how the wheel has now turned full circle! Here, in 1948, under Bradman, the Australians exploited the bouncers to the full (though without the packed leg-field of Jardine), and members of the Nottinghamshire County Committee, the same committee which was forced to apologise to Woodfull and his team in 1934 because Voce had bowled bumpers, now admonished their own spectators for barracking against Australian bumpers. The cricket world, surely, is as crazy and as inconsistent as the outside one.

It was with difficulty that we induced Larwood to come with us to a cricket game for charity which we were playing on the Blackpool ground. He compromised to the extent of promising to come down after afternoon tea. He had not seen either the 1934 or 1938 Australian teams in action. He had not seen his C.-in-C., Douglas Jardine, since Jardine had played in his benefit game in 1935. He had not seen this present Australian team in action, though he had a hankering to see Lindwall bowl. He could not remember the last time he had seen a game on his old home ground, Trent Bridge. Cricket had lost all its appeal for Larwood.

He came to the charity game, forced into it, we thought, by his family who liked to see him with old associates. He told me there a story I loved. It was about Sir Pelham Warner and myself and concerned the bodyline tour. It happened during the Adelaide game, where feeling was tremendously high, and where Woodfull used strong words to Warner over the tactics of the M.C.C. team. That story ran quickly to the Press, and Sir Pelham, jumping to conclusions because I was a pressman, wrongly blamed me for the breach of ethics.

'As we were going out to field in your second innings,' said Larwood, 'Sir Pelham said to me, "Larwood, I will give you a pound if you bowl Fingleton out quickly." If you remember I did, and when I came off the field Sir Pelham was waiting there at the door with a pound note in his hand.'

I will never forget that ball. It was the best ever bowled to me in cricket. At Larwood's top speed, it changed course in the air from leg and, continuing on that course, pitched about the leg and middle stump and took the off-bail. It was absolutely unplayable. A batsman never minds being dismissed by a good ball, even for nothing, as I was that day.

'Ah, well,' said Larwood, 'those days are gone for ever, but here's a pound note. Let's all go and have a drink and we will say it is on Sir Pelham.'

There were times, during the Australian tour of bodyline, when Larwood thought the game not worth the candle. He knew abuse. The tumult was overpowering, the work of fast bowling hard. He has a very sensitive side to his nature and often wondered whether it was worth it, but then he allowed his mind to revert to his coal-mining days before he played cricket and that was sufficient. Strangely, on that tour, his stomach revolted against food. He found that beer, with his occasional pinch of snuff on the field, gave him all the sting he wanted. From the

Australian viewpoint, it gave him more than enough, but he will always be remembered in Australia, tactics of that M.C.C. side apart, as the Prince of Bowlers.

It was a coincidence that very day that Larwood should have received from Australia a long letter from a youth on the art of bowling. It was an interesting letter, asking for advice. It was fitting, even though this lad had never seen Larwood bowl, that he should have written to such a one for advice, though I smiled to myself as I read this delightful piece of youthful folly: 'Do you think, Mr. Larwood,' wrote this ardent theorist, 'that you might have been a better fast bowler if you had begun the swing of your right arm from lower down?' As if any Australian would have wanted Larwood to be better than he was, but perhaps the oddest thing of all about this letter was that it came from Bowral, home town of Bradman. How quaint if Bowral, through Bradman's greatest antagonist on the field, should produce another Larwood!

When we parted we had extracted from him almost a half-promise that he would come to Old Trafford and see and meet the Australians. He wanted to meet O'Reilly; he wanted to see Lindwall particularly, but Larwood never came. I think the inside of an English first-class ground contained too many sad memories for him. He deserved better of the game; he deserved better, particularly, of English cricket because, in tactics, he was only a cog in the wheel. He was, for a certainty, the only bowler who quelled Bradman; the only bowler who made Bradman lose his poise and balance, departing from his set path of easeful centuries into flurried and agitated movements.

I left Blackpool glad that I had seen Larwood, and I think that he, for his part, was pleased again to meet an Australian cricketer, the first since the field of battle in 1932–33. There is something tragic about his finish in cricket and the fact that he wishes to have no ties with the game now at all. It is interesting, too, to look back to those days of 1932–33 and reflect what time has done for the central figures, Bradman and Larwood. The game has been over-kind to one; unkind to the other, but that has ever been the ways of cricket. It is a game, mostly, for batsmen, and I thought of all this as I left Larwood on the note, of all things, of migration. He thinks hard these days of bringing his lovely family of five daughters to settle in a country which once flamed from end to end over his bowling. That, surely, must be the oddest thought of all—Larwood settled in Australia! But he would be doubly welcome. Australia has never held anything against Larwood.

From *Brightly Fades the Don*, 1949.

184

No England fast bowler remotely approached Larwood's figures against Australia for more than twenty years, and when eventually the new destroyer appeared, it was much to the surprise of the cricketing public of both countries, who had not been led to expect any such whirlwind as the one now unleashed by the Northamptonshire fast bowler Frank Holmes Tyson (b. 1930). Among those who witnessed the event at Melbourne on 5 January 1955, was the Oxford blue Alan Ross, at that time cricket correspondent for The Observer.

AT TWENTY minutes past one, that is to say after eighty minutes' further play, the Third Test match, remaining faithful in essentials to its predecessor, even to the result, was all over. Bill Johnston snicked Tyson, and Evans, diving headlong, brought off his second fabulous catch of the morning. England had won by 128 runs. As the players left the field, the crowd broke over the palings and rushed to inspect the wicket. The pitch received during this extraordinary match about as much attention as the play, not altogether undeservedly, for its vagaries and sudden changes of mood persisted to the last. After England's chances on Tuesday evening had seemed to depend almost entirely on Appleyard—the wicket having apparently lost its pace for good and all— Tyson so resurrected its declining vitalities that the remaining eight Australian wickets fell in an hour and twenty minutes for thirty-six runs. There was no need for Appleyard to bowl a ball. It could not this time have been expected of Tyson that he would repeat his triumph of Sydney, for neither in Australia's first innings nor last night did he find the true length for his pace. Today, however, Hutton bowled him from the southern, instead of the Melbourne, end, hoping for the lift that Miller had occasionally managed to obtain. In fact, Tyson got Miller himself with a ball that kicked just enough to find the edge of the bat. For the first half-hour the pitch had definite ambiguities of pace and height, Miller receiving four in a row from Statham that squatted horribly. But once the sweat of night had evaporated in the warm sun the ball came through quite evenly. Suspicion lingered nevertheless, and once again Australian batsmen showed that they are as prone to mistakes of judgment as anybody when faced with bowling of real speed on a fast wicket. Today, they failed generally to play forward, the only honest form of defence when the ball is shooting; instead they preferred to glance, hook or cut, difficult enough strokes to control even on a plumb wicket pitch, let alone on the fifth day, with the wicket not certain to play truly.

Harvey, Benaud and Hole lost their wickets exercising these strokes respectively. Benaud and Archer, on the occasions when they thrust out the left foot, met the ball safely in the middle of the bat, and Archer drove twice with a firmness that suggested the making of 165 runs need not have been unduly difficult. But by then it was too late: Tyson, who in 6.3 overs bowled not one bad ball, had already broken the Australian batting into splinters. He removed Harvey, England's main obstacle, in his first over, and at the end of an hour, during which six wickets fell for twenty-three runs, he had taken five of them for ten. He found his rhythm instantaneously, and length and direction followed. . . .

Haunting images of Tyson's bowling in this match remain. He walks very loosely back to his bowling mark, chewing gum slowly. He has put on weight, making him less angular in movement, and is pleasantly tanned. He turns, moves back a pace, shuffles his feet as if wiping them on a doormat, lopes for three long strides, then quickens up for the climax of the delivery. As he runs he pushes his right hand, with the ball in it, twice from shoulder to waist, in the motions of an auctioneer knocking down an item. His left arm, as he approaches the umpire, is thrown up high and bent back near his right ear. His chest is turned inwards and fully expanded. The left foot, as he comes down on it, points nearer to first slip than long leg, but much less than it used. He has long arms and he brings the ball up from far back. When he is not bowling well, the initial shuffle is more pronounced, and his paces seem too close together for the distance of his run. After letting go the ball, he follows through, drops his shoulders and dangles his arms loosely in front of him, as though completely exhausted. His action is only striking at the moment of delivery; but for the few seconds that count he does most of the important things.

His advances in the control of length and direction can be put down partly to the shortening of his run; though that is more responsible for the great increase in the number of overs which he can now bowl at full pace. The sun has obviously helped considerably, for it has produced the looseness that he has rarely achieved in England. But the main causes seem to lie in the determined application that Tyson has brought to the problems of fast bowling. Intelligence has governed his attitude to them: and he is a man of sensibility, as well as heart.

From *Australia 55*, 1955.

Another spectacular success on that tour was the Tonbridge and Kent bats-
man Michael Colin Cowdrey (b. 1932). When Cowdrey finally retired in
1975 he had reached the coveted mark of a century of centuries and had
played for England more than a hundred times. When he went to Australia
in 1954, however, he was little more than a promising juvenile prodigy, who
benefited from the tutelage of the first professional captain ever to captain
England in a Test series.

I WORKED hard and played well in the nets at Perth whilst we
acclimatised before the matches started. It paid dividends. I got 48 not
out in the two-day up-country match at Bunbury and then went straight
into the opening major game against Western Australia. Here for the
first time I batted with Hutton at the other end. He had already scored
about 70 when I joined him and my concern this time was for him and
not for me. I was petrified at the thought of running him out, which
seemed a distinct possibility as he never called. He simply stroked the
ball away and then ambled up and down. To me it was like flying for the
first time with one of those RAF aerobatic teams. If you took your eye off
your leader, either you were dead, which was bad, or he was dead, which
was infinitely worse. I had no inkling of his intentions. I had to be ready
in case he wanted to pinch a quick third run to keep the strike. At other
times he hit the ball into the covers and stood there watching it. I did not
know whether to watch him or watch the ball. Then he would suddenly
look down the wicket at me with an expression which said, 'Why aren't
you running.' There was no time at all to worry about my own batting.
My entire concentration was focused on not running him out.

We put on 127 for the fourth wicket. I scored 41 and Hutton went on
to make 145 before he retired with a pulled muscle. But it was the
partnership which forged our relationship for the tour. He treated me
almost as if he had been appointed my guardian. Once, half way through
an over from a left-arm fast bowler coming over the wicket, he held up
play for what seemed an eternity, called me into the middle of the pitch
and asked what guard I was taking. I said, 'Leg-stump.' He said 'Um'
and walked slowly back. Two overs later he called me down again. 'I
think you've got to take centre. Move over and play down this bloke's

line.' Occasionally, after that, he would say 'Good shot', as we passed for a run.

For his most junior player, meanwhile, there were few problems. I was enjoying the tour and had little anxiety about the Tests. For a while, at least, there were not going to be any Tests. I missed a couple of games, then failed to make any impression at all in Adelaide as we moved across Australia towards the start of the series. Then, against New South Wales, in Sydney, it happened. Although I had yet to score a century in the County Championship in England I now made two centuries in a match against probably the most powerful of the Australian State sides: 110 in the first innings, 103 in the second.

It was a very significant game for me for more than the obvious reasons. In the first innings I went in number six, after MCC had lost four wickets for 38, and put on 163 in a stand with Hutton. In the second innings I opened. Someone was ill, I think, but whatever the reason Hutton suddenly asked, 'When did you last go in first?' I told him I could not recollect ever having done so. 'Well, you're seeing the ball pretty well,' he said, 'have a go.' I could not argue against his reasoning but I did not relish the prospect. When we batted again, Reg Simpson, who should have been England's opening partner with Hutton, batted badly. I got my second century and I think from that moment Hutton saw me as a certainty for the first Test in Brisbane, possibly as his opening partner. It did not work out that way. In the remaining game before the Tests, against Queensland, I opened again. I got four in the first innings and nought in the second.

I have two other particular recollections from the match against New South Wales. The first was of my demise as a bowler. Earlier, in some up-country game, I had been given a bowl, taken a wicket with my first ball and ended up with something around five for 30. My leg-breaks had impressed the local batsmen but, more to the point, they had impressed Hutton as well, because when we were taking some terrible punishment from the New South Wales batsmen in Sydney a week or so later he suddenly threw the ball to me again. It was my misfortune to bowl to Alan Davidson. He too, was clearly impressed with me because he hit me clean over the stand out of that enormous ground and when I sneaked a look at Wisden now to discover what happened later I find that I was removed from the attack shortly afterwards with an analysis reading: no maidens, thirty-eight runs and no wickets. I did not bowl again.

The other memory is of batting with Hutton on a turning wicket. It was so slow that even Davidson was bowling spinners and Hutton fancied his chances. He asked me to take Richie Benaud at my end while he stayed facing Davidson. His performance after that deserved an Oscar. If the duel had gone on for twenty years Davidson could never have got Hutton out. But Hutton's imitation of a great batsman in trouble was classic. He tied himself into all imaginable knots and then, sportsman that he was, he would nod a little 'Well bowled' to Davidson down the wicket. He kept Davidson on for most of the morning, rationing himself with great restraint to only a boundary every so often.

As we walked off he said: 'How are you then?' I said, 'It's hard work.' His reply was a classic Huttonism. 'Aye, and what's more you're not getting paid for it, are you?'

From *M.C.C.*, 1976.

Stern affairs, and by no means typical of the predicaments in which the first-class cricketer sometimes finds himself. Ernest William Swanton, OBE (b. 1907), cricket correspondent for The Daily Telegraph *from 1946 to 1975, and author of many books on post-war cricket, was also a batsman on the fringe of county standard. One of the several pleasures of his sporting life was to tour with Sir Julien Cahn (1882–1944), a furniture millionaire whose annual expenses of £20,000 a year on cricket included the cost of some arcane equipment.*

JULIEN CAHN was a conspicuous figure in the cricket world of the 'thirties with his own team and two superb grounds, one more or less in Nottingham at West Bridgford, the other in front of his house, Stanford Hall, Loughborough. The wickets were perfect, and the outfields were like bowling greens. Hospitality was on a lavish scale with no shortage of champagne; but there were those who took undue advantage of a bountiful host, and latterly therefore drinks had to be signed for. He had a first-class side, most members of which were accommodated in his furnishing business when they were not playing for him either at home or abroad. He took teams to Jamaica, to the Argentine, to Denmark, to Canada, USA and Bermuda, to Ceylon and Singapore and to New Zealand. His purse was apparently bottomless, and, of course, he gave a vast deal of pleasure to very many people, even though his sides were much too strong for most of their opposition. This didn't worry 'Sir J' —he was first knighted and then accorded a baronetcy for 'service to agriculture and a number of charitable causes'—whose idea of a good game, I suspect, was to see his stars make three or four hundred and then bowl out the enemy quickly enough to avoid too long a spell in the field.

For he played himself, in a manner of speaking, bowling when he felt inclined and sometimes putting himself in first. As a bowler his style is best described as parabolic. It can perhaps be imagined from John Gunn's answer—or it may have been 'Tich' Richmond's—to the question how Sir Julien was bowling that year: 'Up and down, I suppose?' 'Not so mooch oop and down, I'd say, as to and fro'. When I took Crusoe to play once at Stanford he remarked that the chief evidence that Cahn was bowling was a faint whistling in the trees. He was probably hit higher and farther than any bowler before or since, runs, of course, being no object as there were always hundreds to play with. But sometimes he got a wicket, and high was the merriment. The brilliant players who surrounded him made some astonishing catches, one of which at London, Ontario, comes back to me as I write. The batsman hit the cricket equivalent of a full brassie shot, low, down wind, and practically straight. Walter Robins—I think one of the best half-dozen all-round fielders I ever saw—came sprinting in full pelt from the sight-screen as the stroke was made and took the ball right-handed down by his boots. Done in a Test at Lord's it would have won imperishable fame.

It was said, no doubt erroneously, that when the side's averages were made up at the end of the season the scorer by a simple manipulation of the decimal point brought the captain up to the top of the list.

He was the sort of man around whom revolved many such stories. For instance, his pads, which were very large, were said to be blown up with a bicycle pump. The ball certainly bounced readily off them for leg-byes which the umpire sometimes conveniently forgot to signal; but I never saw them inflated, though I did once see the butler, who was in attendance to accoutre Julien in the changing tent at Stanford, rush out with the fielding pads which he had forgotten to strap on. Not a bit abashed, his master paused from leading his team on to the greensward, pulled up his trousers and allowed the matter to be rectified.

Even with his legs thus encased it has to be admitted that Julien was not a brave fielder as many will remember. But if this little weakness is mentioned I must add that as Master of the Pytchley and of the Fernie it was said that no fence was too high for him, and that his intrepidity in the hunting field cost him several broken bones. He was, in fact, even more a mixture than most of us, with an innately kind side to which many a cricketer was indebted, myself included. . . .

So much for Julien Cahn, though I pass on with reluctance from this eccentric open-handed figure who, being something of a hypochondriac, thought nothing of ordering a special train to bring from London the King's physician, Lord Horder, and who took his barber with him round the world. His grounds contained a golf course as well as lawn-tennis and squash courts, bowling and putting greens, swimming pool, besides a lake well stocked with trout and—sublime touch!—a performing seal pond. The last addition to the house before war brought such vanities to a halt was a luxurious theatre seating 350, complete with Wurlitzer organ. He purchased from F. S. Ashley-Cooper, the distinguished historian, the best cricket library ever collected, but thereby hangs a melancholy tale. At his death Lady Cahn offered MCC any items they did not already have, which was a generous gesture considering her husband had enjoyed no more than two years of membership. Later the balance of this unique library was put up for auction, the sale being due to begin at eleven o'clock. However, a considerable collection advertised for sale earlier in the morning was withdrawn at the last moment, the Cahn sale began early, and before serious purchasers arrived, much irreplaceable material went dirt cheap to dealers and has never been located.

From *Sort of a Cricket Person*, 1972.

In spite of Wodehouse's conversion to what is no more than a girl's game played with a hard ball by men wearing pyjamas, cricket remains an indispensable part of the English social scene. Taking into account all the levels at which it is played, the game appears to be more widely popular than ever before. One writer who would have been pleased to hear it is Mary Russell Mitford (1787–1855; Hampshire), whose series of rural essays, published as Our Village *between 1824 and 1832, are represented, most deservedly, in most anthologies of cricket writing.*

A Country Cricket Match

I DOUBT if there be any scene in the world more animating or delight-ful than a cricket-match:—I do not mean a set match at Lord's Ground for money, hard money, between a certain number of gentlemen and players, as they are called—people who make a trade of that noble sport, and degrade it into an affair of bettings, and hedgings, and cheatings, it may be, like boxing or horse-racing; nor do I mean a pretty *fête* in a gentleman's park, where one club of cricketing dandies encounter another such club, and where they show off in graceful costume to a gay marquee of admiring belles, who condescend so to purchase admiration, and while away a long summer morning in partaking cold collations, conversing occasionally, and seeming to understand the game—the whole being conducted according to ball-room etiquette, so as to be exceedingly elegant and exceedingly dull. No! the cricket that I mean is a real solid old-fashioned match between neighbouring parishes, where each attacks the other for honour and a supper, glory and half-a-crown a man. If there be any gentleman amongst them, it is well—if not, it is so much the better. Your gentleman cricketer is in general rather an anomalous character. Elderly gentlemen are obviously good for nothing; and your beaux are, for the most part, hampered and trammelled by dress and habit; the stiff cravat, the pinched-in waist, the dandy-walk—oh, they will never do for cricket! Now, our country lads accustomed to the flail or the hammer (your blacksmiths are capital hitters) have the free use of their arms; they know how to move their shoulders; and they can move their feet too—they can run; then they are so much better made, so much more athletic, and yet so much lissomer—to use a Hampshire phrase, which deserves at least to be good English. Here and there, indeed, one meets with an old Etonian, who retains his boyish love for that game which formed so considerable a branch of his education; some even preserve their boyish proficiency, but in general it wears away like the Greek, quite as certainly, and almost as fast; a few years of Oxford, or Cambridge, or the continent, are sufficient to annihilate both the power and the inclination. No! a village match is the thing—where our highest officer—our conductor (to borrow a musical term) is but a little farmer's second son; where a day-labourer is our bowler, and a blacksmith our long-stop; where the spectators consist of the retired cricketers, the veterans of the green, the careful mothers, the girls, and all the boys of two parishes, together with a few amateurs, little above them in rank, and not at all in pretension; where laughing and shouting, and the very ecstasy of merriment and good-humour prevail: such a match, in short, as I attended yesterday, at the expense of getting twice wet through, and as I would attend tomorrow, at the certainty of having that ducking doubled.

For the last three weeks our village has been in a state of great excitement, occasioned by a challenge from our north-western neighbours, the men of B., to contend with us at cricket. Now, we have not been much in the habit of playing matches. Three or four years ago, indeed, we encountered the men of S., our neighbours south-by-east, with a sort of doubtful success, beating them on our own ground, whilst they in the second match returned the compliment on theirs. This discouraged us. Then an unnatural coalition between a high-church curate and an evangelical gentleman-farmer drove our lads from the Sunday-evening practice, which, as it did not begin before both services were concluded, and as it tended to keep the young men from the ale-house, our magistrates had winked at, if not encouraged. The sport, therefore, had languished until the present season, when under another change of circumstances the spirit began to revive. Half-a-dozen fine active lads, of influence amongst their comrades, grew into men and yearned for cricket; an enterprising publican gave a set of ribands: his rival, mine host of the Rose, an out-doer by profession, gave two; and the clergyman and his lay ally, both well-disposed and good-natured men, gratified by the submission to their authority, and finding, perhaps, that no great good resulted from the substitution of public-houses for out-of-door diversions, relaxed. In short, the practice recommenced, and the hill was again alive with men and boys, and innocent merriment; but farther than the riband matches amongst ourselves nobody dreamed of going, till this challenge—we were modest, and doubted our own strength. The B. people, on the other hand, must have been braggers born, a whole parish of gasconaders. Never was such boasting! such crowing! such ostentatious display of practice! such mutual compliments from man to man—bowler to batter, batter to bowler! It was a wonder they did not challenge all England. It must be confessed that we were a little astounded; yet we firmly resolved not to decline the combat; and one of the most spirited of the new growth, William Grey by name, took up the glove in a style of manly courtesy, that would have done honour to a knight in the days of chivalry.—'We were not professed players,' he said, 'being little better than school-boys, and scarcely older; but, since they had done us the honour to challenge us, we would try our strength. It would be no discredit to be beaten by such a field.'

Having accepted the wager of battle, our champion began forthwith to collect his forces. William Grey is himself one of the finest youths that one shall see—tall, active, slender and yet strong, with a piercing eye full of sagacity, and a smile full of good humour,—a farmer's son by station, and used to hard work as farmers' sons are now, liked by everybody, and admitted to be an excellent cricketer. He immediately set forth to muster his men, remembering with great complacency that Samuel Long, a bowler *comme il y en a peu*, the very man who had knocked down nine wickets, had beaten us, bowled us out at the fatal return match some years ago at S., had luckily, in a remove of a quarter of a mile last Lady-day, crossed the boundaries of his old parish, and actually belonged to us. Here was a stroke of good fortune! Our captain applied to him instantly; and he agreed at a word. Indeed, Samuel Long is a very civilised person. He is a middle-aged man, who looks rather old amongst our young lads, and whose thickness and breadth give no token of remarkable activity; but he is very active, and so steady a player! so safe! We had half gained the match when we had secured him. He is a man of substance, too, in every way; owns one cow, two donkeys, six pigs, and geese and ducks beyond count—dresses like a farmer, and owes no man a shilling—and all this from pure industry, sheer day-labour. Note that your good cricketer is commonly the most industrious man in the parish; the habits that make him such are precisely those which make a good workman—steadiness, sobriety, and activity—Samuel Long might pass for the *beau ideal* of the two characters. Happy were we to possess him! Then we had another piece of good luck. James Brown, a journeyman blacksmith and a native, who, being of a rambling dis-position, had roamed from place to place for half-a-dozen years, had just returned to settle with his brother at another corner of our village, bringing with him a prodigious reputation in cricket and in gallantry—the gay Lothario of the neighbourhood. He is said to have made more conquests in love and in cricket than any blacksmith in the county. To him also went the indefatigable William Grey, and he also consented to play. No end to our good fortune! Another celebrated batter, called Joseph Hearne, had likewise recently married into the parish. He worked, it is true, at the A. mills, but slept at the house of his wife's father in our territories. He also was sought and found by our leader. But he was grand and shy; made an immense favour of the thing; courted courting and then hung back:—'Did not know that he could be spared; had partly resolved not to play again—at least not this season; thought it rash to accept the challenge; thought they might do without him——' 'Truly I think so too,' said our spirited champion; 'we will not trouble you, Mr Hearne.'

Having thus secured two powerful auxiliaries, and rejected a third, we began to reckon and select the regular native forces. Thus ran our list:—William Grey, 1.—Samuel Long, 2.—James Brown, 3.—George and John Simmons, one capital, the other so-so—an uncertain hitter, but a good fieldsman, 5.—Joel Brent, excellent, 6.—Ben Appleton—here was a little pause—Ben's abilities at cricket were not completely ascertained; but then he was so good a fellow, so full of fun and waggery! no doing without Ben. So he figured in the list, 7.—George Harris—a short halt there too! Slowish—slow but sure. I think the proverb brought him in, 8.—Tom Coper—oh, beyond the world, Tom Coper! the red-headed gardening lad, whose left handed strokes send *her* (a cricket-ball, like that other moving thing, a ship, is always of the feminine gender), send her spinning a mile, 9.—Harry Willis, another blacksmith, 10.

We had now ten of our eleven, but the choice of the last occasioned some demur. Three young Martins, rich farmers of the neighbourhood, successively presented themselves, and were all rejected by our independent and impartial general for want of merit—*cricketal* merit. 'Not good enough,' was his pithy answer. Then our worthy neighbour, the half-pay lieutenant, offered his services—he, too, though with some hesitation and modesty, was refused—'Not quite young enough,' was his sentence. John Strong, the exceeding long son of our dwarfish mason, was the next candidate—a nice youth—everybody likes John Strong—and a willing, but so tall and so limp, bent in the middle—a thread-paper, six feet high! We were all afraid that, in spite of his name, his strength would never hold out. 'Wait till next year, John,' quoth William Grey, with all the dignified seniority of twenty speaking to eighteen. 'Coper's a year younger,' said John. 'Coper's a foot shorter,' replied William: so John retired: and the eleventh man remained unchosen, almost to the eleventh hour. The eve of the match arrived, and the post was still vacant, when a little boy of fifteen, David Willis, brother to Harry, admitted by accident to the last practice, saw eight of them out, and was voted in by acclamation.

That Sunday evening's practice (for Monday was the important day) was a period of great anxiety, and, to say the truth, of great pleasure. There is something strangely delightful in the innocent spirit of party. To be one of a numerous body, to be authorised to say *we*, to have a rightful interest in triumph or defeat, is gratifying at once to social feeling and to personal pride. There was not a ten-year old urchin, or a septuagenary woman in the parish who did not feel an additional importance, a reflected consequence, in speaking of 'our side'. An election interests in the same way; but that feeling is less pure. Money is there, and hatred, and politics, and lies. Oh, to be a voter, or a voter's wife, comes nothing near the genuine and hearty sympathy of belonging to a parish, breathing the same air, looking on the same trees, listening to the same nightingales! Talk of a patriotic elector! Give me a parochial patriot, a man who loves his parish! Even we, the female partisans, may partake the common ardour. I am sure I did. I never, though tolerably eager and enthusiastic at all times, remember being in a more delicious state of excitement than on the eve of that battle. Our hopes waxed stronger and stronger. Those of our players who were present were excellent. William Grey got forty notches off his own bat; and that brilliant hitter, Tom Coper, gained eight from two successive balls. As the evening advanced, too, we had encouragment of another sort. A spy, who had been despatched to reconnoitre the enemy's quarters, returned from their practising ground with a most consolatory report. 'Really,' said Charles Grover, our intelligence—a fine old steady judge, one who had played well in his day—'they are no better than so many old women. Any five of ours would beat their eleven.' This sent us to bed in high spirits.

Morning dawned less favourably. The sky promised a series of deluging showers, and kept its word as English skies are wont to do on such occasions; and a lamentable message arrived at the head-quarters from our trusty comrade Joel Brent. His master, a great farmer, had begun the hay-harvest that very morning, and Joel, being as eminent in one field as in another, could not be spared. Imagine Joel's plight! the most ardent of all our eleven! a knight held back from the tourney! a soldier from the battle! The poor swain was inconsolable. At last, one who is always ready to do a good-natured action, great or little, set forth to back his petition; and, by dint of appealing to the public spirit of our worthy neighbour and the state of the barometer, talking alternately of the parish honour and thunder-showers, of lost matches and sopped hay, he carried his point and returned triumphantly with the delighted Joel.

In the meantime we became sensible of another defalcation. On calling over our roll, Brown was missing; and the spy of the preceding night, Charles Grover—the universal scout and messenger of the village, a man who will run half-a-dozen miles for a pint of beer, who does errands for the very love of the trade, who, if he had been a lord, would have been an ambassador—was instantly despatched to summon the truant. His report spread general consternation. Brown had set off at four o'clock in the morning to play in a cricket-match at M., a little town twelve miles off, which had been his last residence. Here was desertion! Here was treachery! Here was treachery against that goodly state, our parish! To send James Brown to Coventry was the immediate resolution; but even that seemed too light a punishment for such delinquency. Then how we cried him down! At ten on Sunday night (for the rascal had actually practised with us, and never said a word of his intended disloyalty) he was our faithful mate, and the best player (take him for all in all) of the eleven. At ten in the morning he had run away, and we were well rid of him; he was no batter compared with William Grey or Tom Coper; not fit to wipe the shoes of Samuel Long, as a bowler; nothing of a scout to John Simmons; the boy David Willis was worth fifty of him—

> 'I trust we have within our realm,
> Five hundred good as he,'

was the universal sentiment. So we took tall John Strong, who, with an incurable hankering after the honour of being admitted, had kept constantly with the players, to take the chance of some such accident—we took John for our *pis-aller*. I never saw any one prouder than the good-humoured lad was of this not very flattering piece of preferment.

John Strong was elected, and Brown sent to Coventry; and when I first heard of his delinquency, I thought the punishment only too mild for the crime. But I have since learned the secret history of the offence (if we could know the secret histories of all offences, how much better the world would seem than it does now!) and really my wrath is much abated. It was a piece of gallantry, of devotion to the sex, or rather a chivalrous obedience to one chosen fair. I must tell my readers the story. Mary Allen, the prettiest girl of M., had, it seems, revenged upon our blacksmith the numberless inconsistencies of which he stood accused. He was in love over head and ears, but the nymph was cruel. She said no, and no, and no, and poor Brown, three times rejected, at last resolved to leave the place, partly in despair, and partly in that hope which often mingles strangely with a lover's despair, the hope that when he was gone he should be missed. He came home to his brother's accordingly; but for five weeks he heard nothing from or of the inexorable Mary, and was glad to beguile his own 'vexing thoughts' by endeavouring to create in his mind an artificial and factitious interest in our cricket-match—all unimportant as such a trifle must have seemed to a man in love. Poor James, however, is a social and warm-hearted person, not likely to resist a contagious sympathy. As the time for the play advanced, the interest which he had at first affected became genuine and sincere: and he was really, when he left the ground on Sunday night, almost as enthusiastically absorbed in the event of the next day as Joel Brent himself. He little foresaw the new and delightful interest which awaited him at home, where, on the moment of his arrival, his sister-in-law and confidante presented him with a billet from the lady of his heart. It had, with the usual delay of letters sent by private hands in that rank of life, loitered on the road, in a degree inconceivable to those who are accustomed to the punctual speed of the post, and had taken ten days for its twelve miles' journey. Have my readers any wish to see this *billet-doux*? I can show them (but in strict confidence) a literal copy. It was addressed,

> 'For mistur jem browne
> 'blaxmith by
> 'S.'

The inside ran thus:—'Mistur browne this is to Inform you that oure parish plays bramley men next monday is a week, i think we shall lose without yew. from your humbell servant to command
> 'MARY ALLEN.'

Was there ever a prettier relenting? a summons more flattering, more delicate, more irresistible? The precious epistle was undated; but, having ascertained who brought it, and found, by cross-examining the messenger, that the Monday in question was the very next day, we were not surprised to find that *Mistur browne* forgot his engagement to us, forgot all but Mary and Mary's letter, and set off at four o'clock the next morning to walk twelve miles, and play for her parish, and in her sight. Really we must not send James Brown to Coventry—must we? Though if, as his sister-in-law tells our damsel Harriet he hopes to do, he should bring the fair Mary home as his bride, he will not greatly care how little we say to him. But he must not be sent to Coventry—True-love forbid!

At last we were all assembled, and marched down to H. common, the appointed ground, which, though in our dominions according to the maps, was the constant practising place of our opponents, and *terra incognita* to us. We found our adversaries on the ground as we expected, for our various delays had hindered us from taking the field so early as we wished; and, as soon as we had settled all preliminaries, the match began.

But, alas! I have been so long settling my preliminaries, that I have left myself no room for the detail of our victory, and must squeeze the account of our grand achievements into as little compass as Cowley, when he crammed the names of eleven of his mistresses into the narrow space of four eight-syllable lines. *They* began the warfare—those boastful men of B. And what think you, gentle reader, was the amount of their innings! These challengers—the famous eleven—how many did they get? Think! imagine! guess!—You cannot?—Well!—they got twenty-two, or, rather, they got twenty; for two of theirs were short notches, and would never have been allowed, only that, seeing what they were made of, we and our umpires were not particular.—They should have had twenty more if they had chosen to claim them. Oh, how well we fielded! and how well we bowled! our good play had quite as much to do with their miserable failure as their bad. Samuel Long is a slow bowler, George Simmons a fast one, and the change from Long's lobbing to Simmons's fast balls posed them completely. Poor simpletons! they were always wrong, expecting the slow for the quick, and the quick for the slow. Well, we went in. And what were our innings? Guess again! —guess! A hundred and sixty-nine! in spite of soaking showers, and wretched ground, where the ball would not run a yard, we headed them by a hundred and forty-seven; and then they gave in, as well they might. William Grey pressed them much to try another innings. 'There was so much chance,' as he courteously observed, 'in cricket, that advantageous as our position seemed, we might, very possibly, be overtaken. The B. men had better try.' But they were beaten sulky, and would not move— to my great disappointment; I wanted to prolong the pleasure of success. What a glorious sensation it is to be for five hours together—winning— winning! always feeling what a whist-player feels when he takes up four honours, seven trumps! Who would think that a little bit of leather, and two pieces of wood, had such a delightful and delighting power!

The only drawback on my enjoyment was the failure of the pretty boy, David Willis, who, injudiciously put in first, and playing for the first time in a match amongst men and strangers, who talked to him, and stared at him, was seized with such a fit of shamefaced shyness, that he could scarcely hold his bat, and was bowled out without a stroke, from actual nervousness. 'He will come off that,' Tom Coper says—I am afraid he will. I wonder whether Tom had ever any modesty to lose. Our other modest lad, John Strong, did very well; his length told in fielding, and he got good fame. Joel Brent, the rescued mower, got into a scrape and out of it again; his fortune for the day. He ran out his mate, Samuel Long; who, I do believe, but for the excess of Joel's eagerness, would have stayed in till this time, by which exploit he got into sad disgrace; and then he himself got thirty-seven runs, which redeemed his reputation. Will Grey made a hit which actually lost the cricket-ball. We think she lodged in a hedge, a quarter of a mile off, but nobody could find her. And George Simmons had nearly lost his shoe, which he tossed away in a passion, for having been caught out, owing to the ball glancing against it. These, together with a very complete somerset of Ben Appleton, our long-stop, who floundered about in the mud, making faces and attitudes as laughable as Grimaldi, none could tell whether by accident or design, were the chief incidents of the scene of action. Amongst the spectators nothing remarkable occurred, beyond the general calamity of two or three drenchings, except that a form, placed by the side of a hedge, under a very insufficient shelter, was knocked into the ditch, in a sudden rush of cricketers to escape a pelting shower, by which means all parties shared the fate of Ben Appleton, some on land and some by water; and that, amidst the scramble, a saucy gipsy of a girl contrived to steal from the knee of the demure and well-apparelled Samuel Long, a smart handkerchief which his careful dame had tied round it to preserve his new (what is the mincing feminine word?)—his new—inexpressibles, thus reversing the story of Desdemona, and causing the new Othello to call aloud for his handkerchief, to the great diversion of the company. And so we parted; the players retired to their supper, and we to our homes; all wet through, all good-humoured and happy—except the losers.

To-day we are happy too. Hats, with ribands in them, go glancing up and down; and William Grey says, with a proud humility, 'We do not challenge any parish; but if we be challenged, we are ready.'

From *Our Village*, 1824–1832.

A hundred years after Miss Mitford, Edmund Blunden (1896–1974) was still celebrating the game in the identical setting. Blunden was a poet and academic once described as 'a frail but intrepid wicketkeeper'. Winner of Hawthornden Prize, 1922; Professor of English Literature, Tokyo University, 1924–26; Fellow and Tutor, English Literature, Merton College, Oxford, 1931–43; Professor of English, Hong Kong, 1955; Professor of Poetry, Oxford, until ill-health forced his retirement in 1968. His only cricketing boast was 'I claim consideration as a wicketkeeper who has taken seven wickets in an innings, out of nine altogether.'

An Ancient Holiday

'NICELY.'

'Pretty stroke.'

'Nice shot, sir.'

And again, a moment later:

'Well hit.'

'Run 'em out.'

'See him open his shoulders to that one.'

It was Saturday afternoon; the place, Harmans Cricket Ground; the occasion a, say rather the, match between Harmans Second Eleven and their inevitable rivals from the next parish, Longley Street. The veterans of the Harmans side, all but 'Tardy' Gibbens, who was as usual at the wicket to open the innings and wear out the enemy with his stolid mahogany-brown pads and bat, were sitting in the small pavilion, putting on their equipment, and talking with the condescending calm expected of veterans. Their comments, chiefly stirred by the batting skill of the young hero Tom Benyon, were registered after murmured repetitions by a number of little boys, who sat with their backs against the pavilion railing; and, while it did not, of course, signify anything to such seasoned spirits, yet the effect of these judicial remarks was to leave in youthful minds the notion, 'I should say old—— had made some runs in his time,' and even though —— never made any nowadays, his name still conveyed the sense of a most valuable cricketer, an old champion. A man who, himself about to enter the arena and face the music, could speak deliberately and coolly of the struggle before him, could forget the enormous responsibilities of the hour in approving or disapproving some technical detail! To John Bowers, seated a little apart from the veterans—the vicar's gardener, the grocer, and general dealer above the bridge, and the '& Son' of the butcher below the bridge—the attitude was not without its quiet tinge of humour; for he knew that, after their probable failure this afternoon, the impassive minds would lapse into a vein of autumn melancholy. Then it would be:

'Ah, Frank, every year after forty counts two.'

But, for the general award, their intrepidity was beyond all question. The cricket ground was among a wide sweep of meadows, which fall easily towards the waters of the Chavender, and at one end of which you may see the church tower, with its 'candle-snuffer' atop of it, of Harmans; at the other, the modest tiled spire of Longley Street retiring among the rich greenery of midsummer. Not only was it as pleasantly situated in a girdle of tall trees, among which rose the red Jacobean chimneys of farmhouses, or the far-off hills, as cricket ground could be; nor was it only for the sake of seeing the white pageantry of the game pass to the cooing of doves in the deep blue shadows of the fir-spinneys near by, that Harmans and district frequented it. I have noticed that it was the Second Eleven which on this day took the field; and the attendance was, from the old, old, very old men who sat on the benches under the oak tree, to the pale mothers who had wheeled their perambulators alongside and rested their no less weary bones a little, in every respect the Second Eleven's attendance. There was, it will have been remarked, a Harmans First Eleven—a fact which explained the reverential care with which the pitch had been prepared, and the out-field grass not left in an intermediate stage between kempt and unkempt as on many a country ground, but mown and rolled with great nicety. The matches of the First Eleven resembled a kind of levees or garden parties, to which fair ladies came flocking, and cars swept in through the opened gates from the byroad to bring the guests, whether more remark-able for blazer, parasol, or the equally resplendent charm of great possessions. Lunch and tea, then, seemed to rob the cricket of its interest; and the cricket itself inclined to be 'to pattern,' sartorial and immaculate.

Some signs of caste might be detected in the Second Eleven's organization. The grocer and general dealer, a man of five-and-thirty, pale, brilliantined, and mincing, would intimate in his manner to the village schoolmaster, that 'clay from clay differs in dignity.' An occasional Malapropism is not much ground lost when he who can present a bill of £20 to him who trembles lest he receive it, is conversing in all Christian charity with that wretch. But these were cloudlets, and no more. Taken at all times and in all its ways, the Harmans Second Eleven was a happy republic, and one that had the chief intention of playing cricket. The game was not to be half-played. It became a battle—indeed, so serious that for some of its members later battles gave less cause for personal anxiety.

And so, here were 'Tardy' and 'Tom,' treating the furious fast bowler at the benches' end and the ancient twisting-handed trundler at the river end with every promise of a noble event. The Longley Street scorer, next to Bowers, was beginning to fret; the Harmans scorer, a youth who frequently set out to keep the book and ended by playing instead of absentees, made no effort to conceal his satisfaction as he croaked, 'Thirty up.' 'Thirty up' was the chorus below the rails, as the nearest youngsters scrambled up to the scoreboard and put up the scratched numeral-plates. 'Benyon seventeen, Gibbens one,' went on the uncertain bass, 'an' twelve extras.' The Longley Street scorer sniffed.

'Ah!' 'O Lord!'

'Tom's out.'

'He shouldn't have nibbled at that.'

'I thought Smith would get him with his off theory,' smirked the Longley Street scorer, and his opposite number looked down his nose.

The gifted and popular Tom Benyon was ruefully walking back into the pavilion. The circle of veterans broke up, as the butcher, thrusting his round felt hat sternly over his eyebrows, took up his bat and, with strides like a parody of the goose-step, clumped forth to the wicket. Bowers, having still leisure enough unless things collapsed, strolled round the boundary with the schoolmaster, Scroggins, a mild man with a family. Scroggins asked, 'Is your father coming to take a look at the game?' Bowers was expecting him there at any minute. 'Some of us hoped,' continued Scroggins, 'that he might have turned out this season. We, I needn't say every one amongst us, would welcome such a return.' 'He says he's finished, except as a spectator and a Wisdenite,' answered Bowers. 'He's fifty this winter, and old for his age, he says, too.' 'O no,' said the elementary schoolmaster, vainly trying to find the right quotation. 'When he said after his game last year that he'd made positively his last appearance, we reminded him of the last appearances of the music-hall favourites. They appear as regularly after those farewells as they did before!' A misfortune had occurred at the wickets.

The butcher had called the rightly named 'Tardy' for a run, and had himself done all the running. 'Tardy' maintained his ground: 'Goo back,' he said, with marble serenity, 'goo back.' It was his error, but he valued the butcher's wicket without sentiment and his own with plenty. The butcher was out, and put out too. 'All right that is, all right, ain't it? Tcha.' He stumped, yet more Prussianly, into the pavilion, asking rhetorically, 'All right, eh? St. Tut-tut-tut.'

Misfortune followed misfortune. The railway clerk, usually reliable for a hard hit or two, and the vicar's gardener had no luck whatever; Scroggins, bland and cautious, turned back to the pavilion as the bailiff from Little Green lashed the ball into the hands of a stout fields-man at square-leg, and was succeeded by the grocer and general dealer. This gentleman had acquired something of the First Eleven's character-istic style, and urbanely placing his bat well forward, saw to his evident surprise the ball glide away behind the wicket. Two runs! ' 'E plays for style, does Mr Kidd,' said a youth in his working clothes, less jacket, who stood ready to follow Scroggins in this career. Again, the ball departed at an angle from the bat of the stylist, and one run ensued. Kidd, thus brought face to face with the old fellow bowling twisters, smoothed his too smooth hair, and, to the disappointment of the expectant boys, omitted to notice the fieldsman moving up behind him, into whose hands he beautifully tipped the ball. 'Bad luck, sir,' every one ventured—and indeed, he returned answer to himself—as he sat down to remove his pads.

John Bowers, senr., came through the clap-gate, frowned at the scoreboard, and made for the pavilion. His old friend, William Dales, captain (the same who kept the 'Swan'), was pacing up and down out-side, bat in hand. 'Why aren't you playing, John?'

'Well, for that matter, Bill, there's one John Bowers playing.'

'There ought to be two.'

'Doing none too well, I see.'

'O, Bill Dales to come in yet, y'know. Bill's to come in yet.'

'And John Bowers.'

'If John Bowers don't bowl the wickets down to-day, John, I—well, I shan't be there at church to-morrow morning.'

The score reached forty before Scroggins departed, and of these forty the indomitable 'Tardy' had made the not remarkable number, two. The stable lad with the broad mustard-coloured belt buffeted the bright air, and Bill Dales reigned in his stead. Jumping—he was a large and red-complexioned man—jumping in at the ball, he was fortunate enough to hit it, and the old men on the benches blinked as something banged against the oak bole just behind them, and leaping back on the green-sward took shape and colour as the cricket ball. The fast bowler, un-accustomed to that sort of indignity, decided on a ball whose speed should surpass that of Jove's thunderbolt. There was a roar from the pavilion as this machination resulted in another mighty blow. The mothers, removing their perambulators from the oak-tree's vicinity, began to hurry. But Bill's life was short, for the next ball happened to be the fatal one, and he came away smiling. 'Some runs, boy, for the love of God,' he said, as John Bowers, junr., passed him. It was the last wicket.

Even cricket could torment John Bowers, junr. He was born with the zest of the game in him; but it implied publicities, and now, walking to the wickets, he felt his usual uncertainties of appearance. He would have liked to simulate calmness, but fearing to do that and give a false impression of *hauteur* he hurried nervously along and allowed those watching to see his true state of mind. The small boys at the pavilion rails detected the nervousness and grinned knowingly as the new batsman left a wide ball alone. That was not the way for the tail end of Harmans Second. He was too timid a batsman, altogether. The ironclad defences of 'Tardy' held out, and Bowers was again the object of criticizing tongues. Why, he had made a hit—there was the ball, racing away! The boys, half-convinced, began to murmur; the veterans, re-assembled, clapped with discrimination.

'Playing 'em with confidence!'

'He's no bat. I never reckoned much of him as a bat.'

Neither did John think much of himself. But that day he felt able to eye the ball steadily and to look round him with purpose. Most days were different touching these points. He made other hits, and the fast bowler, in the last stages of diabolical genius, winked ferociously at the nearest fieldsman, and became a sort of human windmill, twirling his arm as he ran. The ball flew wildly and wide, and the bowler was motioned by his captain into temporary retirement.

By this time, several additions could be seen round the ground. Bowers observed his father and Dales taking out chairs under the shadow of the pavilion shrubbery for the curate and his wife. The curate was evidently preaching—about cricket; for the faces of Bowers senr. and Dales became bright with smiles as they looked out at the new bowler measuring his run. Then there were Mrs Scroggins, in a bulging costume known even to Bowers to be characteristic of earlier periods; and with her, forget-me-not-eyed Miss Wray. Scroggins, in his easiest manner, was explaining the state of the game.

Sixty for nine. Sixty in that stratum of cricket was a fair score, but Longley Green had the three brothers Double, from whom alone sixty might not unreasonably be expected. Then, too, there was a one-armed player, who had so mastered his disability as to be a batsman of great local esteem. The oldest and wisest bowlers were apt to be uncertain what spell to put upon him.

The new bowlers, for both changes were made, were unable to tempt 'Tardy'. Grinning with horrible determination, he met each ball with a barn-door bat, and once or twice the rebound was sufficiently slow and exactly placed to enable him to call Bowers for a run. Bowers, slightly disturbed by the sight of Miss Wray, and the fact that (he thought) she had been looking at him, was becoming reckless, and his narrow escapes caused 'Tardy' to shake his head and demonstrate his own barn-door safety stroke, as though the lesson had not lasted long enough. It was evident by this time to Bowers that luck was with him, and he resolved to settle down to a batsman's innings. The score reached ninety, and the boys round the telegraph had the magic figures for the century ready to hoist, when that innings was ended by a failure to resolve, Bowers attempting to emulate the vigorous Dales, and falling short. The players left the field. 'Tardy's' grin was a little serious at first; he was mildly rebuking Bowers for his foolhardiness; and then, approaching the pavilion, he became overwhelmed with simple joy at his feat of endurance, and grinned with head erect to the chorus of 'What, my old Tardy,' and 'Well played, the old stonewaller.' No words escaped him. He had his glory; the Longley Green team had been unable to move him; and he grinned and grinned like the master of a secret, which in truth had appeared to be little else than the holding of his bat stiff, upright, and not to be moved save an inch or two fore or aft. Bowers, whose score had reached thirty-eight, while 'Tardy's' was five, and would no doubt in eternity become infinity, felt most uncomfortable; he was glad that 'Tardy' was interpreting the position as glowing solely with his own effulgence, but to the choice approbations of the grocer he was somehow inadequate. The grocer honestly meant to praise, but his intention was lost in a self-revealing monologue.

'You made some *dazzling* strokes, Mr Bowers. Quite classical. We never imagined—er, we had had but small conception. Do you know, I myself felt to-day as if I were to assist the fortunes of the side with a long innings? I was never more confident of the forward stroke . . .' He continued to a Bowers hearing an unconnected murmur, which ended, ' 'Ardly the thing of young Sprigg to borrow Mr Tomkins' pads without permission, I think. Noo, 'ardly the thing.'

At the moment when Dales led his Harmanians into the field, it was excitement and tension all round. The result of this ancient annual encounter would crop up in sundry places (especially the 'Grid-iron', the public-house on the edge of Longley Street, and often claimed for Harmans by those who defied the map) throughout the next twelve-month. For the moment, it occupied the whole stage of those engaged in it, and many who watched it. The fates, juggling with the good luck, bad luck, indifferent luck, of this small assembly, were not desired to show their workings in affairs of life and death and Death-in-Life; but what event they had in readiness for the obscure contest of an idle afternoon, was a question which loomed in the shadow of the mossy oak, in the sunny mid-circle, in every part of the field. The decline of imagination can scarcely be upheld, in face of these absorbing rivalries, for what meed?—a transient artificial glory; a stake so far beyond most of our aims, so innocent and honourable, that its pursuance is almost a religion.

Now, out came the pride of Longley Street, the two brothers Double (and the third to follow them duly). They were no novices. Their presence was immediately felt, and the score mounted. The ball seemed, no matter how sent down, to lose its speed on the way to them, or to fall short of its intended pitch. Tom Benyon was without his customary force. Dales, with his special variety of bowling that stops short, or hovers in the air, as it had appeared to do to many a victim, was no more respected by the clean-striking batsmen. Bowers, ordered to take up the story, left it as he found it. The yet grinning 'Tardy', whose arms seemed to be moved by mental levers, abruptly but without variation of extent or time, was able to keep the scoring within bounds, but had no other effect on the stalwart pair. Fifty was due to be signalled in a moment or two when the eldest Double made his first mistake, and the shout of the butcher, who was at present wicket-keeper, was answered by the uplifted finger of the umpire. There was yet a chance.

The excitement, considerable at the opening of this innings, became inhuman as it continued. The match was a match. With 'Soon be back, Alf,' and 'Keep y'r wicket up,' smiling nobly but not too well, the less expert men of Longley Green followed the expert to the wickets (and from the wickets with 'He bowls too straight') until there was one to go in, and still the score was a dozen short of the ninety-six runs notched by Harmans. John Bowers, fielding in the 'gully', could not make the philosophy of 'It'll all be the same in a hundred years' time' cover the possible circumstance of his missing a catch now. Scroggins beside him felt the same, but hid the feeling under a meekly conscious, professional attitude of attention. A ball suddenly sliding between them both, it appeared that Scroggins had stiffened slightly in his alert attitude, for his hand was yards late, and Bowers had contrived to save the runs.

With eight runs separating the combatants, the one-armed batsman, who had held together the fabric almost his accustomed length of time, laid on his best powers to an over-pitched ball. The bowler was John Bowers, and by an extraordinary chance he was now clutching the ball in his right hand stretched out wide; his pose was suggestive of a Grecian dance, and occasioned an intentional dance among the urchins by the pavilion. The last man, a long, thin being, who had kept wicket for Longley Green, came, twisting his head from side to side, to provide the *explicit*. His unconventional purpose, as he met his first ball, seemed to be to scoop the ball over his left shoulder, but it struck his body, rolled to the wicket, and with delicate assurance caused a fatal bail to fall. The long man, casting a melancholy look at this, and repeating his scoop as if to express what might have been, turned away as he had come; the ground rang with clapping, and the bails having been pocketed and stumps drawn by the umpires, the victors came with modest pride from the field.

'A good match.'

'A thundering good catch by that young fellow.'

'Well, it's all over till next year.'

'Pity you didn't catch hold of that one, Smiler.'

'We never had no luck to-day.'

'Mr Double didn't reckon he was out.'

And among the victors, nothing more dramatic was said.

'I didn't half shake when the one-handed chap caught that half-volley of yours.'

'You'll be taking up batting, I 'spect, Mr Bowers.'

'We should have looked middling silly if you hadn't made them runs.'

'I think it's Mr Gibbens who made the runs for me.'

'Come on, Tardy, what you got to say to that?'

'Gentlemen, Mr Gibbens will speak.'

Not he. Grinning again, he shook his head. His increasing deafness had, also, dried up those brief springs of speech which once passed for the prime of simple wisdom. His small son, a crop-headed, hob-nailed imp, carried his brown pads and bat, as he moved towards the exit of the field. To-morrow, with the triumph still flickering radiantly about his grey jaws, 'Tardy' would be ringing the third bell of Harmans' set of six in the fashion of his cricket demeanour. The entering congregation would pass between six shirt-sleeved solemnities, but of these the most automatic, the least animated save for the motion of gripping the bell-pull's red, white, and blue plush in the right hand, the noose at the rope's end with the left, and all the rest, would be 'Tardy', christened Solomon, Gibbens.

From *The Face of England*, 1932.

Schoolboyish attitudes in cricket are by no means confined to schoolboys. Presumably there is something about the game which encourages both the larkiness and the callousness of adolescence. W. G. Grace appears to have disported himself like an errant schoolboy till the day he died, which is indeed why affection for him remains so strong. As to the callousness, the more philistine aspects of life in Victorian Eton had an alarming effect on the subsequent behaviour of some of the sprigs of the nobility. There is something comically appalling about the spectacle of Lord Hams, Governor of Bombay chuckling at the discomfiture of a good friend.

DURING PART of my five years in India my old school-fellow, Lord Wenlock, who had been a Wet Bob at Eton, but was always quite a good cricketer, was Governor of Madras, and we arranged a visit one year of the Madras Eleven to Poona, another, of the Bombay Eleven to Madras. Poor Wenlock had a very serious accident while playing cricket one day. The ball hit him in the mouth, driving his lips through his teeth, and in writing him a letter of sympathy I could not help adding that I should advise him in future not to put his head where his bat ought to be.

From *A Few Short Runs*, 1921.

Lord Harris, however, was not all schoolboy humour, and neither was Grace. If Cardus is right, and there can be no great games without great crowds, then neither can there be great crowds without great men, for which reason Grace remains the most significant figure in English sporting history. It was said of him that he built the cricket pavilions of England, by which is meant that by sheer force of his genius he drew money into the game. No man could wish for a better epitaph, although it has taken a Trinidadian, C. L. R. James, to understand the phenomenon of Grace at its most profound level, and to deliver the most eloquent of all the obsequies.

WHAT MANNER of man was he? The answer can be given in a single sentence. He was in every respect that mattered a typical representative of the pre-Victorian Age.

The evidence for it abounds. His was a Gloucestershire country father who made a good wicket in the orchard and the whole family rose at dawn to get in a few hours of cricket. Their dogs were trained to act as retrievers. They organized clubs and played matches all over their part of the country. W.G. was taking part from the time he was nine. It is 1857, but one is continually reminded of Tom Brown's childhood thirty years before. The back-swording, running and wrestling have been replaced by a game which provides all that these gave in a more organized manner befitting a new age. But the surroundings are the same, the zest, the concentration, the desire to excel, are the same. The Grace family make their own ground at home. I am only surprised that they did not make their own bats, there must have been much splicing and binding. If they try to play according to established principles, well, the father is a trained man of science. Four sons will become doctors. The wicket the father makes is a good one. The boys are taught to play straight. With characteristically sturdy independence, one brother hits across and keeps on hitting across. They let him alone while W.G. and G.F. are encouraged to stick to first principles. Such live and let live was not the Victorian method with youth.

W.G.'s fabulous stamina was not a gift from the gods. Boys of the Grace clan once walked seven miles to school in the morning, seven miles home for lunch, seven miles back to school and seven miles home in the evenings. Decadence was already creeping in and made this seem excessive. So the midday fourteen miles was cut out. That was the breed, reared in the pre-Victorian days before railways. He was not the only pre-Victorian in the family. His elder brother E.M. was even more so than he. The records show that the family in its West Gloucestershire cricketing encounters queried, disputed and did not shrink from fisticuffs. To the end of their days E.M. and W.G. chattered on the field like magpies. Their talking at and even to the batsman was so notorious that young players were warned against them. They were uninhibited with each other and could be furious at fraternal slights or mistakes. They were uninhibited in general. The stories of W.G. which prove this are among the best about him. There is room here for only one.

W.G. enquired about a new bowler from the opposing captain and was told enigmatically, 'He mixes them up.' The Old Man watched the newcomer carefully for a few overs. Then he hit him far away and as he ran between the wickets shouted to his partner: 'Run up. Run up. We'll mix 'em up for him. We'll mix 'em up for him.' It is quite impossible even to imagine anyone shouting such a remark in a big match today. It was most probably out of place already when W.G. made it.

In his attitude to book-learning he belonged entirely to the school of the pre-Arnold Browns. He rebuked a fellow player who was always reading in the dressing-room: 'How do you expect to score if you are always reading?' Then follows this priceless piece of ingenuous self-revelation: 'I am never caught that way.' It would be idle to discount the reputation he gained for trying to diddle umpires, and even on occasions disputing with them. He is credited with inducing a batsman to look up at the sun to see a fictitious flight of birds and then calling on the bowler to send down a fast one while the victim's eyes were still hazy. Yet I think there is evidence to show that his face would have become grave and he would have pulled at his beard if a wicket turned out to be prepared in a way that was unfair to his opponents. Everyone knows such men, whom you can trust with your life, your fortune and your sacred honour, but will peep at your cards when playing bridge at a penny a hundred. His humours, his combativeness, his unashamed wish to have it his own way on the field of play, his manœuvres to encompass this, his delight when he did, his complaints when he didn't, are the rubs and knots of an oak that was sound through and through. Once only was he known to be flustered, and that was when he approached the last few runs of his hundredth century. All who played with him testify that he had a heart of gold, loyal, generous to the end of his life, ready to place his knowledge, his experience and his time at the disposal of young players, even opponents. He is all of one piece, of the same family as the Browns with whom Thomas Hughes begins his book.

W.G. was a pre-Victorian. Yet a man of his stature does not fit easily into one mould. When we look at the family again we see that there was a Victorian in it. The mother was one of those modern women who being born before their time did what was expected of them in the sphere to which they had been called, but made of it a field for the exercise of qualities that would otherwise have been suppressed. The prototype of them all is Florence Nightingale. Mrs Grace's place was in the home, which included the orchard. She mastered the game of cricket, was firm, not to say severe, with W.G. for not catching on quickly enough to her instructions as to how to play a certain stroke. She kept books, the scores of the family in their early matches. She wrote to the captain of the All England XI recommending her son E.M. for a place in his side. She took the opportunity to say a word for W.G., who, she said, would be the best of the Graces—his back-play showed it. The boy, it seems, was *taught* to play forward and back. Until she died the boys wired match scores and their personal scores to her at the end of each day's play. There was much of his mother in W.G.

The three Grace brothers became famous cricketers. The Walker brothers were more than twice as many as the Graces. Yet they do not give the impression of being a clan as the three brothers E.M., W.G. and G.F. (There were two others, Henry and Alfred, who were good, but not great cricketers.) From all accounts E.M. on the cricket field was a card and it would be interesting to know what he was like on the bench: he was a coroner. G.F. appears to have been thoughtful and reserved, and died young. W.G. was close enough to E.M., yet is said to have felt the death of G.F. more than he felt most other bereavements. Linked together, they were yet three individual men. W.G., the greatest of the three, most completely embodied the family qualities. This has been often observed in great men.

We can sum up. He seems to have been one of those men in whom the characteristics of life as lived by many generations seemed to meet for the last, in a complete and perfectly blended whole. His personality was sufficiently wide and firm to include a strong Victorian streak without being inhibited. That I would say was his greatest strength. He was not in any way inhibited. What he lacked he would not need. All that he had he could use. In tune with his inheritance and his environment, he was not in any way repressed. All his physical and spiritual force was at his disposal to do what he wanted to do. He is said on all sides to have been one of the most typical of Englishmen, to have symbolized John

Bull, and so on and so forth. To this, it is claimed, as well as to his deeds, he owed his enormous popularity. I take leave to doubt it. The man usually hailed as representative is never quite typical, is more subtly compounded than the plain up-and-down figure of the stock characteristics. Looking on from outside and at a distance it seems to me that Grace gives a more complex impression than is usually attributed to him. He was English undoubtedly, very much so. But he was typical of an England that was being superseded. He was the yeoman, the country doctor, the squire, the England of yesterday. But he was no relic, nor historical or nostalgic curiosity. He was pre-Victorian in the Victorian Age but a pre-Victorian militant.

There he was using his bat like an axe, building as much of that old world as possible into the new, and fabulously successful at it. The more simple past was battling with the more complex, more dominant, present, and the present was being forced to yield ground and make room. In any age he would have been a striking personality and vastly popular. That particular age he hit between wind and water. Yet, as in all such achievements, he could conquer only by adopting the methods of the new.

Cricket is an art. Like all arts it has a technical foundation. To enjoy it does not require technical knowledge, but analysis that is not technically based is mere impressionism. That W.G. was a pre-Victorian who made a pre-Victorian game a part of the Victorian era appears nowhere so clearly as in the technique he introduced. It had the good fortune (rare with him) to be beautifully stated.

It is as a batsman that he is best known and surely what he did should take its place in the co-ordination which seeks to plot the process by which the arts develop. Batsmen before him were content to specialize in what suited them best. One great player used the forward style. Another was distinguished for his mastery of back-play. Equally the cut as the leg-hit had its particular exponents. There were aggressive players and players defensive. There were players who were good on good wickets. There were others at their best on bad. Whether on the village green or at Lord's, this was in essence cricket of the age of the Browns.

Practically from his very first appearance W.G. put an end to all this categorization. He used all the strokes, he played back or forward, aggressively or defensively, as the circumstances or the occasion required. As he approached forty he confessed to preferring a good slow wicket to a good fast one. In his prime it did not matter to him, and in these days when a jumping or turning wicket is regarded as a reversal of the order of nature, he shares with Victor Trumper and J. B. Hobbs the distinction of being batsmen who at their best were least concerned about the state of the pitch. The crowd at Lord's once rose at him for stopping four shooters in succession. In 1896 on a bad wicket at Sheffield Park the Australian fast bowler Jones frightened out a magnificent batting side. The batsmen went in with the obvious intention of getting out as fast as possible. W.G., then forty-eight, shared with F. S. Jackson the only batting honours of the day. This then, in the classic passage from Ranjitsinhji's *Jubilee Book of Cricket*, was his achievement. I give it in full.

'Before W.G. batsmen were of two kinds, a batsman played a forward game or he played a back game. Each player, too, seems to have made a specialty of some particular stroke. The criterion of style was, as it were, a certain mixed method of play. It was bad cricket to hit a straight ball; as for pulling a slow long-hop, it was regarded as immoral. What W.G. did was unite in his mighty self all the good points of all the good players, and to make utility the criterion of style. He founded the modern theory of batting by making forward- and back-play of equal importance, relying neither on the one nor on the other, but on both. Any cricketer who thinks for a moment can see the enormous change W.G. introduced into the game. I hold him to be, not only the finest player born or unborn, but the maker of modern batting. He turned the old one-stringed instrument into a many-chorded lyre. And, in addition, he made his execution equal his invention. All of us now have the instrument, but we lack his execution. It is not that we do not know, but that we cannot perform. Before W.G. batsmen did not know what could be made of batting. The development of bowling has been natural and gradual; each great bowler has added his quota. W.G. discovered batting; he turned its many narrow straight channels into one great winding river. Anyone who reads his book will understand this. Those who follow may or may not get within measurable distance of him, but it was he who pioneered and made the road. Where a great man has led, many can go afterwards, but the honour is his who found and cut the path. The theory of modern batting is in all essentials the result of W.G.'s thinking and working on the game.'

The age of the Browns is left behind. What they had created is now organized and sublated. Note particularly the words 'thinking and working on the game': remember what he added to bowling. We can be so dazzled by the splendours of his youth that we are apt to forget the mental labours that made him what he was and kept him there.

It is not merely that he cleared the road along which all succeeding batsmen have travelled. He met and conquered such a succession of conditions and bowlers, strategy and tactics, as it has never fallen to the lot of any batsman to face. Late in life he met the googly and was said to be troubled by it. Sir Donald Bradman claims that O'Reilly was a greater bowler than George Lohmann, because O'Reilly bowled the googly and Lohmann did not. All such reasonings and ratings are low tide against the rock of Grace's batsmanship. Trumper used to say that if you got to the pitch of the ball it did not matter which way it was breaking. In his early days W.G. also used to run out of his crease and hit the slow bowlers all over the place. No batsman was more scientific than W.G. and science was his servant, not his master. He was not one who by unusual endowment did stupendously what many others were doing well. He did what no one else had ever done, developed to a degree unprecedented, and till then undreamt of, potentialities inherent in the game. And it was this more than anything else which made possible W.G.'s greatest achievement. It was by modern scientific method that this pre-Victorian lifted cricket from a more or less casual pastime into the national institution which it rapidly became. Like all truly great men, he bestrides two ages. It is at the very least obvious that he was not the rather simple-minded smiter of a cricket ball which is the usual portrayal of him.

So far the best that has been said of W.G. as a historical personage is this, by a bishop:

'Had Grace been born in Ancient Greece the *Iliad* would have been a different book. Had he lived in the Middle Ages he would have been a Crusader and would now have been lying with his legs crossed in some ancient abbey, having founded a great family. As he was born when the world was older, he was the best known of all Englishmen and the King of that English game least spoilt by any form of vice.'

At least it is not unworthy of its subject. Which is precisely why it does W.G. the greatest injustice of all.

When the Bishop implies that W.G.'s gifts would have served him to a more distinguished place in another age he did at least put his finger on the heart of the matter. My contention is that no crusader was more suited to his time than was W.G. to his own; none rendered more service to his world. No other age that I know of would have been able to give him the opportunities the Victorian Age gave him. No other age would have been able to profit so much by him. In the end judgment depends not on what you think of Grace but on the role you give to

217

sports and games in the lives of modern people. As usual, it is Mr Neville Cardus, in his vivid darting style, who has got closest to W.G.: 'The plain, lusty humours of his first practices in a Gloucestershire orchard were to be savoured throughout the man's gigantic rise to a national renown.' Only it was not the plain, lusty humours of an orchard, but of a whole way of life. 'He rendered rusticity cosmopolitan whenever he returned to it. And always did he cause to blow over the fashionable pleasances of St John's. . . .' There they needed it least. It was to bleak Sheffield, to dusty Kennington and to grim Manchester that W.G. brought the life they had left behind. The breezes stirred by his bat had blown in their faces, north, south and east, as well as in the west.

This way of looking at W.G. is not as simple as it may appear. Let me give some idea of what is hidden below the deceptively placid surface.

There are unfortunately none still living who can recall the success of Harriet Beecher Stowe's *Uncle Tom's Cabin* a hundred years ago. Mass emotions have centred on a single figure in no more mystifying quantity and quality than on the figure of Eliza escaping across the ice from slavery to freedom. Melodramas built around this episode played to packed houses in the United States, and the pursuers were shot down to the cheers and tears of thousands who in real life would have nothing whatever to do with such violent disturbances of the established order. The book sold in millions all over Europe. An emotion not dissimilar and no less unaccountable in strictly rational terms seems to have seized vast numbers of people in Britain a generation before, regarding slaves in the West Indies. To many the ferocity of the emotions was inexplicable. American scholarship has found sufficient to give a starting point for investigation.

Industrialism was closing in on an American population that had lived the American version of English rural life. They were aware of their plight in innumerable ways, unverbalized but no less real. To them Eliza was a symbol of escape from furies vague but pursuing. In Europe, where industrialism was adding new pressures to those of an already oppressive feudalism, the hopeful immigrant saw in Eliza's dramatic escape the promise of his own eventual escape to the same wide and hospitable land. What was in the minds and hearts of the people of Victorian England which made them see W.G. as they did I cannot say for certain, as there is much in this sketch that I do not say for certain. But the passions and forces which are embodied in great popular heroes —and W.G. was one of the greatest of popular heroes—these passions and forces do not yield their secrets to the antiquated instruments which the historians still cling to. Wilton St. Hill and Learie Constantine were more than makers of runs and takers of wickets to the people of Trinidad and Tobago. Who will write a biography of Sir Donald Bradman must be able to write a history of Australia in the same period. I have indicated what I think W.G. signified in the lives of the English people, not in what politicians did for them or poets wrote of them or what Carlyle and Ruskin preached to them, but in the lives that they themselves lived from day to day. We shall know more what men want and what they live by when we begin from what they do. They worshipped W.G. That is the fact. And I believe that we have never given this fact the attention it deserves. Some day we shall. Of that I have no doubt. For the time being it is enough to say once more: he brought and made a secure place for pre-industrial England in the iron and steel of the Victorian Age.

We have peered below the surface at what W.G. did for the people. When we try to find what the people did for him we begin with a blank sheet. They went to see him, they cheered him on the field, they walked behind him in the streets. It is accepted that the athlete, the entertainer, the orator, is spurred to excel himself by the applause and excitement of his audience. We apostrophize his marvellous physique. There was more to it than muscle and sinew.

We have seen the state of cricket when he began, with its first tentative attempts at county, not even national, organization. He loved the game passionately and always served it. The proof is in the fact that all the success and all the adulation never turned his head. As he made his tremendous scores he could see the game visibly growing and expanding around him. In 1857 the Cricketers' Fund Friendly Society was started. It could not supply the requirements of the ever-growing body of professionals. W.G. was greatly in demand to play in benefit matches. Their success depended on him and in them he was always at his best. In 1871 he played in three and scored 189 not out, 268 and 217. Thus stimulated by a specific need, he obviously mobilized himself specially to satisfy it. When he made his first triple century in Kent, followed it with a century not out in Gloucestershire and took guard in Yorkshire, I do not see him as merely judging the length, driving and cutting, his personal powers supplying the resources. Such records are not built on such limited premises. He was strong with the strength of men who are filling a social need. Every new achievement made a clearing in the forest, drew new layers of the population, wiped off debts, built pavilions. How warmly the county secretaries and treasurers must have met him at the gates; how happy his fellow Gentlemen must have looked in the dressing-room as they prepared to add another victory over the Players to atone for their long list of defeats; how the crowds must have roared as they saw his gigantic figure with the red-and-yellow cap and black beard emerge from the pavilion to start an innings. The point is that whatever his fatigue, he could not take notice of it. The crowds and the people made of every innings a Test innings. Professor Harbage has boldly written that half the credit for Shakespeare's plays must go to the skilled artisans, the apprentices and the law students (the groundlings), who for twenty years supported him and Burbage against all rivals. Anyone who has participated in an electoral campaign or observed closely key figures in it will have noted how a speaker, eyes red with sleeplessness and sagging with fatigue, will rapidly recover all his power at an uproarious welcome from an expectant crowd. If Grace could be so often and so long at his best it was because so much depended on it, so many hundreds of thousands of people, high and low, were expecting him to be at his best, even to exceed it, as he had so often done in the past. Except for commonplaces and pseudo-scientific misuse of terms (father image), we know as yet very little of the nourishment given to the hero by the crowd. Here it must have been very great—Grace's career was exceptionally long. At times he must have been very tired of it all. Once he even thought of retiring. He didn't. Such a decision could not rest on his individual judgment or inclination.

In the spring of 1895 he was nearly forty-seven. He had scored 98 centuries. Not merely he but the whole country was wondering if, how and when he would add the other two. Eighteen-ninety-four had been a miserable year for everybody. He had scored as well as most of the others, with a total of 1,293 runs, average 29.38, number of centuries three. Only Brockwell with five had scored more. In fact, except for Robert Abel, no one else had scored as many. The centuries scored in the season were 52, no one had scored over 200, there were only five innings which totalled over 400. There had been years in which the Old Man had scored no century at all. His county, Gloucestershire, formerly at the top, was now often at the bottom of the list. As usual he started to practise in March and ran into form early. A whole season and just two more centuries! He had the habit of rising to the occasion and then shooting far above it.

I do not propose to recapitulate in any detail what he did in May. Those who know it know it by heart. Those who don't could spend time worse than in finding out. What I want to stress is that in the words of H. D. G. Leveson-Gower: 'Nothing W. G. Grace ever did, nothing any other champion at any other game ever achieved such widespread and well deserved enthusiasm as his batting in May, 1895, when he was in his forty-eighth year and so burly in figure.'

Burly as the figure was, it was sustained and lifted higher than ever before by what has been and always will be the most potent of all forces in our universe—the spontaneous, unqualified, disinterested enthusiasm and goodwill of a whole community. The spontaneity was only in appearance. Once he had scored the 99th century in the second match of the season, the thirty years of public service and personal achievement gathered themselves together in the generations, willing him to complete the edifice with a crown worthy of it and of them. He did not keep them long. Two modest innings against Yorkshire alone intervened before a magnificent 283. Followed 257 and 73 not out against Kent when he was on the field for every minute of the game, and on the last playing day of May he reached and passed the thousand runs, the first player in the game ever to do so. (It gives us an insight into his mind that in deference to his weight and age he scored heavily by hitting balls on the wicket or outside the off-stump over to the on-side.)

Never since the days of the Olympic champions of Greece has the sporting world known such enthusiasm and never since. That is accepted and it is true and it is important—I am the last to question that. What I take leave to ask even at such a moment is this: On what other occasion, sporting or non-sporting, was there ever such enthusiasm, such an unforced sense of community, of the universal merged in an individual? At the end of a war? A victorious election? With its fears, its hatreds, its violent passions? Scrutinize the list of popular celebrations, the unofficial ones; that is to say, those not organized from above. I have heard of no other that approached this celebration of W.G.'s hundredth century. If this is not social history what is? It finds no place in the history of the people because the historians do not begin from what people seem to want but from what they think the people ought to want.

He finished as grandly as he had begun. That year of 1895 he made nine centuries. Abel was next with five and all the others made fewer still. Next year he was one of the three who scored over 2,000 runs and he made another triple century. As late as 1902 he was still high on the list of heavy scorers for the season. On his fifty-eighth birthday he played for the Gentlemen at the Oval. He made 74 and hit a ball out of the ground. When he hit a stroke for three he could only run one, and the runs were worth a century. Of all his innings this is the one I would choose to see. He had enriched the depleted lives of two generations and millions yet to be born. He had extended our conception of human capacity and in doing all this he had done no harm to anyone. He is excluded from the history books of his country. No statue of him exists.* Yet he continues warm in the hearts of those who never knew him. There he is safe until the whole crumbling edifice of obeisance before Mammon, contempt for Demos and categorizing intellectualism finally falls apart.

From *Beyond a Boundary*, 1963.

---

*The Grace Gate at Lord's, with its chaste inscription 'TO WILLIAM GILBERT GRACE, THE GREAT CRICKETER', is the nearest he has come to a monument.

James, a fiery advocate of West Indian independence, places Grace in his historical context more perceptively than either Trevelyan, or Cole and Postgate, or any of the other social historians who omit Grace from their accounts. But even James omits one of Grace's greatest achievements, which was his sponsorship of a cricketer whose genius was, in its own way, even more remarkable than his own. That Grace took mischievous delight in sponsoring the stupefying heresies of Gilbert Laird Jessop (1874–1955; Cambridge University, Gloucestershire and England), is well-known. On Jessop's county debut, Grace remarked, 'Well, we've found something this time,' and soon after, when challenged to justify his repeated selection of Jessop, Grace answered, 'Ah, you'll soon see what I've got here.' What Grace had 'got here' was the most amazing batsman of all time. Gerald Brodribb came as close as anybody to conveying the effect of Jessop's technique.

HERE IS a description of the spectators' joy at a Jessop innings. It was a Bank Holiday Monday at Bristol in 1910:

'Three Gloucestershire wickets had gone down for nine runs when Jessop joined Mills, and there was a perfect roar of cheers and applause when the Gloucestershire captain was seen on the Pavilion steps. If ever a man could pardonably feel proud that man was G.L.J. on Monday. He was the big strawberry in the basket. The crowd at times was almost hysterical. That was particularly evidenced once when he had scored a five (all run) through the slips. The spectators cheered every run with a crescendo sort of cheer, and the fifth set of cheers reminded one of the finish of a five miles cycle race at Ashley Down in the good old days. And how anxiously they followed his hits when he got into the nineties. They would never have forgiven Braund if he had bowled him when he was 99. But the Bath man did not bowl the darling of the gods. Jessop just swiped him round to the leg boundary and his total was 103. The next ball Jessop undoubtedly swiped at and O. M. Samson who was fielding out near Almondsbury—at least as near there as possible— caught him high up with one hand. A mighty hit and a fine catch. Jessop knew what he was doing. Did Samson?'

In 1907 Jessop made a score of 240 against Sussex at Hove. Here is something from a report in the *Brighton Herald*. After headlines which stated 'Jessop beats Sussex at Bristol', it went on to say that after Gloucestershire had lost four wickets for 68 Jessop rose to the occasion with one of 'those outbursts of volcanic hitting that have given him world-wide reputation, and while the crowd cheered itself hoarse, and the Sussex bowlers seemed helpless, he amassed a score of 240'. When he was eventually out 'the crowd wanted to carry him into the pavilion, but he outpaced them and with the friendly aid of a policeman he encountered nothing more embarrassing than a multitude of pats on the back. When he came out to field later it was noted that he took point's place instead of cover as usual, and had his hand bandaged—a sign of what his innings had cost him in blisters.'

The news that Jessop was batting would cause a frantic dash to any ground, for Jessop was the most complete office-emptier the game has known. W. J. Ford in the last piece he ever wrote puts it well:

'Placard a town or send a "tape" to the clubs: "Rhodes bowling a grand length", "Braund irresistible in the slips", or the like, and how many men will hurry over lunch? But "Jessop not out forty—hitting hard" will make the luncher forgo his coffee and the hansoms will rattle up to Lord's.'

I have letters from those who in their office-boy days were told to stand by to hail cabs if any of the executive had a chance of seeing Jessop in action. When enquiries were made the manager was 'unavoidably absent' on Jessop days. One county court judge admits to being a bit sharp with long-winded lawyers who kept him away from a county match—especially if Jessop was likely to perform. A Bristol correspondent tells me that the omnibuses to Ashley Down would be suddenly crowded to capacity if the news got round that Jessop was batting. One who was once employed as a boy typist would occasionally be given a shilling to go and see Jessop bat, so long as he finished his day's stint, though it might mean working till midnight, for a wage of 9s a week. Another tells me that when a builder was putting a house on the east side of the ground at Hove he achieved a marked speeding up of the work by telling the brickies that if they reached a certain height by the time of the forthcoming match against Gloucester they would be able to see Jessop bat. The work went on so fast that they had built their 'grandstand' by the time of the match. Jessop obliged with a dramatic innings, but one of the brickies fell off in his excitement.

On one occasion, when a certain cabman was charged with illegally parking his cab at a place from where he could see over the wall of the Bristol ground, his defence was that 'Mr Jessop was batting', and the magistrates instantly dismissed the case. . . .

His father was sitting in the pavilion, and as Jessop went into bat he called out, 'Good luck, little Gillie'. Jessop turned and thanked him, and added, 'I'll be sending you up a catch before long, so keep awake.' Not long after, Jessop made a soaring hit which sailed into the pavilion and landed quite near to where his friend was sitting. He had kept his promise. . . .

Henry Grierson recalls how he was staying on holiday at St. Leonards, and hearing that Jessop was batting dashed off on an old horse-bus. As he arrived at the turnstiles a ball landed among the hansoms and cabs parked where the bus station now stands by the Town Hall. Sir Home Gordon tells how during the innings Jessop 'sent more than one ball, driven as though from a gun, into the windows of a chapel on the other side of the road outside the ground, and once hit a ball so hard with the back of his bat that a boundary was scored behind the wicket. . . .'

From *The Croucher*, 1974.

In the lurid light of Jessop's virtuosity, it hardly seems necessary to justify the existence of a game like cricket. Necessary or not, Albert Knight did it, and must surely have been the first writer to see cricket as an expression of national health and a curative for the neuroses of the sedentary life.

CRICKET IN England has suffered probably by contrast with the more vivid and concentrated winter game of Association football, which has been developed and organised so brilliantly during the past decade. In some respects its appeal is to a less hurried race, and to a calmer, quieter frame of mind, than that of a football crowd, yet in the main all games appeal passively or actively, to the sympathies of Englishmen. The ever-widening interest, almost world-wide in its embrace, which the game commands, can never be other than a wholesale strain of mountain air coursing through the depressions to which a life too serious must be subject. The contemplative, meditative mind desired by the philosopher has ever been rare in the world: it is movement and march which men regard as powerful and cheerful things, and they long to press into them. Perhaps in the spectacle of a game we see taking place in real fashion beneath the sun, part of the great allegory of Humanity, the struggle for existence, which was once but a scramble for nuts, attractively symbolised in these delightful and delighting physical activities. We need to preserve the balance of our nature, not to overcheck the great motive energies of our people.

Without the invaluable tonic of games—and the much-derided playing by proxy is a tonic too—the dexterous movements, the rapid swings, the paces of the run, the knocks so gladly borne, the local comradeships and fellow-feeling manifested, life loses at least one of its most valuable stimuli. Without some such open-air delight, thought itself may become a painful restlessness, and the intellect lose the freshness of natural health. To develop the offices of the mind alone may be a rarer error than to develop the feet and limbs alone, but it is probably more disastrous to the individual or the nation exclusively attempting it. The mind which has no care for the body wheels like a swallow through the air: sweeping the grass here, rippling the water there, it finds no abiding strength of fabric but in the nest of a sound body. Where shall this strength be better

226

sought, or rather found by the way, without seeking, than in such a game as cricket? If you consider that the claims of your native land upon your activities and intelligence necessitate a military training, you may prefer the conscription of European methods. Probably for purely muscular development the parade exercise and the drill of a barrack is a more effective instrument than a game pure and simple. It is the method of men who greatly value regulation and prohibition, who endeavour to poise existence on things mechanical, on a dietary which can be accurately compounded in a laboratory. To face the driving winds, to breast the mountain heights, were far better for the making of men.

We do need a great deal more playing: the looking on of the crowds is not half so important a matter. We need many more playing fields in our larger towns. As a nation we suffer greatly by our neglect of an active athleticism. It was not of the great bulk of our people that Matthew Arnold could say that they didn't read books and lived almost wholly out of doors. As a matter of unfortunate fact, the great majority of our townsfolk have not reasonable opportunities to join in the great outdoor game; never have the opportunities to become familiarised with the great emergencies of the cricket-field; never have the sight trained and tested, the muscles hardened and developed, the nerves strengthened, the hearing proved, which is the cricket way of making honest and healthy Englishmen. It is worth noting that for the use of the 450 cricket pitches provided in public parks by the London County Council in 1905, no less than 1,568 clubs made application. We give up these games far too early in life, partly owing to these leagues and competitions which make the winning of matches the all in all, in lieu of the happy, healthy enjoyment of mutual friends, which should be the *raison d'être* of any and every ordinary club. To provide greater opportunities for our national physical pastimes will do more to rehabilitate the nation, to make men and women more wealthy in the long run, than the decrying of athleticism as something which enervates a business nation. Perhaps if athletics were less of a business, its value as a national asset would be far greater than it is. Be that as it may, in every large city the provision of actual playing spaces becomes a more vital problem with every passing year. Without them, our great technical schools will be merely the prison-houses of a people who invert the Master's teaching. 'The body is more than the raiment.'

It is scarcely possible for those engaged in the business of life to devote too much time to games. Almost all the evils of excessive athleticism concern the class entirely devoted to its exploitation, in far less degree do they touch the hundreds of thousands of spectators whose hearts are delivered over to the enthusiasm of it, turned from their own close centre. There are better things in life, one need not doubt, than fine athletic figures and sun-tinted, clear faces, but there is absolutely no reason at all for disparagement of these good attributes. If you had to choose between mental and the bodily manifestations, well and good, but you have not. Those boys and men who idly chatter about cricket and cricketers, who study averages and their decimals, and know from the weirdest of evidence why so and so doesn't get more runs, are harmless votaries of a hobby which might be better and might be far worse. Were they not discussing cricket and football, they would not be at the technical schools, learning how to increase the output and the quality of English manufactures, doing their patriotic best to throttle German competition. I did once know a professional cricketer who recognised in Dante the half-back of a certain football club. He was not a very successful player, and now spends his days pulling the handle of a beer-tap. Cricket kept him from that for quite a long time.

There is no virtue and no mental capacity incompatible with cricket, no life of reasonable service need be hindered by its playing. Provided that the complex administration and business arrangements connected with the game are compatible with honour and a good name, no constituent of the social experiences of our time can exercise a more wholesome and strengthening influence. Cricket makes for tolerance and kindly feeling, for wholesome self-denial and restraint; it smooths out the lines of hard features with the softening touch of joy in natural delight and cultivated skill; it enriches many a close, cabined life with hours of refreshment and relief, and cultivates many a sterile spot. More and more, in these days of mental and physical pressure, when even childhood feels the 'ache of modernity', do we need to preserve these enthusiasms of nature, of our primitive ancestry. More and more do we seem called upon to save our admirations rather than to restrain them, to drink eagerly of the draughts which the childhood of our race knew so well.

Let us hope that the cricket spectacle will long remain among the most living and working powers which go to mould and frame our national life, and that to all of us, as older we grow, it may be that—

> 'The game we have not strength to play
> Seems, somehow, better than before.'

From *The Complete Cricketer*, 1906.

There are, however, less spectacular but just as vital reasons why the English need cricket. For one thing, it can literally shape the contours of a man's life, becoming an instrument of destiny so efficacious as to tickle the fancy of Thomas Hardy himself. E. W. Swanton recounts the heartwarming tale of J. H. Human (b. 1912: Cambridge University, Berkshire and Middlesex).

I OFTEN recall the case of J. H. Human to illustrate how a slice of luck at the right moment can make all the difference to a games-player, and especially perhaps to a cricketer. John Human, a freshman from Repton, had had no trial for Cambridge during the term although no one had got many runs. With only two matches to go before the University Match someone picked up *The Sportsman* in the Cambridge dressing-room at the Oval and said, 'Listen to this. John Human's just made 231 out of 324 for Berks v Herts.' So a wire was sent summoning John to Eastbourne where next day, going in at No. 7, he made 158 not out for the University against 'Shrimp' Leveson-Gower's side, and was promptly given just about the swiftest Blue on record. Doing well against Oxford, John was forthwith made secretary, which was the invariable stepping-stone to the captaincy. This, in turn, led to his being chosen for E. R. T. Holmes's MCC side to New Zealand and Australia.

It happened on the boat out that John fell in love with the daughter of the Lord Mayor of Sydney, whom he married after the tour. So his life was charted, starting from the inconspicuous game between Hertfordshire and Berkshire at Douglas Crossman's ground at Cokenach. But when he was in single figures, as the fielder used to tell and the lucky batsman has often confirmed, John Human gave the easiest possible catch to 'Tommy' Crossman, captain of Herts, on whose father's ground the match was being played. If that catch had been taken John could not have had his Blue as a freshman, and therefore could not have proceeded step by stepswift step to the captaincy, and thence into the Middlesex XI. Thus he could scarcely have put himself in the running for the MCC tour. So no Lord Mayor's daughter and no successful business career in Australia. Mind you, John Human was a highly talented cricketer who but for the war might have played for England. But it needed Tommy Crossman's gaper to set him on the path.

From *Sort of a Cricket Person*, 1972.

Human's story is no doubt destined to find its place in the collected mytho-
logy of a game peculiarly rich in myth. The timelessness which pervades this
mythology removes a story like the one which Swanton tells from its twen-
tieth-century context and replants it in the soil first cultivated two centuries
ago by Nyren and later tended, as here, by E. V. Lucas among others; before
more seasons have passed, Human will become contemporaneous with John
Jackson.

TRENT BRIDGE'S greatest fast bowlers of the past were John Jackson, J. C. Shaw, Martin McIntyre, Fred Morley, Frank Shacklock and Tom Wass, and of these Jackson was in legend the fastest: 'The Demon', in fact, of his day. Jackson, who is celebrated in Prowse's verses—'Jackson's pace is very fearful'—was, however, according to some critics, not the fastest bowler of all, this proud position being given to Brown of Brighton. Next to him was possibly Harvey Fellows, and in our time Stanley Christopherson. But Jackson, who was over six-feet high and weighed fifteen stone, may have been faster than either. At any rate, it was of him that was first told the story of the batsman hit on the ankle, limping away, and, on being informed that he was not out, exclaiming: 'No, but I'm going.'

'His performances against some of the Twenty Twos,' says Caffyn, 'were extraordinary, and many of the players were exceedingly glad to get out and return to the Pavilion without broken bones.' Jackson seemed to have been proud of his menace. 'I never got ten wickets in a first-class match,' he confessed to Old Ebor, 'but I once did something as good. It was in a North v South at Nottingham. I got nine wickets and lamed Johnny Wisden so that he couldn't bat. That was as good as ten, eh?'

It will perhaps be looked upon as an instance of poetic justice when I say that the one-sidedness of Jackson's nose was due to an injury in the nets at Cambridge. On this occasion first-aid was at once brought from the pavilion, in the shape of some brandy, to rub it with. But Jackson knew better than that. 'I drank the brandy,' he told Old Ebor, 'and then went into the pavilion for hot water.'

John Jackson, who was born in Suffolk in 1833, died at Liverpool in 1901. In addition to being known as 'The Demon', he was called 'Jem Crow' and, on account of always blowing his nose resoundingly after he took a wicket, 'The Foghorn'.

From *Cricket All His Life*, 1938.

The seductive nature of cricket's freely adjustable timescale has so besotted at least one writer that he can accept with perfect calm the certitude that he will expire before the game does. It is most impressive that in immolating himself on the fires of his own mortality, Marvin Cohen is careful to exclude cricket from a similar fate.

WHEN I'M dead, will cricket still exist? Yes, but I won't.

Survive me, cricket. Don't mourn me. Carry on, dear game.

England was your birthplace. Favour it, cricket, by retaining your custom there. Be England's quality yet. Not with one-day, limited-over travesties—but with five-day tests, and three-day county matches. Be what we've known. But be your unknown future as well. Be your evolutionary future form—or the many forms foreseen by the possible.

Live on, cricket. Don't mind *me*, if I'm dead. I enjoyed you. Gratify others too. They *deserve* their turn, and claimed the right by being born.

Parallel life. You *are* life, cricket. The life of our race. Only perish if *we* do. But we determine not to, in our huge social aggregate, the collective being of mankind.

Take up your future. Get *all* your innings in. Even to infinitude. For while one player drops, a new one is born, with the instinct to bat, field, bowl. Be more of you, dear cricket. Carry my contributing heart into my body's absence. Widen out the horizons. Consume all our eternity.

Goodby, cricket, I died loving you, playing you. You were my life, in allegory. You gracefully received my poetry. My poetry helped my soul surmount its ordeal. I'm on the other side.

Is there cricket, where I am? My lip is shut, to this forbidden secret. I salute those still living. I'll applaud their centuries, from the members' pavilion, where I own a deathtime membership and wear the sacred tie, in loyalty, and in remembrance.

Is there life after cricket? First go through cricket, to earn the right to this unknown passage. Your discovery may be socially incommunicable: an unplayable wicket.

From *Strangers' Gallery*, 1974.

The sense of time past which pervades so much cricket writing may some-times be expressed through the modest inanimate objects which festoon a cricket pavilion. The eventual fate of Alec Waugh's cricketing regalia is a cautionary tale at once comic and deeply pathetic.

THE THIRD memorable incident during my stay in the Villa Marina was the news from St John's Wood that I had been elected to MCC. I had known that I should be shortly, as I had played the last of my quali-fying matches in the previous summer, and I had learnt that compli-mentary reports upon my play had been sent in to Lord's, but even so the official announcement did represent a genuine achievement. Today it is relatively simple to get elected to MCC. A candidate cannot be entered under the age of fourteen, by which time it can be seen whether or not he has a natural interest in, or aptitude for the game. The seating accomodation has been so enlarged that there is room for a much larger number of members; moreover the cost of the new stands has enforced the need for a larger membership. There are at the moment 15,000. My sons took less than ten years to get elected with no strings being pulled on their behalf. But in the 1920s the waiting list was very long. In those days a male could have his name entered at birth and that was what every far-seeing father did for his son. My father was not far-seeing. He never planned his life in advance. He made instantaneous decisions whenever a new issue arose. Evelyn refers to this trait in him in *A Little Learning*. He speaks of his father's 'deleterious speed'. At Oxford in spite of his love of acting, he never joined the OUDS. He thought it would be too expensive. Actually he could easily have afforded it. Later in London he joined the Savile Club instead of the Garrick. The Savile was at that time in Piccadilly where the Park Lane Hotel now stands—twenty minutes away by bus or tube from his office in Henrietta Street, Covent Garden. The Garrick on the other hand lay between his office and the tube station at Leicester Square, from which he travelled back and forth to his home in Golders Green. The Garrick would have been much more convenient; moreover, he would have found the company there more congenial as it was patronised by prominent actors and producers. At the outbreak of war he resigned from the Savile, as an economy, because he so seldom went there. He did not join another club when the war ended. Had he joined the Garrick in the first place, I do not think he would have resigned in 1914. Through not looking ahead, he deprived himself of many opportunities for conviviality. As regards cricket, he was an enthusiastic follower of the game; he started and nourished my love of it, but he did not enter my name for MCC until 1914; this meant that my contemporaries had a sixteen-year start of me, and I could scarcely hope to be elected until I was over fifty.

During the 1920s, however, there was devised a means by which candidates with reasonable club cricket qualifications could get their election accelerated as playing members. This involved the pulling of certain preliminary strings in order to get one's name on the list of probationary candidates. Then, to justify one's presence there, one had to play in twelve trial games for MCC in which the match manager reported on one's qualities and behaviour. It took me several years even with the backing of P. F. Warner to get on that list. Then I had to play my dozen games. It will be appreciated with what excitement, with what pride I read the announcement of my election. I could now walk into the pavilion not only for Middlesex matches—I was already a member of the county club—but for Test matches, for the Oxford and Cambridge, for the Eton and Harrow matches; I could take a guest in with me. What a pleasure to be able to take my father there. There is no comparison between the view of the play that you get when you are watching behind the bowler's arm and when you are in the members' guest enclosure, the mound or square in the grandstand. It was for this reason that in recent years my father and I had gone more often to the Oval where I was a member. But we both preferred Lord's—the centre and the home of cricket.

As a member of MCC I should be entitled to Rovers' tickets for Test matches, which would allow my friends a choice of seats in the various guests' enclosures. What a valued present that would make. I had known that I should be elected in the spring, but the tangible proof of my election warmed my heart.

I wrote to Peters and asked him to send me out an MCC scarf and tie. The red and yellow in their pristine vividness looked very garish in the Mediterranean sunlight. Eldred viewed it with disfavour. 'Never wear that,' he said, 'except upon the cricket field.' He belonged to a generation that held it to be bad form to wear an old Etonian or a Brigade tie except when you were visiting your old school or attending a reunion dinner. I could see his point. I never thought it good form for debutantes who had been presented at Court to go on to supper at the Ritz with their feathers in their hair, or for men on their way back from Ascot to wear in their buttonholes a Royal Enclosure badge. It was as though the wearers of these insignia were saying 'I may be supping in the same restaurant as you, or walking down the same stretch of pavement, but I am, you will observe, a person belonging to a superior world.'

MCC took a different view of its red and yellow. In the following summer, needing a new blazer, I ordered an MCC one. I was soon made to realise that I had committed a gross solecism and the captain of the side, not in private, but before the other members, warned me that I should cause grave offence to certain veterans who had worn Marylebone blazers in the days of W. G. Grace.

'The old school tie' is the subject of much genial satire. I have been told that the MCC colours came into disrepute because any man whose name was entered at birth could become a member without being a cricketer; and that real cricketers did not like to see 'rabbits' wearing the same colours as themselves. A man of seventy-five wearing a faded MCC blazer could suggest that he had been a member half a century before, in the homeric days of the great doctor.

This snobbery of colours would have made an amusing essay for Max Beerbohm. In the 1930s there was a cartoon in *Punch* by Fougasse, showing an athlete in various forms of sartorial array. 'If you are playing for the old Crundonians,' the caption ran, 'you may wear a Forester scarf, an Incog blazer, an IZ sweater, a Nondescript belt, but the one thing you must not wear is anything Old Crundonian.'

A few years ago in the University match at Lord's, a number of Oxonians went in to bat wearing club and county caps. They were vigorously reproved in *The Daily Telegraph* by E. W. Swanton.

At any rate I did not wear my MCC blazer again upon the cricket field. I took it around with me on cruises and on beaches: in the Riviera and the Caribbean. It was a familiar sight in St Thomas in the 1950s when it was surmounted by a wide-brimmed cha-cha hat. I used it as a writing coat, and several press interviews recorded my wearing of it at my desk in the Algonquin. Finally it fell to pieces in the Macdowell Colony in the early '60s. It embarrassed me on the cricket field, but it was a good friend, the companion of many contented hours.

From *A Year to Remember*: *1931*, 1975.

In an essay entitled 'Ours is the Real Cricket' (1931), the novelist Hugh de Selincourt suggested that of all forms of the English game, village cricket is the purest. Not everyone agreed, then or now, but it was easy enough to see why de Selincourt believed that it was in the uncluttered, private setting of a village match, where the contest has a communal significance which can be savoured only by the members of that community, that quiddity of character is most naturally expressed. A few seasons earlier, in 1924, de Selincourt had achieved the classic which had been theoretically possible ever since Nyren, and the guidelines which were so skilfully laid down by Miss Mitford, a novel which expresses both a sense of character and a sense of place by describing a village match. De Selincourt's exquisite book ends in the same way as his later novel, The Saturday Match *does, with nightfall and sleep. No writer has better expressed the idea of cricket as a benediction.*

The Evening Passes and Night Falls

THE STUMPS had been pulled up and stored with the umpires' torn coats in the locker; the seats and benches had been carried into the Pavilion; the large shutters had been lowered; the doors of the Pavilion barred and locked. The cricket ground, in the light of the sinking sun, looked as desolate as the two worn patches by the bowlers' creases, which were now the only visible signs that a match had been played.

Players and spectators straggled up the road to the village in thick, gossiping throngs, through which young Trine in his two-seater (giving Waite a lift) slowly made his way, tooting his horn and wishing 'goodnight' to players and others whom he knew, at any rate, by sight. Sid Smith met his wife and children at the gate and persuaded her to come back into the village to listen to the band, which would play that evening in the Square. Keen eyes of women gave Mrs Sid three months before her next came; but there, you could never be certain! In her best clothes and in his own happy humour after the match Sid had a glimpse of the fine lass, Liz, he had wooed before the swamp of domesticity had closed over their heads. He pushed the perambulator up the hill in the vain but valiant hope of regaining that girl, a hope that glimmered dimly and dumbly in some remote corner of his consciousness.

Old John, Ted Bannister and Teddie White slowed up as they came to 'The Dog and Duck'. Old John, in a more benevolent mood even than usual, was much affected by the sight of the small family party, Sid pushing the pram, with two small boys hanging on to his jacket. He came hurrying to Mrs Smith:

'You must let your husband join us,' he said. 'We've had such a glorious nice match; the best match as I've ever played in, I do verily believe.'

All smiles, Mrs Sid answered: 'Now don't you keep him long, Mr McLeod, mind.'

'Long, bless me, no, Mrs Smith! But your good man'll be as parched as a day in the desert.'

'Oh, no! That's all right; I'll stay here,' said Sid, protesting. But Ted Bannister took one arm and old John the other, and he was dragged into 'The Dog and Duck', not, it must be owned, too reluctantly. A friendly but vigorous argument ensued between John and Ted Bannister as to who should stand treat, which was won by Ted Bannister, John grumbling that he never knew such a chap.

'Go on, put that inside yourself, mate,' said Ted handing him a pint of old Burton, for which 'The Dog and Duck' had a name.

Nothing is quite so refreshing as a long, cool drink of good old ale after a hot afternoon's cricket; each man took a long, appreciative draught after wishing each other, 'Well, here's luck!' and then in silence allowed the pleasant effect of that drink to permeate quietly through him before enjoying another good pull at the big pewter mug. John's face was a study of happy comfort as he slowly tilted his pot and, emptying it, set it down on the counter, carefully drawing a deep, comfortable sigh. Beaming, he watched the others follow his excellent example and then said, as though inspired by a sudden novel idea of extreme brilliancy:

'How about another small one?'

The men smiled. In a most businesslike manner John asked Jock, the barman, for another half-pint each, and over that the men, their first parched thirst a little quenched, were able to chat. They discussed the great question who had really done the most to win the match for Tillingfold, and after dismissing the claims, first of one man, then of another, came to the conclusion that every man in the side had done his share. 'Ah! that's the beauty of cricket!' declared old John heartily, wiping his face all over with a large handkerchief, 'that's the glorious beauty of cricket. Every single man-jack of us helped, one way or another to win that game.'

'Yes!' said Ted Bannister, with the utmost composure: 'if there is a better game than cricket I should like to know it.' And he surveyed the company as a man does who has said the last word.

What would have been Gauvinier's thoughts had he heard him say it?

II

Gauvinier, as a matter of fact, was quietly absorbing with Francis Allen, the scorer, a tap of old beer which he preferred to that to be obtained at 'The Dog and Duck'. The pub was at the end of the village, more retired perhaps and secluded.

'It adds to the life of the place, a game like that, this afternoon,' said Gauvinier.

'It'll be a pity if we can't get another field for football and cricket should have to stop. The turf must have a rest.'

'Yes; it's just got going proper-like since the war.'

'All the grousing and chat really is only a sign of keenness, don't you think?'

'No use payin' any heed to that, man,' said old Francis encouragingly, pouring his beer down.

'I wonder why one is so mad on cricket. It's only a game, after all.'

'Here! you'd better have another half-pint to wash that duck of yours off your chest.' He ordered it, while Paul laughed.

'I'd like to have made a few today. Your young Horace batted well. He should be a fine cricketer one day.'

'They're nice people, the whole lot of 'em,' said Francis appreciatively. 'The nipper wanted to play today—just a little. I had some fun with 'un this morning.' He paused, savouring the reminiscence. 'Wouldn't let on I had a message for 'un. He pretty nigh bust hisself wanting to know.'

'The kid's not an atom conceited. I'd as soon have him on a side as any man I've ever played with.'

Francis looked very pleased.

'Except, perhaps, Mr Waite, eh? Or Ted Bannister,' he slyly suggested.

'You are an old devil. Who's ever told you . . . '

'Who's told me! You hide your blummin' feelings too well.'

'Oh, damn it! I try to,' said Gauvinier guiltily. 'But that catch . . . ' he began to shake with laughter.

'Pretty near scared the life out of him. Mind now, or you'll spill the beer over your trousies. I could see his scared look from the score box.'

Gauvinier managed to finish his beer without a catastrophe.

'The joke is that half Tillingfold will think him a class fielder now.'

'Well, why not?'

'Oh, no reason, of course, only it's rather funny. So damnably like the world.'

'It takes all sorts to make a world, if it comes to that.'

'You're right, Francis, you're right. One's little job is to find the place for the Bannocks and the Bannisters, that's all.'

There was a silence.

'Oh, well,' said Gauvinier, 'I must push along, I suppose.'

'Yes, musn't sit here all evening makin' beasts of ourselves.'

They slowly 'got a move on', and Gauvinier mounted his bicycle and rode home into the glory of the evening. Even the cricket match was forgotten for a little while as he looked at the blaze of colour which celebrated the close of the day. He rode slowly lingering as at a majestic rite. The whole vast sky glowed red and orange; the trees shone rosy in the reflected light which touched the hills. No breath of wind stirred the glowing stillness. His heart worshipped God and colour and life.

And night was treading softly from the woods where the little owls were beginning to cry.

III

In the Square the band gradually assembled and put on their instruments and began to play. For miles around their music carried; and so clear and so still was the air of the evening that farmers on the hills coming from their stables stood still for a moment and remarked: 'Ah! there's the band then! Hear it plain tonight,' and they were answered, after a listening pause, 'Yes, there's the band. You're right. Hear it plain too.'

People from all the villages round walked in little groups to Tillingfold to shop and drink and gossip. They stood thickly about in the main street, making reluctant room for the motors which every Saturday throughout the summer seemed to pass through the village in greater numbers.

Jim Saddler and Sam Bird edged carefully about in the crowd to collect two others for a quiet game of solo in the Village Room. Old Francis, who had declined John's invitation, they got for one, and deciding to pick up their fourth in the room, they set off down the street just as the band began to play its last piece. They saw Sid ahead of them who was pushing the pram, packed, somehow, with both tired little boys, and the sleeping baby.

'Rather him than me!' said Sam Bird mysteriously. They passed Teddie White, properly stiff and uncomfortable in his best suit and boots, on his way to the jollification—with his wife—his wife not quite walking with him, whether owing to her modesty or his, being uncertain.

Just about the time that Sid reached home after a morning's work, an afternoon's strenuous game, and a mile's shove home of a heavy pram, very glad to sit down and take his boots off, Mrs Cairie leaned out of the window and called out to Horace, who had made his father come out on the lawn and bowl at a stump with him, that she insisted upon his coming to bed *at once*, and Mrs Trine patted her son Edgar's face as she left him to smoke a cigar with his father and two visiting men after dinner, saying how glad she was that he had had a nice game, and begging him not to let the gentlemen sit too long before joining the ladies—a ceremony which the Trines liked to maintain, though all the ladies smoked.

At this time, too, Dick Fanshawe climbed on to his bicycle to go and discuss the game with his friend, Paul Gauvinier—with life and art and morals thrown in, of course.

At length the band stopped playing and dispersed, the gossiping groups broke up and straggled away, some singing unuproarious catches along the still lanes. Slowly the square emptied, the colour went out of the sky, and night descended peacefully upon the village of Tillingfold.

Rich and poor, old and young, were seeking sleep.

From *The Cricket Match*, 1924.

Perhaps after all no Englishman can perceive fully the nature of what Edmund Blunden has described as 'our most beautiful and subtle game'. Throughout his life the Englishman is so close to cricket that it becomes virtually impossible for him to attain the required perspective, and so, just as it has taken a Trinidadian like C. L. R. James to explain to the professional historians who Dr Grace was, so Arthur Grimble made the interesting discovery that it demanded a South Sea Island savage to explain to us what sort of a game cricket is.

BUT I like best of all the dictum of an old man of the Sun clan, who once said to me, 'We old men take joy in watching the *kirikiti* of our grandsons, because it is a fighting between factions which makes the fighters love each other.' We had not been talking of cricket up to that moment, but of the savage land-feuds in which he had taken a sanguinary part himself before the hoisting of the British flag in 1892. The talk had run mainly on the family loyalties which had held his faction together. His remark, dropped out of a reflective silence at the end, meant that cricket stood, in his esteem, for all the fun of fighting, and all the discipline needed for unity in battle, plus a broad fellowship in the field more valuable than anything the old faction wars had ever given his people. I doubt if anyone of more sophisticated culture has ever summed up the spiritual value of cricket in more telling words than his. 'Spiritual' may sound over-sentimental to a modern generation, but I stand by it, as everyone else will who has witnessed the moral teaching-force of the game in malarial jungle, or sandy desolation, or the uttermost islands of the sea.